Risk Management

Risk Management

Edwin McGregor

Willford Press
www.willfordpress.com

Published by Willford Press,
118-35 Queens Blvd., Suite 400,
Forest Hills, NY 11375, USA

ISBN: 978-1-68285-989-6

Cataloging-in-Publication Data

Risk management / Edwin McGregor.
p. cm.
Includes bibliographical references and index.
ISBN 978-1-68285-989-6
1. Risk management. 2. Industrial management. 3. Management. I. McGregor, Edwin.
HD61 .R57 2022
658.155--dc23

For information on all Willford Press publications
visit our website at www.willfordpress.com

Willford Press

TABLE OF CONTENTS

PREFACE

This book aims to help a broader range of students by exploring a wide variety of significant topics related to this discipline. It will help students in achieving a higher level of understanding of the subject and excel in their respective fields. This book would not have been possible without the unwavered support of my senior professors who took out the time to provide me feedback and help me with the process. I would also like to thank my family for their patience and support.

The identification, evaluation and prioritization of risks is referred to as risk management. It also involves the application of resources to minimize, control and monitor the probability and impact of unfortunate events. Risks can come from a number of different sources such as uncertainty in financial markets, natural causes and disasters, deliberate attack from adversaries, threats from project failures and credit risk. There are some guiding principles for risk management. These state that risk management should create value, be tailorable, take human factors into account and be dynamic. The strategies that are used to manage threats include reducing the negative effect or probability of the threat, avoiding the threat, and retaining some or all of the potential or actual consequences of threat. Most of the topics introduced in this book cover new techniques and the applications of risk management. It presents the complex subject of risk management in the most comprehensible and easy to understand language. The book is appropriate for students seeking detailed information in this area as well as for experts.

A brief overview of the book contents is provided below:

Chapter - Business Risks and its Types

Business risk refers to the possibility of a company making inadequate profits due to varied reasons. Some of these factors are sales volume, per-unit price, input costs, competition, and the overall economic climate and government regulations, etc. Common types of business risks include financial risk, strategic risk, operational risk, reputational risk, etc. This chapter sheds light on business risks and its types to provide a thorough understanding of the subject.

Chapter - Risk Management: Types and Processes

The process of identifying, evaluating and prioritizing of risks by using various resources for minimization and control of such unprofitable events and opportunities is known as risk management. Financial risk management, operational risk management, enterprise risk management, etc. are a few of its types. This chapter discusses the processes and types of risk management in detail.

Chapter - Risk Analysis

The identification and assessment of the factors that may negatively impact the success of a project is known as risk analysis. Hillier tree analysis, value tree analysis, event tree analysis, break-even analysis, etc. are some of the concepts studied within it. The topics in this chapter will help in gaining a better perspective about these related concepts of risk analysis.

Chapter - Market Risk

The risk of losses arising due to fluctuations in market prices is referred to as market risk. Equity risk, credit risk, foreign exchange risk, liquidity risk, commodity risk, etc. are some common forms of the market risks. This chapter has been carefully written to provide an easy understanding of these market risks.

Chapter - Financial Risk

A few of the diverse aspects related to risk management are risk breakdown structure, network theory, event chain methodology, value at risk, control self-assessment, risk pool, contingency plan, etc. This chapter carefully examines these diverse aspects of risk management to provide an extensive understanding of the subject.

Chapter - Quality Related Risks

Financial risk deals with various types of risks related to financial transactions of a company. Some of its concepts include macro risk, valuation risk, volatility risk, model risk, total return swap, etc. The topics elaborated in this chapter will help in gaining a better perspective of these concepts of financial risk.

Chapter - Diverse Aspects of Risk Management

Quality refers to the value of a product. Quality risk is the potential loss of value of a product due to failure in adhering to minimum specifications. Quality Risk Management includes development, manufacturing, distribution and inspection of products. All these aspects of quality related risks have been carefully analyzed in this chapter.

Chapter - Risk Management Software

There are many software that are used to increase the working efficiency of risk management and optimization of business performance. GRC Envelop, Avanon, Lockpath, SAS, Qualys, Cura, Optial, etc. are some examples of these software. This chapter has been carefully written to provide an easy understanding of these risk management software.

Edwin McGregor

Business Risks and its Types

1

CHAPTER

Business risk refers to the possibility of a company making inadequate profits due to varied reasons. Some of these factors are sales volume, per-unit price, input costs, competition, and the overall economic climate and government regulations, etc. Common types of business risks include financial risk, strategic risk, operational risk, reputational risk, etc. This chapter sheds light on business risks and its types to provide a thorough understanding of the subject.

BUSINESS RISK

Business risk is the exposure a company or organization has to factors that will lower its profits or lead it to fail.

Anything that threatens a company's ability to meet its target or achieve its financial goals is called business risk. These risks come from a variety of sources, so it's not always the company head or a manager who's to blame. Instead, the risks may come from other sources within the firm or they may be external—from regulations to the overall economy.

While a company may not be able to shelter itself from risk completely, there are ways it can help protect itself from the effects of business risk, primarily by adopting a risk management strategy.

Business risk is associated with the overall operation of a business entity. These are things that impair its ability to provide investors and stakeholders with adequate returns. For example, a business manager may make certain decisions that affect its profits or he may not anticipate certain events in the future, causing the business to incur losses or fail.

Business risk is influenced by a number of different factors including:

- Consumer preferences, demand, and sales volumes.
- Per-unit price and input costs.
- Competition.
- The overall economic climate.
- Government regulations.

The company is also exposed to financial risk, liquidity risk, systematic risk, exchange-rate risk, and country-specific risk. These make it increasingly important to minimize business risk.

A company with a higher amount of business risk should choose a capital structure with a lower debt ratio to ensure it can meet its financial obligations at all times. When revenues drop, the company may not be able to service its debt, which may lead to bankruptcy. On the other hand, when revenues increase, it experiences larger profits and is able to keep up with its obligations.

To calculate risk, analysts use four simple ratios: contribution margin, operation leverage effect, financial leverage effect, and total leverage effect. For more complex calculations, analysts can incorporate statistical methods. Business risk usually occurs in one of four ways: strategic risk, compliance risk, operational risk, and reputational risk.

Factors affecting Business Risk

Every business is subject to risks that affect cash flows and profitability. Some come from internal weaknesses; some come from external threats; and some arise from positive sources, such as expansion and growth opportunities. Although risks change over time and vary between businesses and industries, the factors that affect business risks generally remain the same. To successfully mitigate and manage business risks, it's vital to understand these factors.

Internal Factors

Human, technological and physical factors both cause and affect internal business risks. Human factors can include your employees, vendors and customers. Technological factors include computers, information technology and business processes that rely on technology to remain cost effective and efficient. Physical factors can include equipment malfunctions, downtime and eventual obsolescence. Brick and mortar businesses also face risks relating to building maintenance and losses the business may incur due to slips, falls or other accidents. Internal factors are generally those you can predict, plan for and control.

External Factors

External economic, natural and political factors are those over which you have little or no control. As a result, the risks these factors pose can affect your business to a great degree. On the other hand, external factors most often aren't business-specific, so when an external factor affects your business, it's most likely also affecting the competition. The key to mitigating external risks lies in constantly monitoring your customers, the economy, pending legislation and your competitors. An emergency plan can mitigate risks that a fire, flood or a tornado might pose.

Cash Management

Cash-handling policies and procedures, purchasing decisions and budget allotments can all affect cash flow risks. Risks pertaining to fraud and employee theft increase without strong cash controls, including separation of duties, an authorization system and regular transaction reviews. A weak or nonexistent procurement policy can lead to poor purchase decisions, vendor favoritism and overpayment risks. Without regular monitoring, even well thought out budget allotments can go awry when market conditions change.

Personal Factors

Personal conflicts and complacency are additional factors that can affect business risks, according to the U.S. Small Business Administration. For example, balancing work with personal and family obligations can affect both you and your employees. A common scenario occurs when a key employee submits a time-off request for the busiest day of the month. Complacency can lead to missing opportunities for growth and increased profitability because you're satisfied with the status quo.

FINANCIAL RISK

Financial risk is a term that can apply to businesses, government entities, the financial market as a whole, and the individual. This risk is the danger or possibility that shareholders, investors, or other financial stakeholders will lose money.

There are several specific risk factors that can be categorized as a financial risk. Any risk is a hazard that produces damaging or unwanted results. Some more common and distinct financial risks include credit risk, liquidity risk, and operational risk.

Financial risk is a type of danger that can result in the loss of capital to interested parties.

- For governments, this can mean they are unable to control monetary policy and default on bonds or other debt issues.
- Corporations also face the possibility of default on debt they undertake but may also experience failure in an undertaking the causes a financial burden on the business.
- Individuals face financial risk when they make decisions that may jeopardize their income or ability to pay a debt they have assumed.
- Financial markets face financial risk due to various macroeconomic forces, changes to the market interest rate, and the possibility of default by sectors or large corporations.

Financial risks are everywhere and come in many different sizes, affecting everyone. You should be aware of all financial risks. Knowing the dangers and how to protect yourself will not eliminate the risk, but it will mitigate their harm.

Financial Risks for Businesses

It is expensive to build a business from the ground up. At some point, in any company's life, they will need to seek outside capital to grow. This need for funding creates a financial risk to both the business and to any investors or stakeholders invested in the company.

Credit risk— also known as default risk—is the danger associated with borrowing money. Should the borrower become unable to repay the loan, they will default. Investors affected by credit risk suffer from decreased income from loan repayments, as well as lost principal and interest. Creditors may also experience a rise in costs for collection of the debt.

When only one or a handful of companies are struggling it is known as a specific risk. This danger, related to a company or small group of companies, includes issues related to capital structure, financial transactions, and exposure to default. The term is typically used to reflect an investor's uncertainty of collecting returns and the accompanying potential for monetary loss.

Businesses can experience operational risk when they have poor management or flawed financial reasoning. Based on internal factors, this is the risk of failing to succeed in its undertakings.

Financial Risks for Governments

Financial risk also refers to the possibility of a government losing control of their monetary policy and being unable or unwilling to control inflation and defaulting on its bonds or other debt issues. Governments issue debt in the form of bonds and note to fund wars, build bridges and other infrastructure and pay for its general day-to-day operations. The U.S. government debt known as Treasurys and considered one of the safest investments in the world.

The list of governments that have defaulted on debt they issued includes Russia, Argentina, Greece, and Venezuela. Sometimes these entities will only delay debt payments or pay less than the agreed upon amount, either way, it causes financial risk to investors and other stakeholders.

Financial Risks for the Market

Several types of financial risk are tied to financial markets. Many circumstances can impact the financial market. As demonstrated during the 2007-2008 global financial crisis, when a critical sector of the market struggles it can impact the monetary well-being of the entire marketplace. During this time, businesses closed, investors lost fortunes, and governments were forced to rethink their monetary policy. However, many other events also impact the market.

Volatility brings uncertainty about the fair value of market assets. Seen as a statistical measure, volatility reflects the confidence of the stakeholders that market returns match the actual valuation of individual assets and the marketplace as a whole. Measured as implied volatility (IV) and represented by a percentage, this statistical value indicates the bullish or bearish—market on the rise versus the market in decline—view of investments. Volatility or equity risk can cause abrupt price swings in shares of stock.

Default and changes in the market interest rate can also pose a financial risk. Defaults happen mainly in the debt or bond market as companies or other issuers fail to pay their debt obligations, harming investors. Changes in the market interest rate can push individual securities into being unprofitable for investors, forcing them into lower paying debt securities or facing negative returns.

Asset-backed risk is the chance that asset-backed securities—pools of various types of loans—may become volatile if the underlying securities also change in value. Sub-categories of asset-backed risk involve prepayment—the borrower paying off a debt early, thus ending the income stream from repayments—and significant changes in interest rates.

Financial Risks for Individuals

Individuals can face financial risk when they make poor decisions. This hazard can have wide-ranging causes from taking an unnecessary day off of work to investing in highly speculative investments. Every undertaking has exposure to pure risk—dangers that cannot be controlled, but some are done without fully realizing the consequences.

Liquidity risk comes in two flavors for investors to fear. The first involves securities and assets that cannot be purchased or sold quickly enough to cut losses in a volatile market. Known as market liquidity risk this is a situation where there are few buyers but many sellers. The second risk is funding or cash flow liquidity risk. Funding liquidity risk is the possibility that a corporation will not have the capital to pay its debt, forcing it to default, and harming stakeholders.

Speculative risk is one where a profit or gain has an uncertain chance of success. Perhaps the investor did not conduct proper research before investing, reached too far for gains, or invested too large of a portion of their net worth into a single investment.

Investors holding foreign currencies are exposed to currency risk because different factors, such as interest rate changes and monetary policy changes, can alter the calculated worth or the value of their money. Meanwhile, changes in prices because of market differences, political changes, natural calamities, diplomatic changes, or economic conflicts may cause volatile foreign investment conditions that may expose businesses and individuals to foreign investment risk.

Tools to Control Financial Risk

Luckily there are many tools available to individuals, businesses, and governments that allow them to calculate the amount of financial risk they are taking on.

The most common methods that investment professionals use to analyze risks associated with long-term investments—or the stock market as a whole—include fundamental analysis, technical analysis, and quantitative analysis.

- Fundamental analysis is the process of measuring a security's intrinsic value by evaluating all aspects of the underlying business including the firm's assets and its earnings.
- Technical analysis is the process of evaluating securities through statistics and looks at historical returns, trade volume, share prices, and other performance data.
- Quantitative analysis is the evaluation of the historical performance of a company using specific financial ratio calculations.

For example, when evaluating businesses, the debt-to-capital ratio measures the proportion of debt used given the total capital structure of the company. A high proportion of debt indicates a risky investment. Another ratio, the capital expenditure ratio, divides cash flow from operations by capital expenditures to see how much money a company will have left to keep the business running after it services its debt.

In terms of action, professional money managers, traders, individual investors, and corporate investment officers use hedging techniques to reduce their exposure to various risks. Hedging against investment risk means strategically using instruments—such as options contracts—to offset the chance of any adverse price movements. In other words, you hedge one investment by making another.

Pros and Cons of Financial Risk

Financial risk, in itself, is not inherently good or bad but only exists to different degrees. Of course, "risk" by its very nature has a negative connotation, and financial risk is no exception. A risk can spread from one business to affect an entire sector, market, or even the world. Risk can stem from uncontrollable outside sources or forces, and it is often difficult to overcome.

While it isn't exactly a positive attribute, understanding the possibility of financial risk can lead to better, more informed business or investment decisions. Assessing the degree of financial risk associated with a security or asset helps determine or set that investment's value. Risk is the flip side of the reward. One could argue that no progress or growth can occur, be it in a business or a portfolio, without the assumption of some risk. Finally, while financial risk usually cannot be controlled, exposure to it can be limited or managed.

Pros:

- Encourages more informed decisions
- Helps assess value (risk-reward ratio)
- Can be identified using analysis tools

Cons:

- Can arise from uncontrollable or unpredictable outside forces
- Risks can be difficult to overcome
- Ability to spread and affect entire sectors or markets

STRATEGIC RISK

Strategic risks are those that arise from the fundamental decisions that directors take concerning an organisation's objectives. Essentially, strategic risks are the risks of failing to achieve these business objectives. A useful subdivision of strategic risks is:

- Business risks: Risks that derive from the decisions that the board takes about the products or services that the organisation supplies. They include risks associated with developing and marketing those products or services, economic risks affecting product sales and costs, and risks arising from changes in the technological environment which impact on sales and production.
- Non-business risks: Risks that do not derive from the products or services supplied. For example, risks associated with the long-term sources of finance used. Strategic risk levels link in with how the whole organisation is positioned in relation to its environment and are not affected solely by what the directors decide. Competitor actions will affect risk levels in product markets, and technological developments may mean that production processes, or products, quickly become out-of-date.

Strategic risks are determined by board decisions about the objectives and direction of the organisation. Board strategic planning and decision-making processes, therefore, must be thorough. The UK Cadbury report recommends that directors establish a formal schedule of matters that are reserved for their decision. These should include significant acquisitions and disposals of assets, investments, capital projects, and treasury policies.

To take strategic decisions effectively, boards need sufficient information about how the business is performing, and about relevant aspects of the economic, commercial, and technological environments. To assess the variety of strategic risks the organisation faces, the board needs to have a breadth of vision; hence governance reports recommend that a board be balanced in skills, knowledge, and experience.

However, even if the board follows corporate governance best practice concerning the procedures for strategic decision making, this will not necessarily ensure that the directors make the correct decisions.

For example, the severe problems that the UK's Northern Rock bank faced were not caused by a lack of formality. Northern Rock's approach to risk management conformed to banking regulations, but its strategy was based on the assumption that it would continually be able to access the funds it required. In 2007, its funding was disrupted by the global credit crunch resulting from problems in the US subprime mortgage market, and UK Government action was required to rescue the bank.

The report Enterprise Governance – Getting the Balance Right, published by the Chartered Institute of Management Accountants (CIMA) and the International Federation of Accountants (IFAC) highlighted choice and clarity of strategy, and strategy execution, as key issues underlying strategic success and failure. Other issues identified in the report were the ability to respond to abrupt changes or fast-moving conditions, and (the most significant issue in strategy-related failure) the undertaking of unsuccessful mergers and acquisitions.

Managing Strategic Risks

Strategic risks are often risks that organisations may have to take in order (certainly) to expand, and even to continue in the long term. For example, the risks connected with developing a new product may be very significant – the technology may be uncertain, and the competition facing the organisation may severely limit sales. However, the alternative strategy may be to persist with products in mature markets, the sales of which are static and ultimately likely to decline.

An organisation may accept other strategic risks in the short term, but take action to reduce or eliminate those risks over a longer timeframe. A good example of this sort of risk, would include fluctuations in the world supply of a key raw material used by a company in its production. For instance, the problem can be global, the business may be unable to avoid it, in the short term, by changing supplier. However, by redesigning its production processes over the longer term, it could reduce or eliminate its reliance on the material.

Ultimately, some risks should be avoided and some business opportunities should not be accepted, either because the possible impacts could be too great (threats to physical safety, for example) or because the probability of success could be so low that the returns offered are insufficient to warrant taking the risk. Directors may make what are known as 'go errors' when they unwisely pursue opportunities, risks materialise, and losses exceed returns.

However, directors also need to be aware of the potentially serious consequences of 'stop errors' – not taking opportunities that should have been pursued. A competitor may take up these opportunities, and the profits made could boost its business.

OPERATIONAL RISK

Operational risk summarizes the uncertainties and hazards a company faces when it attempts to do its day-to-day business activities within a given field or industry. A type of business risk, it can result from breakdowns in internal procedures, people and systems—as opposed to problems incurred from external forces, such as political or economic events, or inherent to the entire market or market segment, known as systematic risk.

Operational risk can also be classified as a variety of unsystematic risk, which is unique to a specific company or industry.

Operational risk focuses on how things are accomplished within an organization and not necessarily what is produced or inherent within an industry. These risks are often associated with active decisions relating to how the organization functions and what it prioritizes. While the risks are not guaranteed to result in failure, lower production, or higher overall costs, they are seen as higher or lower depending on various internal management decisions.

Because it reflects man-made procedures and thinking processes, operational risk can be summarized as a human risk; it is the risk of business operations failing due to human error. It changes from industry to industry and is an important consideration to make when looking at potential investment decisions. Industries with lower human interaction are likely to have lower operational risk.

Examples of Operational Risk

One area that may involve operational risk is the maintenance of necessary systems and equipment. If two maintenance activities are required, but it is determined that only one can be afforded at the time, making the choice to perform one over the other alters the operational risk depending on which system is left in disrepair. If a system fails, the negative impact is associated directly with the operational risk.

Other areas that qualify as operational risk tend to involve the personal element within the organization. If a sales-oriented business chooses to maintain a subpar sales staff, due to its lower salary costs or any other factor, this behavior is considered an operational risk. The same can be said for failing to properly maintain a staff to avoid certain risks. In a manufacturing company, for example, choosing not to have a qualified mechanic on staff, and having to rely on third parties for that work, can be classified as an operational risk. Not only does this impact the smooth functioning of a system, but it also involves additional time delays.

The willing participation of employees in fraudulent activity may also be seen as operational risk. In this case, the risk involves the possibility of repercussions if the activity is uncovered. Since individuals make an active decision to commit fraud, it is considered a risk relating to how the business operates.

Operational Risk vs. Financial Risk

In a corporate context, financial risk refers to the possibility that a company's cash flow will prove inadequate to meet its obligations—that is, its loan repayments and other debts. Although this inability could relate to or result from decisions made by management (especially company finance professionals), as well as the performance of the company products, financial risk is considered distinct from operational risk. It is most often related to the company's use of financial leverage and debt financing, rather than the day-to-day efforts of making the company a profitable enterprise.

COMPLIANCE RISK

Compliance risk is exposure to legal penalties, financial forfeiture and material loss an organization faces when it fails to act in accordance with industry laws and regulations, internal policies or prescribed best practices.

Compliance risk is also sometimes known as *integrity risk*. Many compliance regulations are enacted to ensure that organizations operate fairly and ethically. For that reason, compliancerisk is also known as integrity risk.

Compliance risk management is part of the collective governance, risk management and compliance (GRC) discipline. The three fields frequently overlap in the areas of incident management, internal auditing, operational riskassessment, and compliance with regulations such as the Sarbanes-Oxley Act. Penalties for compliance violations include payments for damages, fines and voided contracts, which can lead to the organization's loss of reputation and business opportunities, as well as the devaluation of its franchises.

REPUTATIONAL RISK

Reputational risk is a threat or danger to the good name or standing of a business or entity. Reputational risk can occur in the following ways:

- Directly, as the result of the actions of the company itself.
- Indirectly, due to the actions of an employee or employees.
- Tangentially, through other peripheral parties, such as joint venture partners or suppliers.

In addition to having good governance practices and transparency, companies need to be socially responsible and environmentally conscious to avoid or minimize reputational risk.

Reputational risk is a hidden danger that can pose a threat to the survival of the biggest and best-run companies. It can often wipe out millions or billions of dollars in market capitalization or potential revenues and can occasionally result in a change at the uppermost levels of management.

Reputational risk can also arise from the actions of errant employees, such as egregious fraud or massive trading losses disclosed by some of the world's biggest financial institutions. In an increasingly globalized environment, reputational risk can arise even in a peripheral region far away from home base.

In some instances, reputational risk can be mitigated through prompt damage control measures, which is essential in this age of instant communication and social media networks. In other instances, this risk can be more insidious and last for years. For example, gas and oil companies have been increasingly targeted by activists because of the perceived damage to the environment caused by their extraction activities.

Example of Reputational Risk

Reputational risk exploded into full view in 2016 when the scandal involving the opening of millions of unauthorized accounts by retail bankers (and encouraged or coerced by certain supervisors) was exposed at Wells Fargo.

The CEO, John Stumpf, and others were forced out or fired. Regulators subjected the bank to fines and penalties, and a number of large customers reduced, suspended, or discontinued altogether doing business with the bank. Wells Fargo's reputation was tarnished, and the company continues to rebuild its reputation and its brand into 2019.

ROLE OF THE BOARD IN RISK MANAGEMENT

In decades past, boards could rely solely on management to oversee and manage risk. The 2008 financial crisis, also known as the global financial crisis, was considered to be the worst financial crisis since the Great Depression. Harsh economic times hit boards of directors squarely, as they came face to face with complex legal issues and failing businesses. The financial downfall, along with the subsequent fallout, was an abrupt wake-up call for boards of directors to delve deeper into their organization's risk management practices.

The pervasiveness of risk in the workings of everyday business means that boards must factor risk as an integral part of organizational strategy. Technology has increased the pace of business transactions globally, which has increased the volume and speed of product cycles. Today's businesses are wrought with complexities and litigiousness like never before—issues that hold the potential to destroy organizations overnight.

Increased Scrutiny over Risk

In addition to management, boards are increasingly being held accountable for managing risk. Corporate governance rules and credit rating agencies are taking a stronger role in corporate risk by forming policies that address risk management policies. These emerging trends are forcing boards to assess past organizational exposures to risks. Economic trends also demand boards to be forward-thinking with regard to overseeing current financial risks and exposures to minimize the impact of financial crises.

Since the 2008 financial crisis, the New York Stock Exchange's corporate governance rules now require that risk assessment and risk management be included in audit committee discussions. Corporate credit ratings now include an assessment of commercial risk management processes, as required by commercial credit rating agencies, such as Standard and Poor's. These changes mean that risk management items are becoming staples of board agendas.

Potential Loss Areas

Exposures to financial loss can include real and personal property, as well as property that is tangible and intangible, and personnel losses. Revenues can be lost by profit margins or expense increases. Poor risk management exposes organizations to civil and statutory offences, which can result in fines or other legal complications. The result of not managing risks can quickly deplete an organization's reserves. Examples of risks with financial impact include:

- Retained losses: Insurance deductibles, retention amounts, or exclusions.
- Net insurance proceeds.

- Costs for loss control measures.
- Claim management expenses.
- Administrative costs to manage programs.

Finding the Balance between Taking and Managing Risks

Board members, executive directors, managers, and stakeholders know that there are strategic advantages to taking risks and that realizing growth requires some degree of risk. While managing complex business transactions, managers struggle to strike a balance between adding value while managing risks.

Development of Policies, Procedures and Awareness

The board should not take a direct role in managing risks. The board's role should be limited to risk oversight of management and corporate issues that affect risk. Without becoming directly involved in managing risk, boards can fulfill their role in risk oversight by:

- Developing policies and procedures around risk that are consistent with the organization's strategy and risk appetite.
- Following up on management's implementation of risk management policies and procedures.
- Following up to be assured that risk management policies and procedures function as they are intended.
- Taking steps to foster risk awareness.
- Encourage an organizational culture of risk adjusting awareness.

Areas of Risk Management Oversight

Boards should be looking at areas that either may be subject to risk or may be out of compliance with established best practices on risk management, from a domestic and global standpoint. Specific areas that boards should review include:

- Fiduciary duties.
- Federal and state laws and regulations.
- Stock exchange listing requirements.
- Established and evolving best practices, domestic and worldwide.

Risk management may fall under more than one committee, which may be the risk management committee or the audit committee. To effectively cover all areas of risk, committees should be coordinated so that communication between them regarding risk occurs horizontally and vertically. Committees report back to the board regarding the adequacy of risk management measures so that the board has confidence that management can support them.

Risk Management Oversight from a Broad Perspective

Board members need to have a good understanding of risk management, even when they lack expertise in that area. Boards may lean on the expertise of outside consultants to help them review company risk management systems and analyze business specific risks. Boards should perform a formal review of risk management systems, annually.

As part of the annual review, boards should review risk oversight policies and procedures at the board and committee levels and assess risk on an ongoing basis. It's helpful to familiarize the board with expectations within the industry or regulatory bodies that the organization operates in by arranging for a formal annual presentation on risk management best practices. The annual risk management review should include communication from management about lessons learned from past mistakes.

Risk management issues have been at an all-time high. Boards can continue to expect risk management to be an increasingly challenging part of board decision-making. There is a lot at stake with poor risk management practices. The impact will be felt from the top to the bottom and transcend across the board, management, and stakeholders. Taking a focused approach to risk management should be more than a compliance mechanism. Risk management needs to be an integral part of the organization's culture, strategy, and day-to-day business operations. Of all the risk management challenges that boards face, the greatest challenge is in navigating organizational growth while protecting the organization from unnecessary risk, so that it doesn't impact the business negatively. Today's commercial and economic climate demands that boards step up their game with an intense focus on risk management.

References

- Businessrisk: investopedia.com, Retrieved 14 May, 2019
- Factors-affecting-business-risk-7416741: bizfluent.com, Retrieved 24 August, 2019
- Strategic-and-operational-risks, exam-support-resources-professional-exams-study-resources-strategic-business-leader-technical-articles: accaglobal.com, Retrieved 23 January, 2019
- Operational-risk: investopedia.com, Retrieved 09 April, 2019
- Compliance-risk: searchcompliance.techtarget.com, Retrieved 17 July, 2019
- Reputational-risk: investopedia.com, Retrieved 06 July, 2019
- Role-of-the-board-in-risk-management: boardeffect.com, Retrieved 07 February, 2019

Risk Management: Types and Processes

CHAPTER 2

The process of identifying, evaluating and prioritizing of risks by using various resources for minimization and control of such unprofitable events and opportunities is known as risk management. Financial risk management, operational risk management, enterprise risk management, etc. are a few of its types. This chapter discusses the processes and types of risk management in detail.

RISK MANAGEMENT

Business Risk management is a subset of risk management used to evaluate the business risks involved if any changes occur in the business operations, systems and process. It identifies, prioritizes and addresses the risk to minimize penalties from unexpected incidents, by keeping them on track. It also enables an integrated response to multiple risks, and facilitates a more informed risk-based decision making capability.

Businesses today are unpredictable, volatile and seem to become more complex every day. By its very nature, it is filled with risk. Businesses have viewed risk as an evil that should be minimized or mitigated, whenever possible. However, risk assessment provides a mechanism for identifying which risks represent opportunities and which represent potential pitfalls. Risks can have negative impact, positive impact, or both. Risks with a negative impact can prevent value creation or erode existing value. Risks with positive impact may offset negative impacts or represent opportunities.

The risk management process involves:

- Identifying risks: Spotting the evolving risks by studying internal and external factors that impact the business objectives.
- Analyzing risks: It includes the calibration and, if possible, creation of probability distributions of outcomes for each material risk.
- Responding to risk: After identifying and analyzing the potential risk, appropriate strategy needs to be incorporated. Either by establishing new processes or eliminating, depending on kind and severity of the risk.
- Monitoring risk and opportunities: Continually measuring the risks and

opportunities of the business environment. Also keep a check on performance of management strategies.

Types of Risks

- Hazard risk: A hazard is anything in the workplace that has the potential to harm people. Hazard risk includes factors which are not under the control of business environment, such as fallout of machinery or dangerous chemical, natural calamities.
- Financial risk: A large number of businesses take risk with their financial assets, quite regularly. Sometimes choosing a wrong supplier or distributor can backfire. Financial risk also includes risk in pricing, currency exchange and during liquidation of any asset. Business risk management should say how much risk is too much in financial relationship.
- Operational risk: Evaluation of risk loss resulting from internal process, system, people or due to any external factor through which a company operates.
- Strategic risks: Might arise from making poor or wrong business plans and losing the competition in the market. Failure to respond to changes in the business environment or inadequate capital allocation also represents strategic risk.

Techniques to Deal with Identified Risks

- Risk Avoidance: This is the process by which you reduce the risk exposure by avoiding or eliminating the activities.
- Risk Loss Reduction: This is reducing the risk by reducing the maximum amount of probable loss; utilizing other venues, personnel, equipment, etc., for the activity.
- Risk acceptance: This is accepting the risk as it cannot be cost effectively reduced. However, all necessary attempts should be taken to monitor any increases in risk exposure to a preestablished level. Once that level is reached, there will be no other option but total removal of the personnel at risk.
- Risk Transference: This is the use of contracts, insurance, disclaimers, and/or releases of claims to transfer the liability for the expected loss to other parties involved.
- Risk Spreading: This is simply spreading the largest amount of risk over a larger part of the organization or activity by manipulating the sequence or size of the events or activities.

Insurance

This is the transfer of risk from one party to another in which the insurer is obligated to indemnify the insured for an economic loss caused by an unexpected event during a period of time covered by such insurance. Types of insurance vary from liability to crime/theft losses and fire. Rates are governed based on the frequency of claims and cost of each claim.

- Risk Mitigation Strategies.
- Risk avoidance.
  - Removal.
- Risk reduction.
  - Decrease potential.
- Risk spreading.
  - Spread the risk.
- Risk transfer.
  - Insurance.
- Risk acceptance.
  - Acceptance.
- Risk Avoidance.

Risk is avoided when the organization refuses to accept it. The exposure is not permitted to come into existence. This is accomplished by simply not engaging in the action that gives rise to risk. If you do not want to risk losing your savings in a hazardous venture, then pick one where there is less risk. If you want to avoid the risks associated with the ownership of property, the do not purchase property but lease or rent instead. If the use of a particular product is hazardous, then do not manufacture or sell it. This is a negative rather than a positive technique. It is sometimes an unsatisfactory approach to dealing with many risks. If risk avoidance were used extensively, the business would be deprived of many opportunities for profit and probably would not be able to achieve its objectives.

Risk Reduction

Risk can be reduced in 2 ways—through loss prevention and control. Examples of risk reduction are medical care, fire departments, night security guards, sprinkler systems, burglar alarms—attempts to deal with risk by preventing the loss or reducing the chance that it will occur. Some techniques are used to prevent the occurrence of the loss, and other techniques like sprinkler systems are intended to control the severity of the loss if it does happen. No matter how hard we try, it is impossible to prevent all losses. The loss prevention technique cannot cost more than the losses.

Risk Retention

Risk retention is the most common method of dealing with risk. Organizations and individuals face an almost unlimited number of risks, and in most cases nothing is done about them. When some positive action is not taken to avoid, reduce, or transfer the risk, the possibility of loss involved in that risk is retained. Risk retention can be conscious or unconscious. Conscious risk retention takes place when the risk is perceived and not transferred or reduced. When the risk is not recognized, it is unconsciously retained—the person retains the financial risk without realizing that he or she is doing so. Risk retention may be voluntary or involuntary. Voluntary risk retention is when the risk is recognized and there is an agreement to assume the losses involved. This is done when there are no alternatives that are more attractive. Involuntary risk retention takes place when risks are unconsciously retained or when the risk cannot be avoided, transferred, or reduced. Risk retention may be the best way. Everyone decides which risks to retain and which to avoid or transfer. A person may not be able to bear the loss. What may be a financial disaster for one may be handled by another. As a general rule, the only risks that should be retained are those that can lead to relatively small certain losses.

Risk Transfer

Risk may be transferred to someone who is more willing to bear the risk. Transfer may be used to deal with both speculative and pure risk. One example is hedging; hedging is a method of risk transfer accomplished by buying and selling for future delivery so that dealers and processors protect themselves against a decline or increase in market price between the time they buy a product and the time they sell it. Pure risks may be transferred through contracts, like a hold-harmless agreement where one individual assumes another's possibility of loss. Contractual agreements are common in the construction industry. They are also used between manufacturers and retailers about product liability exposure. Insurance is also a means of transferring risk. In consideration of a payment or premium, by one party, the second party contracts to indemnify the first party up to a certain limit for the specified loss.

Risk Sharing

This is a special case of risk transfer and retention. When risks are shared, the possibility of loss is transferred form the individual to the group. A corporation is a good example of risk sharing—a number of investors pool their capital, and each only bears a portion of the risk that the enterprise may fail.

A TRA will incorporate a combination of mitigation tools into the TRA.

RISK MANAGEMENT PROCESS

Implementing a risk management process is vital for any organization. Good risk management doesn't have to be resource intensive or difficult for organizations to undertake or insurance brokers to provide to their clients. With a little formalization, structure, and a strong understanding of the organization, the risk management process can be rewarding.

Risk management does require some investment of time and money but it does not need to be substantial to be effective. In fact, it will be more likely to be employed and maintained if it is implemented gradually over time.

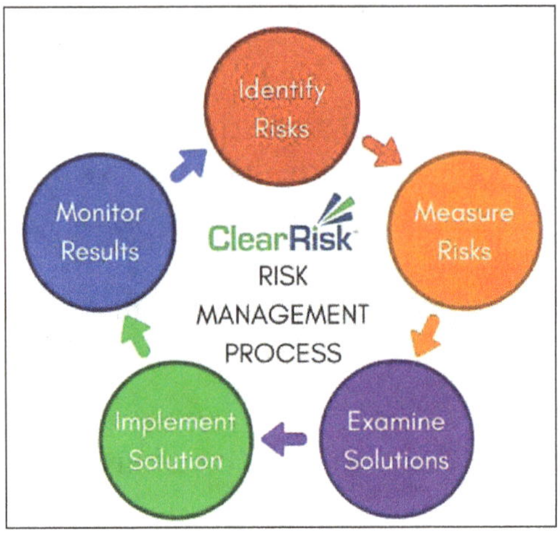

The key is to have a basic understanding of the process and to move towards its implementation.

The 5 Step Risk Management Process are:

Identify Potential Risks

The four main risk categories of risk are hazard risks, such as fires or injuries; operational risks, including turnover and supplier failure; financial risks, such as economic recession; and strategic risks, which include new competitors and brand reputation. Being able to identify what types of risk you have is vital to the risk management process.

An organization can identify their risks through experience and internal history, consulting with industry professionals, and external research. They may also try interviews or group brainstorming.

It's important to remember that the risk environment is always changing, so this step should be revisited regularly.

Measure Frequency and Severity

Many organizations use a heat map to measure their risks on this scale. A risk map is a visual tool that details which risks are frequent and which are severe (and thus require the most resources). This will help you identify which are very unlikely or would have low impact, and which are very likely and would have a significant impact.

Knowing the frequency and severity of your risks will show you where to spend your time and money, and allow your team to prioritize their resources.

Examine Alternative Solutions

What are the potential ways to treat the risk and of these, which strikes the best balance between being affordable and effective? Organizations usually have the options to accept, avoid, control, or transfer a risk.

Accepting the risk means deciding that some risks are inherent in doing business and that the benefits of an activity outweigh the potential risks.

To avoid a risk, the organization simply has to not participate in that activity.

Risk control involves prevention (reducing the likelihood that the risk will occur) or mitigation, which is reducing the impact it will have if it does occur.

Risk transfer involves giving responsibility for any negative outcomes to another party, as is the case when an organization purchases insurance.

Decide which solution to use and Implement it

Once all reasonable potential solutions are listed, pick the one that is most likely to achieve desired outcomes.

Find the needed resources, such as personnel and funding, and get the necessary buy-in. Senior management will likely have to approve the plan, and team members will have to be informed and trained if necessary.

Set up a formal process to implement the solution logically and consistently across the organization, and encourage employees every step of the way.

Monitor Results

Risk management is a process, not a project that can be "finished" and then forgotten about. The organization, its environment, and its risks are constantly changing, so the process should be consistently revisited.

Determine whether the initiatives are effective and whether changes or updates are required. Sometimes, the team may have to start over with a new process if the implemented strategy is not effective.

If an organization gradually formalizes its risk management process and develops a risk culture, it will become more resilient and adaptable in the face of change. This will also mean making more informed decisions based on a complete picture of the organization's operating environment and creating a stronger bottom line over the long-term.

FINANCIAL RISK MANAGEMENT

Financial risk management is the practice of economic value in a firm by using financial instruments to manage exposure to risk: operational risk, credit risk and market risk, foreign exchange risk, shape risk, volatility risk, liquidity risk, inflation risk, business risk, legal risk, reputational risk, sector risk etc. Similar to general risk management, financial risk management requires identifying its sources, measuring it, and plans to address them.

Financial risk management can be qualitative and quantitative. As a specialization of risk management, financial risk management focuses on when and how to hedge using financial instruments to manage costly exposures to risk.

In the banking sector worldwide, the Basel Accords are generally adopted by internationally active banks for tracking, reporting and exposing operational, credit and market risks.

Uses of Financial Risk Management

Finance theory (i.e., financial economics) prescribes that a firm should take on a project if it increases shareholder value. Finance theory also shows that firm managers cannot create value for shareholders, also called its investors, by taking on projects that shareholders could do for themselves at the same cost.

When applied to financial risk management, this implies that firm managers should not hedge risks that investors can hedge for themselves at the same cost. This notion was captured by the so-called "hedging irrelevance proposition": In a perfect market, the firm cannot create value by hedging a risk when the price of bearing that risk within the firm is the same as the price of bearing it outside of the firm. In practice, financial markets are not likely to be perfect markets.

This suggests that firm managers likely have many opportunities to create value for shareholders using financial risk management, wherein they have to determine which risks are cheaper for the firm to manage than the shareholders. Market risks that result in unique risks for the firm are commonly the best candidates for financial risk management.

The concepts of financial risk management change dramatically in the international realm. Multinational Corporations are faced with many different obstacles in overcoming these challenges. There has been some research on the risks firms must consider when operating in many countries, such as the three kinds of foreign exchange exposure for various future time horizons: transactions exposure, accounting exposure, and economic exposure.

OPERATIONAL RISK MANAGEMENT

Operational Risk Management is a methodology for organizations looking to put into place real oversight and strategy when it comes to managing risks. Every business faces circumstances or fundamental changes in their situation that can be seen as presenting varying levels of risk to that business, from minor inconveniences to potentially putting its very existence in jeopardy.

The Basel Committee on Banking Supervision has described operational risk as: "the risk of loss resulting from inadequate or failed internal processes, people, and systems, or from external events. As such, operational risk captures business continuity plans, environmental risk, crisis management, process systems, and operations risk, people related risks and health and safety, and information technology risks."

All of these risks need to be managed and the more sophisticated the approach to risk management, the more chance the business has to thrive and grow.

The Benefits of Operational Risk Management

Before you decide whether or not you want to investigate how Operational Risk Management works and what you need to do to implement it, you will want to know what the potential benefits of it are.

These will help to convince those with sign-off on the decision that it is the right move for your organization, so here are the main benefits of Operational Risk Management:

- Improving the reliability of business operations.
- Improving the effectiveness of the risk management operations.
- Strengthening the decision-making process where risks are involved.
- Reduction in losses caused by poorly-identified risks.
- Early identification of unlawful activities.
- Lower compliance costs.
- Reduction in potential damage from future risks.

There are plenty more benefits as well as a few challenges, as with any major business process, but Operational Risk Management is an essential step for every company that is looking to avoid potentially damaging issues.

Working of Operational Risk Management

The first stage of any Operational Risk Management strategy is of course to understand the nature of your business and the particular risks associated with it. If you manage a company that runs water ski lessons, there will be risks your business will face that are very different to a company that creates technology for vending machines. Spending time worrying about risks that are nothing to do with you is just wasting time.

There are three levels of Operational Risk Management that you can choose to embark upon, and these are as follows:

- In-depth: As the name suggests, this is the kind of risk management that we would all be undertaking in an ideal world, as it will deliver the best results and practically make risk a thing of the past (not completely, of course, as not every risk is foreseeable). We don't live in an ideal world, but there are still many situations when you can take the time to plan for a new project or business venture with in-depth Operational Risk Management, which can include staff training or and the implementation of new policies and procedures.
- Deliberate: This is still not 'panic stations' in the world of risk management but is undertaken at various stages during the life cycle of a project or a business and can come in the form of routine safety checks or performance reviews.
- Time-Critical: This kind of Operational Risk Management involves more urgency as it is usually done in the midst of operational change when there is only a limited amount of time for it to be done before the potential consequences of any non-identified risks might start to be felt. The US Navy has the following processes for time-critical ORM: Assess the situation; Balance your resources: Communicate risks and intentions; and do and debrief.

Stages of Operational Risk Management

Those were the stages the Navy uses for time-critical Operational Risk Management, but for a more standard risk management process these are the usual stages you will need to undertake:

- Risk Identification: Understanding the risks specific to your business is key, but there are also many potential risks that affect any kind of business and you need to identify all of them, both those that are recurring and those that can be one-off events. The identification process needs to involve staff from all levels of the business if possible, bringing a variety of backgrounds and experiences to make a cohesive result. Risks that can be identified by work floor staff will be very different and no less critical than those identified from the boardroom.

- Risk Assessment: Once the risks have been identified, they need to be assessed. This needs to be done from both a quantitative and qualitative perspective and factors like the frequency and severity of occurrence need to be taken into consideration. The assessment needs to prioritize the management of these risks in relation to those factors.
- Measurement and Mitigation: Mitigating these risks (if not actually eliminating them altogether) is the next stage, with controls put in place that should limit the company's exposure to the risks and the potential damage caused by them.
- Monitoring and Reporting: Any Operational Risk Management plan must have something in place for the ongoing monitoring and reporting of these risks if only to demonstrate how effective the plan has been. Most of all, it's to ensure that the solutions put in place are continuing to be effective and doing their job in managing the risks.

There are other processes and models out there, particularly in the banking world, but most follow similar approaches to the one listed above.

ENTERPRISE RISK MANAGEMENT

Enterprise risk management (ERM) in business includes the methods and processes used by organizations to manage risks and seize opportunities related to the achievement of their objectives. ERM provides a framework for risk management, which typically involves identifying particular events or circumstances relevant to the organization's objectives (risks and opportunities), assessing them in terms of likelihood and magnitude of impact, determining a response strategy, and monitoring process. By identifying and proactively addressing risks and opportunities, business enterprises protect and create value for their stakeholders, including owners, employees, customers, regulators, and society overall.

ERM can also be described as a risk-based approach to managing an enterprise, integrating concepts of internal control, the Sarbanes–Oxley Act, data protection and strategic planning. ERM is evolving to address the needs of various stakeholders, who want to understand the broad spectrum of risks facing complex organizations to ensure they are appropriately managed. Regulators and debt rating agencies have increased their scrutiny on the risk management processes of companies.

The point of enterprise risk management is not to create more bureaucracy, but to facilitate discussion on what the really big risks are.

ERM Frameworks

There are various important ERM frameworks, each of which describes an approach for identifying, analyzing, responding to, and monitoring risks and opportunities, within the internal and external environment facing the enterprise. Management selects a *risk response strategy* for specific risks identified and analyzed, which may include:

- Avoidance: exiting the activities giving rise to risk.
- Reduction: taking action to reduce the likelihood or impact related to the risk.
- Alternative Actions: deciding and considering other feasible steps to minimize risks.
- Share or Insure: transferring or sharing a portion of the risk, to finance it.
- Accept: no action is taken, due to a cost/benefit decision.

Monitoring is typically performed by management as part of its internal control activities, such as review of analytical reports or management committee meetings with relevant experts, to understand how the risk response strategy is working and whether the objectives are being achieved.

Casualty Actuarial Society Framework

In 2003, the Casualty Actuarial Society (CAS) defined ERM as the discipline by which an organization in any industry assesses, controls, exploits, finances, and monitors risks from all sources for the purpose of increasing the organization's short- and long-term value to its stakeholders." The CAS conceptualized ERM as proceeding across the two dimensions of *risk type* and *risk management processes*. The risk types and examples include:

- Hazard risk: Liability torts, Property damage, Natural catastrophe
- Financial risk: Pricing risk, Asset risk, Currency risk, Liquidity risk
- Operational risk: Customer satisfaction, Product failure, Integrity, Reputational risk; Internal Poaching; Knowledge drain
- Strategic risks: Competition, Social trend, Capital availability

The risk management process involves:

- Establishing Context: This includes an understanding of the current conditions in which the organization operates on an internal, external and risk management context.
- Identifying Risks: This includes the documentation of the material threats to

the organization's achievement of its objectives and the representation of areas that the organization may exploit for competitive advantage.

- Analyzing/Quantifying Risks: This includes the calibration and, if possible, creation of probability distributions of outcomes for each material risk.
- Integrating Risks: This includes the aggregation of all risk distributions, reflecting correlations and portfolio effects, and the formulation of the results in terms of impact on the organization's key performance metrics.
- Assessing/Prioritizing Risks: This includes the determination of the contribution of each risk to the aggregate risk profile, and appropriate prioritization.
- Treating/Exploiting Risks: This includes the development of strategies for controlling and exploiting the various risks.
- Monitoring and Reviewing: This includes the continual measurement and monitoring of the risk environment and the performance of the risk management strategies.

COSO ERM Framework

The COSO "Enterprise Risk Management-Integrated Framework" published in 2004 (New edition COSO ERM 2017 is not Mentioned and the 2004 version is outdated) defines ERM as a "process, effected by an entity's board of directors, management, and other personnel, applied in strategy setting and across the enterprise, designed to identify potential events that may affect the entity, and manage risk to be within its risk appetite, to provide reasonable assurance regarding the achievement of entity objectives".

The COSO ERM Framework has eight Components and four objectives categories. It is an expansion of the COSO Internal Control-Integrated Framework published in 1992 and amended in 1994. The eight components - additional components highlighted - are:

- Authority and pledge to the ERM.
- Risk Management policy.
- Mixer of ERM in the institution.
- Risk Assessment.
- Risk Response.
- Communication and reporting.
- Information and communication.
- Monitoring.

The four objectives categories are:

- Strategy: High-level goals, aligned with and supporting the organization's mission.
- Operations: Effective and efficient use of resources.
- Financial Reporting: Reliability of operational and financial reporting.
- Compliance: Compliance with applicable laws and regulations.

ISO 31000: The new International Risk Management Standard

ISO 31000 is an International Standard for Risk Management which was published on 13 November 2009. An accompanying standard, ISO 31010 - Risk Assessment Techniques, soon followed together with the updated Risk Management vocabulary ISO Guide 73.

RIMS Risk Maturity Model

The RIMS Risk Maturity Model (RMM) for Enterprise Risk Management, published in 2006, is an umbrella framework of content and methodology that detail the requirements for sustainable and effective enterprise risk management. The RMM model consists of twenty-five competency drivers for seven attributes that create ERM's value and utility in an organization. The 7 attributes are:

- ERM-based approach.
- ERM process management.
- Risk appetite management.
- Root cause discipline.
- Uncovering risks.
- Performance management.
- Business resiliency and sustainability.

The model was developed by Steven Minsky, CEO of LogicManager, and published by the Risk and Insurance Management Society in collaboration with the RIMS ERM Committee. The Risk Maturity Model is based on the Capability Maturity Model, a methodology founded by the Carnegie Mellon University Software Engineering Institute (SEI) in the 1980s.

Implementing an ERM program

Goals of an ERM program

Organizations by nature manage risks and have a variety of existing departments or functions ("risk functions") that identify and manage particular risks. However, each risk function varies in capability and how it coordinates with other risk functions. A central goal and challenge of ERM is improving this capability and coordination, while integrating the output to provide a unified picture of risk for stakeholders and improving the organization's ability to manage the risks effectively.

Typical Risk Functions

The primary risk functions in large corporations that may participate in an ERM program typically include:

- Strategic planning: Identifies external threats and competitive opportunities, along with strategic initiatives to address them.
- Marketing: Understands the target customer to ensure product/service alignment with customer requirements.
- Compliance and Ethics: Monitors compliance with code of conduct and directs fraud investigations.
- Accounting/Financial compliance: Directs the Sarbanes-Oxley Section 302 and 404 assessment, which identifies financial reporting risks.
- Law Department: Manages litigation and analyzes emerging legal trends that may impact the organization.
- Insurance: Ensures the proper insurance coverage for the organization.
- Treasury: Ensures cash is sufficient to meet business needs, while managing risk related to commodity pricing or foreign exchange.
- Operational Quality Assurance: Verifies operational output is within tolerances
- Operations management: Ensures the business runs day-to-day and that related barriers are surfaced for resolution.
- Credit: Ensures any credit provided to customers is appropriate to their ability to pay.
- Customer service: Ensures customer complaints are handled promptly and root causes are reported to operations for resolution.
- Internal audit: Evaluates the effectiveness of each of the above risk functions and recommends improvements.

Common Challenges in ERM Implementation

Various consulting firms offer suggestions for how to implement an ERM program.

Common topics and challenges include:

- Identifying executive sponsors for ERM.
- Establishing a common risk language or glossary.
- Describing the entity's risk appetite (i.e., risks it will and will not take)
- Identifying and describing the risks in a "risk inventory".
- Implementing a risk-ranking methodology to prioritize risks within and across functions.
- Establishing a risk committee and or Chief Risk Officer (CRO) to coordinate certain activities of the risk functions.
- Establishing ownership for particular risks and responses.
- Demonstrating the cost-benefit of the risk management effort.
- Developing action plans to ensure the risks are appropriately managed.
- Developing consolidated reporting for various stakeholders.
- Monitoring the results of actions taken to mitigate risk.
- Ensuring efficient risk coverage by internal auditors, consulting teams, and other evaluating entities.
- Developing a technical ERM framework that enables secure participation by 3rd parties and remote employees.

Internal Audit Role

In addition to information technology audit, internal auditors play an important role in evaluating the risk-management processes of an organization and advocating their continued improvement. However, to preserve its organizational independence and objective judgment, Internal Audit professional standards indicate the function should not take any direct responsibility for making risk management decisions for the enterprise or managing the risk-management function.

Internal auditors typically perform an annual risk assessment of the enterprise, to develop a plan of audit engagements for the upcoming year. This plan is updated at various frequencies in practice. This typically involves review of the various risk assessments performed by the enterprise (e.g., strategic plans, competitive benchmarking, and SOX 404 top-down risk assessment), consideration of prior audits, and interviews with a variety of senior management. It is designed for identifying audit projects, not to identify, prioritize, and manage risks directly for the enterprise.

Current Issues in ERM

The risk management processes of corporations worldwide are under increasing regulatory and private scrutiny. Risk is an essential part of any business. Properly managed, it drives growth and opportunity. Executives struggle with business pressures that may be partly or completely beyond their immediate control, such as distressed financial markets; mergers, acquisitions and restructurings; disruptive technology change; geopolitical instabilities; and the rising price of energy.

Sarbanes-oxley Act Requirements

Section 404 of the Sarbanes-Oxley Act of 2002 required U.S. publicly traded corporations to utilize a control framework in their internal control assessments. Many opted for the COSO Internal Control Framework, which includes a risk assessment element. In addition, new guidance issued by the Securities and Exchange Commission (SEC) and PCAOB in 2007 placed increasing scrutiny on top-down risk assessment and included a specific requirement to perform a fraud risk assessment. Fraud risk assessments typically involve identifying scenarios of potential (or experienced) fraud, related exposure to the organization, related controls, and any action taken as a result.

NYSE Corporate Governance Rules

The New York Stock Exchange requires the Audit Committees of its listed companies to "discuss policies with respect to risk assessment and risk management." The related commentary continues: "While it is the job of the CEO and senior management to assess and manage the company's exposure to risk, the audit committee must discuss guidelines and policies to govern the process by which this is handled. The audit committee should discuss the company's major financial risk exposures and the steps management has taken to monitor and control such exposures. The audit committee is not required to be the sole body responsible for risk assessment and management, but, as stated above, the committee must discuss guidelines and policies to govern the process by which risk assessment and management is undertaken. Many companies, particularly financial companies, manage and assess their risk through mechanisms other than the audit committee. The processes these companies have in place should be reviewed in a general manner by the audit committee, but they need not be replaced by the audit committee".

ERM and Corporate Debt Ratings

Standard & Poor's (S&P), the debt rating agency, plans to include a series of questions about risk management in its company evaluation process. This will rollout to financial companies in 2007. The results of this inquiry is one of the many factors considered in debt rating, which has a corresponding impact on the interest rates lenders charge companies for loans or bonds. On May 7, 2008, S&P also announced that it would begin including an ERM assessment in its ratings for non-financial companies starting in 2009, with initial comments in its reports during Q4 2008.

IFC Performance Standards

IFC Performance Standard focuses on the management of Health, Safety, Environmental and Social risks. The third edition was published on January 1, 2012 after a two-year negotiation process with the private sector, governments and civil society organisations. It has been adopted by the Equator Banks, a consortium of over 90 commercial banks in 37 countries.

Data Privacy

Data privacy rules, such as the European Union's General Data Protection Regulation, increasingly foresee significant penalties for failure to maintain adequate protection of individuals' personal data such as names, e-mail addresses and personal financial information, or alert affected individuals when data privacy is breached. The EU regulation requires any organization--including organizations located outside the EU--to appoint a Data Protection Officer reporting to the highest management level if they handle the personal data of anyone living in the EU.

STRATEGIC RISK MANAGEMENT

Strategic risk management enables top management to link strategy with risk management in highly uncertain environment. Achievement of goals described in the strategy requires identification and dealing with risks. The strategic risk management is part of enterprise risk management (ERM) as defined by COSO (Committee of Sponsoring Organizations of the Treadway Commission) in *Enterprise Risk Management—Integrated Framework*in 2004.

As the environment becomes more and more turbulent, and long-term planning gets shorter and shorter due to inability to predict future, the strategic risk management becomes a necessary tool for managers. It helps extend planning and increase its accuracy, which translated into decline in losses related to bad strategic decisions.

Principles of Strategic Risk Management

M.L. Frigo and R.J. Anderson defined six principles of strategic risk management in relation to ERM:

- It's a process for identifying, assessing, and managing both internal and external events and risks that could impede the achievement of strategy and strategic objectives.

- The ultimate goal is creating and protecting shareholder and stakeholder value.
- It's a primary component and necessary foundation of the organization's overall enterprise risk management process.
- As a component of ERM, it is by definition effected by boards of directors, management, and others.
- It requires a strategic view of risk and consideration of how external and internal events or scenarios will affect the ability of the organization to achieve its objectives.
- It's a continual process that should be embedded in strategy setting, strategy execution, and strategy management.

Strategic Risk Management Process

The strategic risk management process was proposed by M. Tonello:

- Achieve a deep understanding of the strategy of the organization
- Gather views and data on strategic risks.
- Prepare a preliminary strategic risk profile.
- Validate and finalize the strategic risk profile.
- Develop a strategic risk management action plan.
- Communicate the strategic risk profile and strategic risk management action plan.
- Implement the strategic risk management action plan.

Implementation of SRMedit

Implementation of SRM in the enterprise requires to deal with four main issues:

- Corporate governance.
- Personnel.
- Reward mechanisms.
- Organization size, structure and culture.

If the goals of top management are different than those of enterprise owners, the increased exposure to risks is inevitable. The risk level accepted by managers can be lowered if they are also owners of the company. If the power of investors is low, the managers tend to take higher risks. Therefore, effective corporate governance is necessary for SRM to work properly.

The personnel should be prepared for risk events to avoid panic and wrong decisions. The managers should teach personnel how to behave in case of crisis situations. They should also create a set of procedures and risk management plans. The personnel and managers should be rewarded for good decisions related to risks. Some add that they should bc also punished for bad ones.

The whole implementation of SRM usually requires change in the organizational culture. In case of risk management, the communication systems should be fast and reliable, personnel must not be afraid of taking about risks. This helps to identify all the risks related to enterprise strategy.

PROJECT RISK MANAGEMENT

Project risk management is an important aspect of project management. Project risk is defined by PMI as, "an uncertain event or condition that, if it occurs, has a positive or negative effect on a project's objectives."

Project risk management remains a relatively undeveloped discipline, distinct from the risk management used by Operational, Financial and Underwriters' risk management. This gulf is due to several factors: Risk Aversion, especially public understanding and risk in social activities, confusion in the application of risk management to projects, and the additional sophistication of probability mechanics above those of accounting, finance and engineering.

With the above disciplines of Operational, Financial and Underwriting risk management, the concepts of risk, risk management and individual risks are nearly interchangeable; being either personnel or monetary impacts respectively. Impacts in project risk management are more diverse, overlapping monetary, schedule, capability, quality and engineering disciplines. For this reason, in project risk management, it is ncccssary to specify the differences (paraphrased from the "Department of Defense Risk, Issue, and Opportunity Management Guide for Defense Acquisition Programs"):

- Risk Management: Organizational policy for optimizing investments and (individual) risks to minimize the possibility of failure.
- Risk: The likelihood that a project will fail to meet its objectives.
- A risk: A single action, event or hardware component that contributes to an effort's "Risk."

An improvement on the PMBOK definition of risk management is to add a future date to the definition of a risk. Mathematically, this is expressed as a probability multiplied by an impact, with the inclusion of a future impact date and critical dates. This addition of future dates allows predictive approaches.

Good Project Risk Management depends on supporting organizational factors, having clear roles and responsibilities, and technical analysis.

Chronologically, Project Risk Management may begin in recognizing a threat, or by examining an opportunity. For example, these may be competitor developments or novel products. Due to lack of definition, this is frequently performed qualitatively, or semi-quantitatively, using product or averaging models. This approach is used to prioritize possible solutions, where necessary.

In some instances it is possible to begin an analysis of alternatives, generating cost and development estimates for potential solutions.

Risk Register

Identify		Analyze				Plan Response	Monitor and Control	
ID	Description	Category	Probability	Estim. Impact	Add. Workload, days	Status	Response Cost	Costs
1	Scope creep	Scope	0.25	5200	3	Response Planned	600	600
2	Initial plan mistake	Schedule	0.2	[illegible]	1	Occurred (issue)	[illegible]	[illegible]
3	The server with the project management software breaks down.	Operational	0.05	4700	0	Response Planned	1300	1300
4	Supplier increases the price	Financial	0.05	200	0	Response Planned	1200	1200
5	Supplier delays the delivery of major components	External	0.1	0	5	Not Treated	-	-
6	Product quality does not correspond to the initial requirements.	Quality	0.15	4500	1	Response Planned	2000	2000
7	People receive other priorities from their line managers.	Resource	0.25	1100	1	Response Planned	800	800
8	Lack of management support	Resource	0.2	0	4	Response Planned	-	-
9	Key people are unavailable	Resource	0.2	0	5	Not Treated	-	-

An example of the Risk Register that includes 4 steps: Identify, Analyze, Plan Response, Monitor and Control.

Once an approach is selected, more familiar risk management tools and a general project risk management process may be used for the new projects:

- A Planning risk management.
- Risk identification and monetary identification.
- Performing qualitative risk analysis.
- Communicating the risk to stakeholders and the funders of the project.
- Refining or iterating the risk based on research and new information.
- Monitoring and controlling risks.

Finally, risks must be integrated to provide a complete picture, so projects should be integrated into enterprise wide risk management, to seize opportunities related to the achievement of their objectives.

Project Risk Management Tools

In order to make project management effective, the managers use risk management tools. It is necessary to assume the measures referring to the same risk of the project and accomplishing its objectives.

The project risk management (PRM) system should be based on the competences of the employees willing to use them to achieve the project's goal. The system should track down all the processes and their exposure which occur in the project, as well as the circumstances that generate risk and determine their effects. Nowadays, the Big Data (BD) analysis appears an emerging method to create knowledge from the data being generated by different sources in production processes. According to Górecki, the BD seems to be the adequate tool for PRM.

COMPLIANCE RISK MANAGEMENT

Compliance risk management is the process of managing corporate compliance to meet regulations within a workable timeframe and budget. Not every regulated company manages this particularly well, and some even consider noncompliance fines as a normal cost of doing business. Their philosophy is that the fines are far cheaper than deploying and maintaining a compliance process.

This thinking is not limited to smaller and less sophisticated companies. Even very large companies may be aware of noncompliant activities, but if those activities are making a great deal of money than the organization may decide to look the other way. Wells Fargo is the poster child for this type of thinking.

However, as Wells Fargo found out approach is high risk. Regulators such as US attorneys are becoming more aggressive both by shortening compliance investigation timelines, and slapping on higher fines. In addition, noncompliance can be embarrassingly public, which leads to civil lawsuits, investor exodus, the eroding reputation.

Managing Compliance Risk

Managing compliance risk means having a workable plan, procedures, and technology to oversee compliance efforts. Taking the above four categories, let's look at managing risk by company sophistication and compliance levels:

- Little to no compliance risk management: If necessary, build the business case around the high risk of noncompliance. Form a compliance team to identify compliance needs and requirements, assess the existing compliance program, build a phased budget for objectives, and assign resources to reach the objectives.
- Aging compliance process and technology: Assess compliance and objectives, and invest in new technology. You may want to invest in one product for the entire corporation or point products for a few well-defined hot spots. Choices range from unified GRC frameworks to compliance point products such as financial reporting for SOX, compliant cloud storage for HIPAA, outgoing email checking, or auditing software.
- Active compliance program but millions of documents to review: Some compliance investigations require organizations to analyze and review millions of documents within a few weeks. Start now to research eDiscovery machine learning and automated compliance workflows. These platforms are not cheap but they save large amounts of money on the review process, and companies can leverage them for all legal and compliance discovery.
- Valuable IP is at risk without proactive compliance: It's much more effective to interrupt potential noncompliance before it turns into a violation. Digital communications monitoring analyzes suspicious patterns in digital messaging, such as employee texting and email patterns, social media, or chat.

You are never too far behind to become compliant, or too advanced that you don't need to worry about it anymore. Build in annual assessments to your compliance processes, and make sure that your compliance officers understand the changing regulations that might impact your industry. Also track the compliance technology industry for continual advancements and breakthroughs.

HEDGE

A hedge is an investment position intended to offset potential losses or gains that may be incurred by a companion investment. A hedge can be constructed from many types of financial instruments, including stocks, exchange-traded funds, insurance, forward contracts, swaps, options, gambles, many types of over-the-counter and derivative products, and futures contracts.

Public futures markets were established in the 19th century to allow transparent, standardized, and efficient hedging of agricultural commodity prices; they have since expanded to include futures contracts for hedging the values of energy, precious metals, foreign currency, and interest rate fluctuations.

Examples:

Agricultural Commodity Price Hedging

A typical hedger might be a commercial farmer. The market values of wheat and other crops fluctuate constantly as supply and demand for them vary, with occasional large moves in either direction. Based on current prices and forecast levels at harvest time, the farmer might decide that planting wheat is a good idea one season, but the price of wheat might change over time. Once the farmer plants wheat, he is committed to it for an entire growing season. If the actual price of wheat rises greatly between planting and harvest, the farmer stands to make a lot of unexpected money, but if the actual price drops by harvest time, he is going to lose the invested money.

Due to the uncertainty of future supply and demand fluctuations, and the price risk imposed on the farmer, the farmer in this example may use different financial transactions to reduce, or hedge, their risk. One such transaction is the use of forward contracts. Forward contracts are mutual agreements to deliver a certain amount of a commodity at a certain date for a specified price and each contract is unique to the buyer and seller. For this example, the farmer can sell a number of forward contracts equivalent to the amount of wheat he expects to harvest and essentially lock in the current price of wheat. Once the forward contracts expire, the farmer will harvest the wheat and deliver it to the buyer at the price agreed to in the forward contract. Therefore, the farmer has reduced his risks to fluctuations in the market of wheat because he has already guaranteed a certain number of bushels for a certain price. However, there are still many risks associated with this type of hedge. For example, if the farmer has a low yield year and he harvests less than the amount specified in the forward contracts, he must purchase the bushels elsewhere in order to fill the contract. This becomes even more of a problem when the lower yields affect the entire wheat industry and the price of wheat increases due to supply and demand pressures. Also, while the farmer hedged all of the risks of a price decrease away by locking in the price with a forward contract, he also gives up the right to the benefits of a price increase. Another risk associated with the forward contract is the risk of default or renegotiation. The forward contract locks in a certain amount and price at a certain future date. Because of that, there is always the possibility that the buyer will not pay the amount required at the end of the contract or that the buyer will try to renegotiate the contract before it expires.

Future contracts are another way our farmer can hedge his risk without a few of the risks that forward contracts have. Future contracts are similar to forward contracts except they are more standardized (i.e. each contract is the same quantity and date for everyone). These contracts trade on exchanges and are guaranteed through clearinghouses. Clearinghouses ensure that every contract is honored and they take the opposite side of every contract. Future contracts typically are more liquid than forward contracts and move with the market. Because of this, the farmer can minimize the risk he faces in the future through the selling of future contracts. Future contracts also differ from forward contracts in that delivery never happens. The exchanges and clearinghouses allow the buyer or seller to leave the contract early and cash out. So tying back into the farmer selling his wheat at a future date, he will sell short futures contracts for the amount that he predicts to harvest to protect against a price decrease. The current (spot) price of wheat and the price of the futures contracts for wheat converge as time gets closer to the delivery date, so in order to make money on the hedge, the farmer must close out his position earlier than then. On the chance that prices decrease in the future, the farmer will make a profit on his short position in the futures market which offsets any decrease in revenues from the spot market for wheat. On the other hand, if prices increase, the farmer will generate a loss on the futures market which is offset by an increase in revenues on the spot market for wheat. Instead of agreeing to sell his wheat to one person on a set date, the farmer will just buy and sell futures on an exchange and then sell his wheat wherever he wants once he harvests it.

Hedging a Stock Price

A common hedging technique used in the financial industry is the long/short equity technique.

A stock trader believes that the stock price of Company A will rise over the next month, due to the company's new and efficient method of producing widgets. He wants to buy Company A shares to profit from their expected price increase, as he believes that shares are currently underpriced. But Company A is part of a highly volatile widget industry. So there is a risk of a future event that affects stock prices across the whole industry, including the stock of Company A along with all other companies.

Since the trader is interested in the specific company, rather than the entire industry, he wants to *hedge out* the industry-related risk by short selling an equal value of shares from Company A's direct, yet weaker competitor, Company B.

The first day the trader's portfolio is:

- Long 1,000 shares of Company A at $1 each.
- Short 500 shares of Company B at $2 each.

The trader has sold short the same value of shares (the value, number of shares × price, is $1000 in both cases).

If the trader was able to short sell an asset whose price had a mathematically defined relation with Company A's stock price (for example a put option on Company A shares), the trade might be essentially riskless. In this case, the risk would be limited to the put option's premium.

On the second day, a favorable news story about the widgets industry is published and the value of all widgets stock goes up. Company A, however, because it is a stronger company, increases by 10%, while Company B increases by just 5%:

- Long 1,000 shares of Company A at $1.10 each: $100 gain.
- Short 500 shares of Company B at $2.10 each: $50 loss (in a short position, the investor loses money when the price goes up).

The trader might regret the hedge on day two, since it reduced the profits on the Company A position. But on the third day, an unfavorable news story is published about the health effects of widgets, and all widgets stocks crash: 50% is wiped off the value of the widgets industry in the course of a few hours. Nevertheless, since Company A is the better company, it suffers less than Company B:

Value of long position (Company A):

- Day 1: $1,000.
- Day 2: $1,100.
- Day 3: $550 => ($1,000 – $550) = $450 loss.

Value of short position (Company B):

- Day 1: –$1,000.
- Day 2: –$1,050.
- Day 3: –$525 => ($1,000 – $525) = $475 profit.

Without the hedge, the trader would have lost $450 (or $900 if the trader took the $1,000 he has used in short selling Company B's shares to buy Company A's shares as well). But the hedge – the short sale of Company B net a profit of $25 during a dramatic market collapse.

Stock/futures Hedging

The introduction of stock market index futures has provided a second means of hedging risk on a single stock by selling short the market, as opposed to another single or selection of stocks. Futures are generally highly fungible and cover a wide variety of potential investments, which makes them easier to use than trying to find another stock which somehow represents the opposite of a selected investment. Futures hedging is widely used as part of the traditional long/short play.

Hedging Employee Stock Options

Employee stock options (ESOs) are securities issued by the company mainly to its own executives and employees. These securities are more volatile than stocks. An efficient way to lower the ESO risk is to sell exchange traded calls and, to a lesser degree, to buy puts. Companies discourage hedging the ESOs but there is no prohibition against it.

Hedging Fuel Consumption

	Absense of hedging instrument	Presence of Hedging Instrument
Increase in Oil Price	Decrease in Revenue	Appreciation in Revenue due to the Change in Price of the Hedging Instrument
No Movement in Oil Price	No Change	Decrease in Revenue by the Cost of Hedging Instrument

Airlines use futures contracts and derivatives to hedge their exposure to the price of jet fuel. They know that they must purchase jet fuel for as long as they want to stay in business, and fuel prices are notoriously volatile. By using crude oil futures contracts to hedge their fuel requirements (and engaging in similar but more complex derivatives transactions), Southwest Airlines was able to save a large amount of money when buying fuel as compared to rival airlines when fuel prices in the U.S. rose dramatically after the 2003 Iraq war and Hurricane Katrina.

Hedging Emotions

As an emotion regulation strategy, people can bet against a desired outcome. A New England Patriots fan, for example, could bet their opponents to win to reduce the negative emotions felt if the team loses a game. People typically do not bet against desired outcomes that are important to their identity, due to negative signal about their identity that making such a gamble entails. Betting against your team or political candidate, for example, may signal to you that you are not as committed to them as you thought you were.

Types of Hedging

Hedging can be used in many different ways including foreign exchange trading. The stock example above is a "classic" sort of hedge, known in the industry as a pairs trade due to the trading on a pair of related securities. As investors became more sophisticated, along with the mathematical tools used to calculate values (known as models), the types of hedges have increased greatly.

Examples of hedging include:

- Forward exchange contract for currencies.
- Currency future contracts.
- Money Market Operations for currencies.

- Forward Exchange Contract for interest.
- Money Market Operations for interest.
- Future contracts for interest.
- Covered Calls on equities.
- Short Straddles on equities or indexes.
- Bets on elections or sporting events.

Hedging Strategies

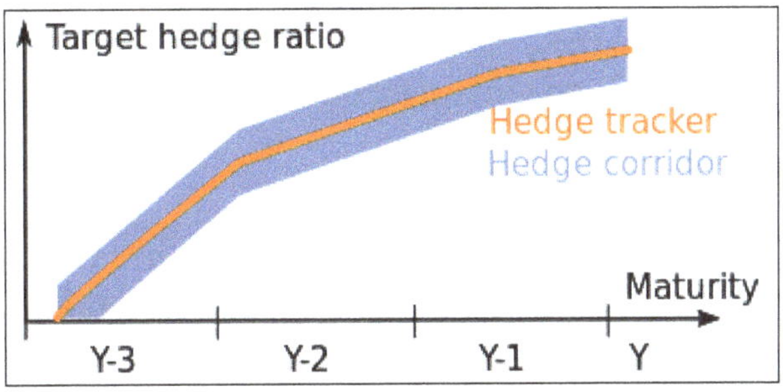

Tracker hedging. The fraction of open positions has to be within the (grey-blue) hedging corridor at every instance of time.

A hedging strategy usually refers to the general risk management policy of a financially and physically trading firm how to minimize their risks. As the term hedging indicates, this risk mitigation is usually done by using financial instruments, but a hedging strategy as used by commodity traders like large energy companies, is usually referring to a business model (including both financial *and* physical deals).

In order to show the difference between these strategies, consider the fictional company *BlackIsGreen Ltd* trading coal by buying this commodity at the wholesale market and selling it to households mostly in winter.

Back-to-back hedging

Back-to-back (B2B) is a strategy where any open position is immediately closed, e.g. by buying the respective commodity on the spot market. This technique is often applied in the commodity market when the customers' price is directly calculable from visible forward energy prices at the point of customer sign-up.

If *BlackIsGreen* decides to have a B2B-strategy, they would buy the exact amount of coal at the very moment when the household customer comes into their shop and signs the contract. This strategy minimizes many commodity risks, but has the drawback that it has a large volume and liquidity risk, as *BlackIsGreen* does not know whether it can find enough coal on the wholesale market to fulfill the need of the households.

Tracker Hedging

Tracker Hedging is a pre-purchase approach, where the open position is decreased the closer the maturity date comes.

If *BlackIsGreen* knows that most of the consumers demand coal in winter to heat their house, a strategy driven by a tracker would now mean that *BlackIsGreen* buys e.g. half of the expected coal volume in summer, another quarter in autumn and the remaining volume in winter. The closer the winter comes, the better are the weather forecasts and therefore the estimate, how much coal will be demanded by the households in the coming winter.

Retail customers' price will be influenced by long-term wholesale price trends. A certain *hedging corridor* around the pre-defined tracker-curve is allowed and fraction of the open positions decreases as the maturity date comes closer.

Delta Hedging

Delta-hedging mitigates the financial risk of an option by hedging against price changes in its underlying. It is called like that as Delta is the first derivative of the option's value with respect to the underlying instrument's price. This is performed in practice by buying a derivative with an inverse price movement. It is also a type of market neutral strategy.

Only if *BlackIsGreen* chooses to perform *delta-hedging* as strategy, actual financial instruments come into play for hedging (in the usual, stricter meaning).

Risk Reversal

Risk reversal means simultaneously buying a call option and selling a put option. This has the effect of simulating being long on a stock or commodity position.

Natural Hedges

Many hedges do not involve exotic financial instruments or derivatives such as the married put. A natural hedge is an investment that reduces the undesired risk by matching cash flows (i.e. revenues and expenses). For example, an exporter to the United States faces a risk of changes in the value of the U.S. dollar and chooses to open a production facility in that market to match its expected sales revenue to its cost structure.

Another example is a company that opens a subsidiary in another country and borrows in the foreign currency to finance its operations, even though the foreign interest rate may be more expensive than in its home country: by matching the debt payments to expected revenues in the foreign currency, the parent company has reduced its foreign currency exposure. Similarly, an oil producer may expect to receive its revenues in U.S. dollars, but faces costs in a different currency; it would be applying a natural hedge if it agreed to, for example, pay bonuses to employees in U.S. dollars.

One common means of hedging against risk is the purchase of insurance to protect against financial loss due to accidental property damage or loss, personal injury, or loss of life.

Categories of Hedgeable Risk

There are varying types of financial risk that can be protected against with a hedge. Those types of risks include:

- Commodity risk is the risk that arises from potential movements in the value of commodity contracts, which include agricultural products, metals, and energy products.
- Credit risk is the risk that money owing will not be paid by an obligor. Since credit risk is the natural business of banks, but an unwanted risk for commercial traders, an early market developed between banks and traders that involved selling obligations at a discounted rate.
- Currency risk (also known as Foreign Exchange Risk hedging) is used both by financial investors to deflect the risks they encounter when investing abroad and by non-financial actors in the global economy for whom multi-currency activities are a necessary evil rather than a desired state of exposure.
- Interest rate risk is the risk that the relative value of an interest-bearing liability, such as a loan or a bond, will worsen due to an interest rate increase. Interest rate risks can be hedged using fixed-income instruments or interest rate swaps.
- Equity risk is the risk that one's investments will depreciate because of stock market dynamics causing one to lose money.
- Volatility risk is the threat that an exchange rate movement poses to an investor's portfolio in a foreign currency. Volume risk is the risk that a customer demands more or less of a product than expected.

Hedging Equity and Equity Futures

Equity in a portfolio can be hedged by taking an opposite position in futures. To protect your stock picking against systematic market risk, futures are shorted when equity is purchased, or long futures when stock is shorted.

One way to hedge is the market neutral approach. In this approach, an equivalent dollar amount in the stock trade is taken in futures – for example, by buying 10,000 GBP worth of Vodafone and shorting 10,000 worth of FTSE futures (the index in which Vodafone trades).

Another way to hedge is the beta neutral. Beta is the historical correlation between a stock and an index. If the beta of a Vodafone stock is 2, then for a 10,000 GBP long position in Vodafone an investor would hedge with a 20,000 GBP equivalent short position in the FTSE futures.

Futures contracts and forward contracts are means of hedging against the risk of adverse market movements. These originally developed out of commodity markets in the 19th century, but over the last fifty years a large global market developed in products to hedge financial market risk.

Futures Hedging

Investors who primarily trade in futures may hedge their futures against synthetic futures. A synthetic in this case is a synthetic future comprising a call and a put position. Long synthetic futures means long call and short put at the same expiry price. To hedge against a long futures trade a short position in synthetics can be established, and vice versa.

Stack hedging is a strategy which involves buying various futures contracts that are concentrated in nearby delivery months to increase the liquidity position. It is generally used by investors to ensure the surety of their earnings for a longer period of time.

Contract for Difference

A contract for difference (CFD) is a two-way hedge or swap contract that allows the seller and purchaser to fix the price of a volatile commodity. Consider a deal between an electricity producer and an electricity retailer, both of whom trade through an electricity market pool. If the producer and the retailer agree to a strike price of $50 per MWh, for 1 MWh in a trading period, and if the actual pool price is $70, then the producer gets $70 from the pool but has to rebate $20 (the "difference" between the strike price and the pool price) to the retailer.

Conversely, the retailer pays the difference to the producer if the pool price is lower than the agreed upon contractual strike price. In effect, the pool volatility is nullified and the parties pay and receive $50 per MWh. However, the party who pays the difference is "out of the money" because without the hedge they would have received the benefit of the pool price.

Basis Risk

Basis risk in finance is the risk associated with imperfect hedging. It arises because of the difference between the price of the asset to be hedged and the price of the asset serving as the hedge, or because of a mismatch between the expiration date of the hedge asset and the actual selling date of the asset (calendar basis risk), or—as in energy—due to the difference in the location of the asset to be hedged and the asset serving as the hedge (locational basis risk).

Under these conditions, the spot price of the asset, and the futures price, do not converge on the expiration date of the future. The amount by which the two quantities differ measures the value of the basis risk.

- Basis = Futures price of contract – Spot price of hedged asset.
- Basis risk is not to bc confused with another type of risk known as price risk.

Examples:

Some examples of basis risks are:

- Treasury bill future being hedged by two year Bond, there lies the risk of not fluctuating as desired.
- Foreign currency exchange rate (FX) hedge using a non-deliverable forward contract (NDF): the NDF fixing might vary substantially from the actual available spot rate on the market on fixing date.
- Over-the-counter (OTC) derivatives can help minimize basis risk by creating a perfect hedge. This is because OTC derivatives can be tailored to fit the exact risk needs of a hedger.

Shape Risk

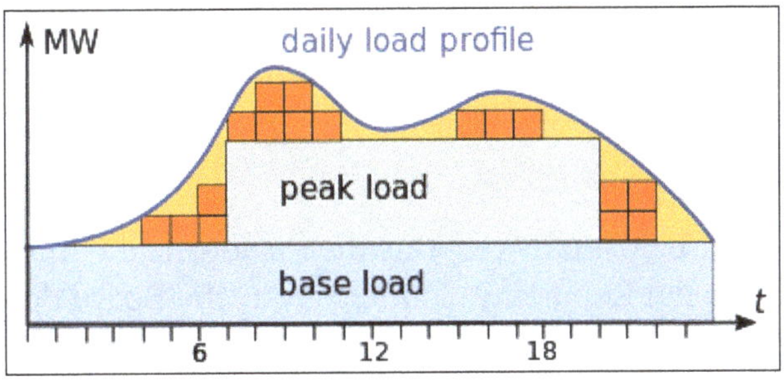

Forecasted load shape profile (in dark blue) and forward contracts for base load, peak load and several hourly contracts (in orange) bought under the assumption that buying energy on the spot market is cheaper than selling. The remaining (beige) shape exposure cannot be captured by contracts.

Shape risk in finance is a type of basis risk when hedging a load profile with standard hedging products having a lower granularity. In other words a commodity supplier wants to pre-purchase supplies for expected demand, but can only buy in fixed amounts that are bigger than the demand forecasted. This means it has to either over order or under order and make up the difference at the time of delivery at the spot price which might be much higher. Shape risk is also related to commodity risk.

For example an electricity provider has to produce or buy electricity in advance in order to distribute to its consumers based on forecasts i.e. how much energy will be consumed every minute on the following day. Such forecasts are usually based on the average historical consumption of the same set of customers; however, the provider can only produce e.g. only hourly blocks of electricity of 1MWh, and not smaller quantities. There is a certain financial risk that the provider produces too less energy and thus has to buy the remaining power from a market opponent for a high spot price to be able to fulfill the need of its customers.

RISK APPETITE

In risk management, risk appetite is the level of risk an organization is prepared to accept.

Risk appetite constraints are not easy to define; every organization can tolerate different levels of risk. It is important, however for the organization to establish a common understanding of risk and be prepared for the likelihood and impact of known threats. Organizations should define the maximum level of risk tolerance in each area of risk before taking action.

Organizations sometimes express their risk appetite through the creation of a risk appetite statement, a document that helps guide organizational risk management activities. The statement should be based on a review of the perspectives and concerns of all stakeholders and address the implications of current corporate strategies and practices.

Levels

The Board of Directors are normally responsible for setting an organisation's risk appetite. In the UK the Financial Reporting Council says: "the Board determines the nature, and extent, of the significant risks the company is willing to embrace." The appropriate level will depend on the nature of the work undertaken and the objectives pursued. For example, where public safety is critical (e.g. operating a nuclear power station) appetite will tend to be low, while for an innovative project (e.g. early development on an innovative computer program) it may be very high, with the acceptance of short term failure that could pave the way to longer term success.

Below are examples of broad approaches to setting risk appetite that a business may adopt to ensure a response to risk that is proportionate given their business objectives.

- Averse: Avoidance of risk and uncertainty is a key organization objective.
- Minimal: Preference for ultra-safe options that are low risk and only have a potential for limited reward.
- Cautious: Preference for safe options that have a low degree of risk and may only have limited potential for reward.

- Open: Willing to consider all potential options and choose the one most likely to result in successful delivery, while also providing an acceptable level of reward and value for money.
- Hungry: Eager to be innovative and to choose options offering potentially higher business rewards, despite greater inherent risk.

The appropriate approach may vary across an organization, with different parts of the business adopting an appetite that reflects their specific role, with an overarching risk appetite framework to ensure consistency.

Measurement

Precise measurement is not always possible and risk appetite will sometimes be defined by a broad statement of approach. An organization may have an appetite for some types of risk and be averse to others, depending on the context and the potential losses or gains.

However, often measures can be developed for different categories of risk. For example, it may aid a project to know what level of delay or financial loss it is permitted to bear. Where an organization has standard measures to define the impact and likelihood of risks, this can be used to define the maximum level of risk tolerable before action should be taken to lower it.

Purpose and Benefits

By defining its risk appetite, an organization can arrive at an appropriate balance between uncontrolled innovation and excessive caution. It can guide people on the level of risk permitted and encourage consistency of approach across an organisation.

Defined acceptable levels of risk also means that resources are not spent on further reducing risks that are already at an acceptable level.

Main Areas

In literature there are six main areas of risk appetite:

- Financial,
- Health,
- Recreational,
- Ethical,
- Social,
- Information.

There is often a confusion between *risk management* and *risk appetite*, with the rigor of the former now recovering some of its lost ground from the vagueness of the latter. Derived correctly the risk appetite is a consequence of a rigorous risk management analysis not a precursor. Simple risk management techniques deal with the impact of hazardous events, but this ignores the possibility of collateral effects of a bad outcome, such as for example becoming technically bankrupt. The quantity that can be put at risk depends on the cover available should there be a loss, and a proper analysis takes this into account. The "appetite" follows logically from this analysis. For example an organization should be "hungry for risk" if it has more than ample cover compared with its competitors and should therefore be able to gain greater returns in the market from high risk ventures.

RISK AVOIDANCE

Risk avoidance is the elimination of hazards, activities and exposures that can negatively affect an organization's assets.

Whereas risk management aims to control the damages and financial consequences of threatening events, risk avoidance seeks to avoid compromising events entirely.

While the complete elimination of all risk is rarely possible, a risk avoidance strategy is designed to deflect as many threats as possible in order to avoid the costly and disruptive consequences of a damaging event. A risk avoidance methodology attempts to minimize vulnerabilities which can pose a threat. Risk avoidance and mitigation can be achieved through policy and procedure, training and education and technology implementations.

RISK INTELLIGENCE

Risk intelligence (RQ) is the ability of an organization to gather information that will successfully identify uncertainties in the workplace.

An important goal of risk intelligence is to help the organization achieve a competitive advantage. Organizations with high risk intelligence tend to make more informed business and security decisions than those with low RQ.

Financial executive and Columbia University professor Leo Tilman defined risk intelligence. According to Tilman, risk intelligence is "the organizational ability to think holistically about risk and uncertainty, speak a common risk language and effectively use forward-looking risk concepts and tools in making better decisions, alleviating threats, capitalizing on opportunities and creating lasting value".

RISK ASSESSMENT

Risk assessment is the identification of hazards that could negatively impact an organization's ability to conduct business. These assessments help identify these inherent business risks and provide measures, processes and controls to reduce the impact of these risks to business operations.

Companies can use a risk assessment framework(RAF) to prioritize and share the details of the assessment, including any risks to their information technology (IT) infrastructure. The RAF helps an organization identify potential hazards and any business assets put at risk by these hazards, as well as potential fallout if these risks come to fruition.

In large enterprises, the risk assessment process is usually conducted by the Chief Risk Officer (CRO) or a Chief Risk Manager (CRM).

Risk Assessment Steps

How a risk assessment is conducted varies widely depending on the risks unique to the type of business, the industry that business is in and the compliance rules applied to that given business or industry. However, there are five general steps that companies can follow regardless of their business type or industry.

- Step 1: Identify the hazards. The first step in a risk assessment is to identify any potential hazards that, if they were to occur, would negatively influence the organization's ability to conduct business. Potential hazards that could be considered or identified during risk assessment include natural disasters, utility outages, cyberattacks and power failure.
- Step 2: Determine what, or who, could be harmed. After the hazards are identified, the next step is to determine which business assets would be negatively influenced if the risk came to fruition. Business assets deemed at risk to these hazards can include critical infrastructure, IT systems, business operations, company reputation and even employee safety.
- Step 3: Evaluate the risks and develop control measures. A risk analysis can help identify how hazards will impact business assets and the measures that can be put into place to minimize or eliminate the effect of these hazards on business assets. Potential hazards include property damage, business interruption, financial loss and legal penalties.
- Step 4: Record the findings. The risk assessment findings should be recorded by the company and filed as easily accessible, official documents. The records should include details on potential hazards, their associated risks and plans to prevent the hazards.

- Step 5: Review and update the risk assessment regularly. Potential hazards, risks and their resulting controls can change rapidly in a modern business environment. It is important for companies to update their risk assessments regularly to adapt to these changes.

Risk assessment tools, such as risk assessment templates, are available for different industries. They might prove useful to companies developing their first risk assessments or updating older assessments.

Quantitative vs. Qualitative

Risk assessments can be quantitative or qualitative. In a quantitative risk assessment, the CRO or CRM assigns numerical values to the probability an event will occur and the impact it would have. These numerical values can then be used to calculate an event's risk factor, which, in turn, can be mapped to a dollar amount.

Quantitative Risk Assessment Example

EVENT	LIKLIHOOD(A)	IMPACT (B)	RISK FACTOR(A xB)
Fire in data center	0.7	0.9	0.63
Loss of power	0.5	0.8	0.40
Staff illness	0.6	0.5	0.30
Huricane	0.4	0.9	0.36
Water leak	0.3	0.5	0.15
Employee forgot to log off	0.8	0.3	0.24

Qualitative risk assessments, which are used more often, do not involve numerical probabilities or predictions of loss. The goal of a qualitative approach is to simply rank which risks pose the most danger.

The Goal of Risk Assessments

Similar to risk assessment steps, the specific goals of risk assessments will likely vary based on industry, business type and relevant compliance rules. An information security risk assessment, for example, should identify gaps in the organization's IT security architecture, as well as review compliance with infosec-specific laws, mandates and regulations.

Some common goals and objectives for conducting risk assessments across industries and business types include the following:

- Developing a risk profile that provides a quantitative analysis of the types of threats the organization faces.

- Developing an accurate inventory of IT assets and data assets.
- Justifying the cost of security countermeasures to mitigate risks and vulnerabilities.
- Developing an accurate inventory of IT assets and data assets.
- Identifying, prioritizing and documenting risks, threats and known vulnerabilities to the organization's production infrastructure and assets.
- Determining budgeting to remediate or mitigate the identified risks, threats and vulnerabilities.
- Understanding the return on investment, if funds are invested in infrastructure or other business assets to offset potential risk.

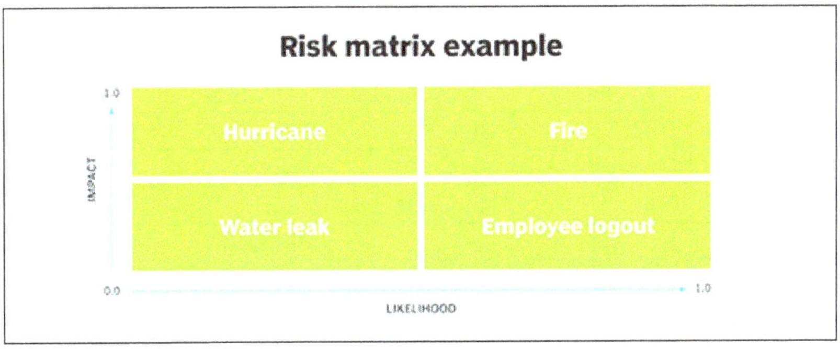

The ultimate goal of the risk assessment process is to evaluate hazards and determine the inherent risk created by those hazards. The assessment should not only identify hazards and their potential effects, but should also identify potential control measures to offset any negative impact on the organization's business processes or assets.

RISK MATRIX

A Risk Matrix is a matrix that is used during risk assessment to define the level of risk by considering the category of probability or likelihood against the category of consequence severity. This is a simple mechanism to increase visibility of risks and assist management decision making.

Risk is the lack of certainty about the outcome of making a particular choice. Statistically, the level of downside risk can be calculated as the product of the probability that harm occurs (e.g., that an accident happens) multiplied by the severity of that harm (i.e., the average amount of harm or more conservatively the maximum credible amount of harm). In practice, the risk matrix is a useful approach where either the probability or the harm severity cannot be estimated with accuracy and precision.

Although standard risk matrices exist in certain contexts (e.g. US DoD, NASA, ISO), individual projects and organizations may need to create their own or tailor an existing risk matrix. For example, the harm severity can be categorized as:

- Catastrophic: Multiple deaths.
- Critical: One death or multiple severe injuries.
- Marginal: One severe injury or multiple minor injuries.
- Negligible: One minor injury.

The probability of harm occurring might be categorized as 'certain', 'likely', 'possible', 'unlikely' and 'rare'. However it must be considered that very low probabilities may not be very reliable.

The resulting risk matrix could be:

	Negligible	Marginal	Critical	Catastrophic
Certain	High	High	Extreme	Extreme
Likely	Moderate	High	High	Extreme
Possible	Low	Moderate	High	Extreme
Unlikely	Low	Low	Moderate	Extreme
Rare	Low	Low	Moderate	High

The company or organization then would calculate what levels of risk they can take with different events. This would be done by weighing the risk of an event occurring against the cost to implement safety and the benefit gained from it.

Example Matrix

The following is an example matrix of possible personal injuries, with particular accidents allocated to appropriate cells within the matrix:

	Negligible	Marginal	Critical	Catastrophic
Certain	Stubbing Toe			
Likely		Fall		
Possible			Major Car Accident	
Unlikely			Aircraft crash	
Rare				Major Tsunami

Problems

Tony Cox argues that risk matrices experience several problematic mathematical features making it harder to assess risks. These are:

- Poor resolution. Typical risk matrices can correctly and unambiguously compare only a small fraction (e.g., less than 10%) of randomly selected pairs of hazards. They can assign identical ratings to quantitatively very different risks ("range compression").

- Errors. Risk matrices can mistakenly assign higher qualitative ratings to quantitatively smaller risks. For risks with negatively correlated frequencies and severities, they can be "worse than useless," leading to worse-than-random decisions.

- Suboptimal resource allocation. Effective allocation of resources to risk-reducing countermeasures cannot be based on the categories provided by risk matrices.

- Ambiguous inputs and outputs. Categorizations of severity cannot be made objectively for uncertain consequences. Inputs to risk matrices (e.g., frequency and severity categorizations) and resulting outputs (i.e., risk ratings) require subjective interpretation, and different users may obtain opposite ratings of the same quantitative risks. These limitations suggest that risk matrices should be used with caution, and only with careful explanations of embedded judgments.

Thomas, Bratvold, and Bickel demonstrate that risk matrices produce arbitrary risk rankings. Rankings depend upon the design of the risk matrix itself, such as how large the bins are and whether or not one uses an increasing or decreasing scale. In other words, changing the scale can change the answer.

Douglas W. Hubbard and Richard Seiersen take the general research from Cox, Thomas, Bratvold, and Bickel, and provide specific discussion in the realm of cybersecurity risk. They point out that since 61% of cyber security professionals use some form of risk matrix, this can be a serious problem. Hubbard and Seiersen consider these problems in the context of other measured human errors and conclude that "The errors of the experts are simply further exacerbated by the additional errors introduced by the scales and matrices themselves. There is no need for cybersecurity (or other areas of risk analysis that also use risk matrices) to reinvent well-established quantitative methods used in many equally complex problems".

Risk Assessment Framework

A risk assessment framework (RAF) is a strategy for prioritizing and sharing information about the security risks to an information technology (IT) infrastructure.

A good RAF organizes and presents information in a way that both technical and non-technical personnel can understand. It has three important components: a shared vocabulary, consistent assessment methods and a reporting system.

The common view an RAF provides helps an organization see which of its systems are at low risk for abuse or attack and which are at high risk. The data an RAF provides is useful for addressing potential threats pro-actively, planning budgets and creating a culture in which the value of data is understood and appreciated.

There are several risk assessment frameworks that are accepted as industry standards including:

- Risk Management Guide for Information Technology Systems (NIST guide) from the National Institute of Standards.
- Operationally Critical Threat, Asset, and Vulnerability Evaluation (OCTAVE) from the Computer Emergency Readiness Team.
- Control Objectives for Information and related Technology (COBIT) from the Information Systems Audit and Control Association.

To create a risk management framework, an organization can use or modify the NIST guide, OCTAVE or COBIT or create a framework inhouse that fits the organization's business requirements. However the framework is built, it should:

- Inventory and categorize all IT assets.
- Assets include hardware, software, data, processes and interfaces to external systems.
- Identify threats.
- Natural disasters or power outages should be considered in addition to threats such as malicious access to systems or malware attacks.
- Identify corresponding vulnerabilities.
- Data about vulnerabilities can be obtained from security testing and system scans. Anecdotal information about known software and/or vendor issues should also be considered.
- Prioritize potential risks.
- Prioritization has three sub-phases: evaluating existing security controls, determining the likelihood and impact of a breach based on those controls, and assigning risk levels.
- Document risks and determine action.
- This is an on-going process, with a pre-determined schedule for issuing reports. The report should document the risk level for all IT assests, define what level of risk an organization is willing to tolerate and accept and identify procedures at each risk level for implementing and maintaining security controls.

BENEFITS OF RISK MANAGEMENT

Fewer Surprises

The whole aim of risk management is to identify threats. What every organization needs is a robust system where threats are addressed in a timely fashion and are mitigated by relevant personnel. Managing and addressing risks will, at the end of the day, lead to less expense and unnecessary publicity that can be damaging to a company's reputation.

A simple example of this is introducing a new product to market. Mercedes Benz spends on average six years developing one of their cars before launching it, whereas Alfa Romeo launched the Giulia in just two and a half years. This is something that could have been avoided if they had planned out the process of bringing a new product to market, and taken into consideration the potential risks involved.

Realistic Expectations

Great risk management helps senior management to be realistic when it comes to forecasting the possibilities of success. By setting achievable goals, an organization's leadership also helps to improve the morale of the whole team and support productivity.

Efficient Decisions Made

One of the chief benefits of enterprise risk management is that your decisions are powered by good information. A robust risk management system will be intuitive and comprehensive, offering you data right across the board so you can make more effective decisions. Ideally, a risk management system works best when linked to a project management dashboard with real-time data.

A prime example of this was when Tata Motors offered to buy Jaguar and Land Rover from the Ford Motor Company in 2008. Nine years later in 2017, Jaguar and Land Rover finished the year with record sales volumes. Tata Motors had clearly done its homework, knowing the various risks involved in purchasing both brands and forecasting correctly.

Escalation

Another benefit of risk management services is that tiers can be created so that risks, depending on their severity, can be escalated from junior management to middle management and, finally, to senior management. Low-level risks are something that shouldn't take up the time, effort and energy of higher management who will have more important things to consider and pursue.

An easy-to-understand global example would be the risk assessment of a tsunami based on geographical location. This document by UNESCO – Tsunami risk assessment and mitigation for the Indian Ocean – and what to do about it – gives a comprehensive outline of what a tsunami is, why it happens, and what measures you can take to safeguard yourself from it.

UNESCO reviews tsunami warning systems, UNESCO.

Focused on Risk

The benefits of a risk management plan and the benefits of risk management in projects are vast. But one of the main advantages is that they create a culture that's focused on risk. This means that a conversation on risk and how it can be mitigated is started on all levels of the company structure; something that is highly desired since proactive ideas and mechanisms can be discussed and put in place.

References

- Business-risk-management: whatissixsigma.net, Retrieved 25 March, 2019
- Risk-avoidance, computer-science: sciencedirect.com, Retrieved 28 May, 2019
- The-risk-management-process-in-5-steps, risk-management-blog-47395: clearrisk.com, Retrieved 14 April, 2019
- Operational-risk-management: tallyfy.com, Retrieved 08 June, 2019
- Strategic-risk-management: ccopcdia.org, Retrieved 23 July, 2019
- What-is-compliance-risk-management: enterprisefeatures.com, Retrieved 19 May, 2019
- Risk-intelligence-RQ: searchcompliance.techtarget.com, Retrieved 12 January, 2019
- Risk-assessment-framework-RAF: searchcio.techtarget.com, Retrieved 29 August, 2019

Risk Analysis

3 CHAPTER

The identification and assessment of the factors that may negatively impact the success of a project is known as risk analysis. Hillier tree analysis, value tree analysis, event tree analysis, break-even analysis, etc. are some of the concepts studied within it. The topics in this chapter will help in gaining a better perspective about these related concepts of risk analysis.

Risk analysis is the review of the risks associated with a particular event or action. It is applied to projects, information technology, security issues and any action where risks may be analyzed on a quantitative and qualitative basis. Risk analysis is a component of risk management.

Risks are part of every IT project and business endeavor. As such, risk analysis should occur on a recurring basis and be updated to accommodate new potential threats. Strategic risk analysis minimizes future risk probability and damage.

The risk management process involves a few key steps. First, potential threats are identified. For example, risks are associated with individuals using a computer either incorrectly or inappropriately, which creates security risks. Risks are also related to projects that are not completed in a timely manner, resulting in significant costs.

Next, quantitative and/or qualitative risk analysis is applied to study identified risks. Quantitative risk analysis measures expected risk probability to forecast estimated financial losses from potential risks. Qualitative risk analysis does not use numbers but reviews threats, and determines and establishes risk mitigation methods and solutions.

A contingency plan may be used during risk analysis. If a risk is presented, contingency plans help minimize damage.

RISK ANALYSIS TECHNIQUES

The purpose of the risk analysis technique is to identify all the uncertainties that may have an impact on your initiative. Risks can come up whether or not you decide to take action in a specific direction. For instance, there could be risks associated with doing nothing.

Risk estimation or analysis is a process of forecasting the likelihood or probability of future events using data from previous events and/or details of the design of the plant in question. At its simplest level it can be the estimation of the unreliability of essential equipment. Reliability techniques have been under development for most of this century particularly in the aircraft and defence industries. However, since the 1970s the nuclear industry has taken the lead in developing risk analysis techniques. An early example was NRC's Reactor Safety Study[5] in which the probability of nuclear accidents and their consequences were estimated. Since then, probabilistic techniques have been used as part of the design process, as at Sizewell "B" for example, and as an aid to determining the acceptability of a given design or design change.

- Failure modes and effects analysis (FMEA).
- Event tree analysis.
- Fault tree analysis.

The first step in any analysis, however, is to set down details of the overall plant, possibly in functional block diagram form if the system is complex. In a functional block diagram each part of the plant carrying out a particular function is represented by a single building block, the diagram then showing the interrelationships between the various blocks. All activities and processes need to be understood including details of any protective features.

The next step carefully and systematically identifies all the potential hazards and all the ways that the hazard can be generated. FMEA can be used to determine the initiating events or causes which could lead to the hazard. The technique is described as "bottom-up" since individual failures are traced forward to the final effect.

The results of an FMEA are summarized in truth or decision tables. The results are categorized according to their severity and estimates obtained of their probability of occurrence. This enables priorities for corrective action to be undertaken at the design stage. In practice, however, FMEA is primarily used to determine the effect of component failures, whether electrical, mechanical or structural, on a single system and not on the whole of a complex plant. The significance of failure of each component is then studied in turn. FMEA is an effective way of identifying all single faults which could cause system failure.

The event tree approach is used on a complex plant and is similar to an FMEA in that all possible sequences, following any postulated initiating event, are constructed. It is often convenient to group together similar initiating events. A simple event tree can be illustrated by considering the example shown in figure.

Figure represents a hypothetical fire protection system provided to extinguish any fire which might occur in a particular room in a building. Two electric pumps are provided to deliver water to a sprinkler system through an electrically operated valve. Water is taken from a reservoir. An automatic fire sensing system starts the pumps. The design intent is that one pump suffices. In this example the nonreturn valves in the system are assumed always to work. As a further line of defence to stop any fire spreading and causing extensive damage outside the room a fire door is provided, electrically driven, but manually operated. The fire door and the sprinkler system are each assumed to be 100% effective if they operate. Note, the example is not meant to be representative of any practical arrangement. One way of drawing the corresponding event tree is shown in figure.

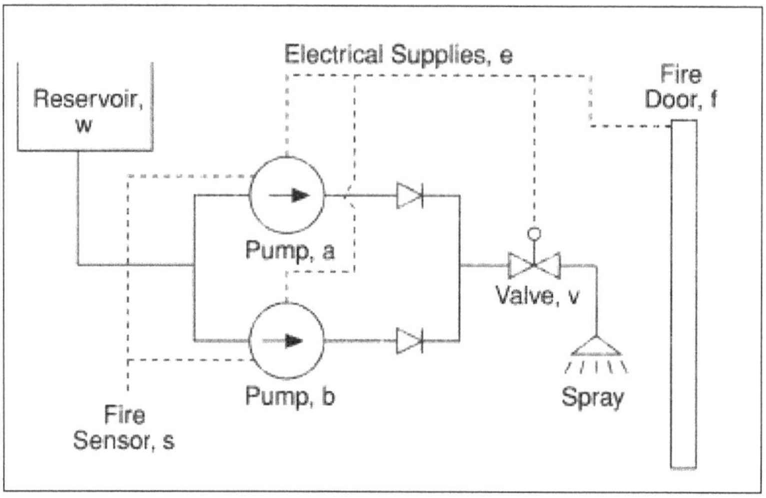

Hypothetical fire protection system.

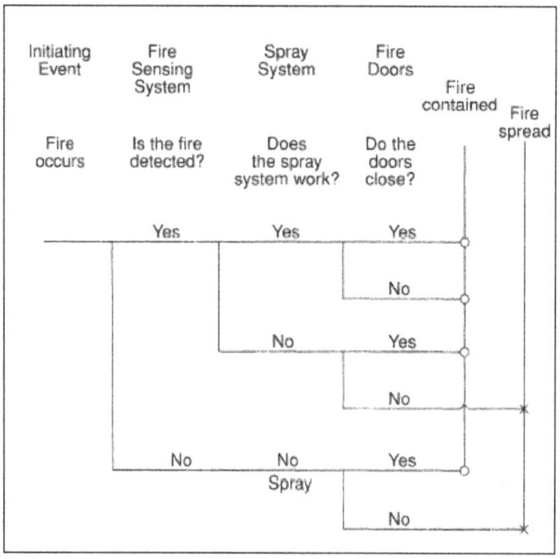

Event tree.

Along the top are listed all the items which should work. Starting with the initiating event, the fire, the first question asked is whether the automatic fire sensing system has worked. If it has then that is a success and the branch continues straight across; a step down indicates failure. Each branch then leads to a further question. The top branch leads do the question "does the spray system work?" The answer "yes" leads straight across; the answer "no" is represented by the branch which steps down. In this way is developed a tree of all possible sequences. In this example, the sequences whose end points are marked with a circle are deemed a success, although any success states claimed have to be demonstrated by calculation or other evidence. Those with a cross are failures. The probability of failure at each branch could also be added and hence the probability of each sequence evaluated. The total probability of failure is then obtained by summing all the failure sequence probabilities. In this example the failure probability of the overall spray system has to be input; this can be obtained from a fault tree analysis or, if desired, the event tree can be expanded to represent individual components. In general, the event tree is particularly useful in identifying those sequences which have to be shown by subsequent analysis to be acceptable because of their high probability.

Event trees, however, are usually constructed at a level with systems represented by blocks. Care has to be exercised to ensure that dependencies are correctly represented. In the example shown, if electrical failure is the main cause of spray system failure then it would equally stop the fire door from being closed, and an optimistic result could occur if the two events were assumed unrelated. The problem could be overcome by giving the question of electrical failure its own branch point in the tree.

It may be, however, that the consequences are not defined in such a simplistic way as in the above example. Sequences are continued until any risk is fully identified. In the case of a chemical plant or nuclear power station the risk to be established could be the risk of death to an individual, or societal risk from a release of toxic chemicals or radioactive material. The aim of any risk analysis would be to show that any residual risk was sufficiently low as to be deemed tolerable. Methods of analyzing the probability of release of harmful releases are specific to particular industries.

The fault tree approach treats any problem in a "top-down" manner. Whereas event trees identify a range of possible outcomes, fault trees identify ail contributors towards one specified outcome—the "top event". It is a logic diagram used to determine how a defined risk can occur either at the component level or at the system level. Consider again the system shown in figure. Using capital letters to designate failure states a fault tree can be drawn for this system as shown in figure, using symbols based upon those used in the NRC study. The top event is the event we are interested in—the possibility of fire spread outside the equipment room. The AND gate underneath shows that the top event will only occur if all the input events, namely, the fire door not having been closed and the sprinkler system having failed to extinguish the fire. The AND gate at the next level down shows that the sprinkler system is only ineffective if there is no flow from pump "a" and no flow from pump "b". An OR gate defines the situation if one or more of the input events exist. Thus, the tree shows that the fire door remains open if either the electrical supply fails or if it fails because it jams (or because the operator failed to act). The branches end at a "basic" event which needs no further development because failure rate data are known or are assumed.

Using capital letters to represent the failure probability of the corresponding item, the probability of the top event, T, can be set down using the notation of Boolean algebra. The symbol for "and" is a dot, and for "or" the plus sign, +. This gives:

$$T = \{(A + E + W + V + S).(B + E + W + V + S)\}.(F + E)$$

This expression can be simplified by applying the logical rules of Boolean algebra[6]. For example, A.A = A = A + A.B and so on. In this way the expression is reduced to:

$$T = F.A.B + F.W + F.V + FS + E$$

Boolean reduction automatically takes into account the fact that loss of electrics is a contributing factor to the failure of a number of items. Component failure probabilities can be substituted to obtain system failure probability. (F.A.B), (F.W), (F.V), (F.S) and (E) are "Minimal Cut Sets" of components. In any minimal cut set all the component failures of which it consists must occur to result in system failure, but no other simultaneous failure is necessary. A "Non-minimal Cut Set" includes components whose failures can be tolerated. Boolean algebra identifies all the minimal cut-sets.

Only relatively simple systems can be analyzed by hand. Complex systems require the use of computer codes. Such codes can have a significant commercial value and new codes offering greater flexibility are continually appearing.

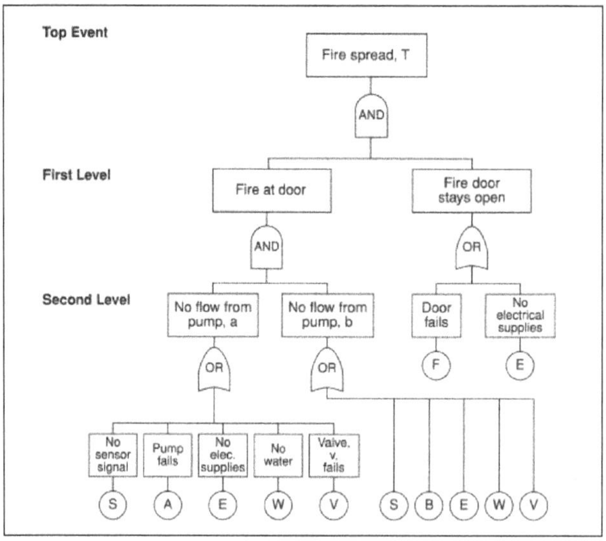

Fault tree

The value of any risk analysis obviously depends upon its completeness and whether all important initiating events and fault sequences have been identified. Certain aspects are difficult to model, such as the effect of human intervention, which may be either beneficial or harmful. When low probability risks are being evaluated the contribution from outside hazards such as aircraft crashing on the plant, earthquakes or extreme environmental conditions may be important. Failure rate data may not always be available or directly applicable and so judgements regarding its applicability may have to be applied. A particular difficulty can be the treatment of common cause failures. A common cause failure is an event which could cause simultaneous failure on a number of similar components and hence eliminate any benefit from redundancy or even diversity. A failure mode affecting similar components is sometimes referred to as a common mode failure.

It follows that there can be uncertainties associated with any risk analysis, and that judgement need to be exercised in using the results. A risk calculation may be carried out at the design stage or on a completed plant or piece of equipment. The mere process of carrying out a risk assessment at the design stage is valuable, however, since it can identify ways of improving the design and reducing the risk.

SENSITIVITY ANALYSIS

Sensitivity analysis is the quantitative risk assessment of how changes in a specific model variable impacts the output of the model. It is also a key result of Monte Carlo simulations of project schedules. Often referred to as a Tornado chart, sensitivity analysis shows which task variables (Cost, Start and Finish Times, Duration, etc) have the greatest impact on project parameters.

A sensitivity analysis determines how different values of an independent variable affect a particular dependent variable under a given set of assumptions. In other words, sensitivity analyses study how various sources of uncertainty in a mathematical model contribute to the model's overall uncertainty. This technique is used within specific boundaries that depend on one or more input variables.

Sensitivity analysis is used in the business world and in the field of economics. It is commonly used by financial analysts and economists, and is also known as a what-if analysis.

Working of Sensitivity Analysis

Sensitivity analysis is a financial model that determines how target variables are affected based on changes in other variables known as input variables. This model is also referred to as what-if or simulation analysis. It is a way to predict the outcome of a decision given a certain range of variables. By creating a given set of variables, an analyst can determine how changes in one variable affect the outcome.

Both the target and input—or independent and dependent—variables are fully analyzed when sensitivity analysis is conducted. The person doing the analysis looks at how the variables move as well as how the target is affected by the input variable.

Sensitivity analysis can be used to help make predictions in the share prices of public companies. Some of the variables that affect stock prices include company earnings, the number of shares outstanding, the debt-to-equity ratios (D/E), and the number of competitors in the industry. The analysis can be refined about future stock prices by making different assumptions or adding different variables. This model can also be used to determine the effect that changes in interest rates have on bond prices. In this case, the interest rates are the independent variable, while bond prices are the dependent variable.

Sensitivity analysis allows for forecasting using historical, true data. By studying all the variables and the possible outcomes, important decisions can be made about businesses, the economy, and about making investments.

Example of Sensitivity Analysis

Assume Sue is a sales manager who wants to understand the impact of customer traffic on total sales. She determines that sales are a function of price and transaction volume. The price of a widget is $1,000, and Sue sold 100 last year for total sales of $100,000. Sue also determines that a 10% increase in customer traffic increases transaction volume by 5%. This allows her to build a financial model and sensitivity analysis around this equation based on what-if statements. It can tell her what happens to sales if customer traffic increases by 10%, 50%, or 100%. Based on 100 transactions today, a 10%, 50%, or 100% increase in customer traffic equates to an increase in transactions by 5%, 25%, or 50% respectively. The sensitivity analysis demonstrates that sales are highly sensitive to changes in customer traffic.

Benefits and Limitations of Sensitivity Analysis

Conducting sensitivity analysis provides a number of benefits for decision-makers. First, it acts as an in-depth study of all the variables. Because it's more in-depth, the predictions may be far more reliable. Secondly, It allows decision-makers to identify where they can make improvements in the future. Finally, it allows for the ability to make sound decisions about companies, the economy, or their investments.

But there are some disadvantages to using a model such as this. The outcomes are all based on assumptions because the variables are all based on historical data. This means it isn't exactly accurate, so there may be room for error when applying the analysis to future predictions.

Sensitivity Analysis in Project Management

In a very simple example, you have 2 materials with their most likely estimated low and high ranges.

- Material A: $1000 ($750 – $1500).
- Material B: $10,000 ($9950 – $10, 100).
- Total Base Cost is $11, 000.

We want to understand how variances in the cost of specific materials impacts the variance of the total project costs. If we can identify what is causing the most cost variance, it may be possible to manage this risk in such a way to provide higher level of confidence in the expected cost of the project.

If we run a Monte Carlo risk analysis, we will see that expected cost can range from a low of $10,500 and a high of $12000, a $1500 possible variance. the goal of the sensitivity analysis is not to identify which input "costs" the most, but which one has strongest relationship between the its cost and the $1500 range we get from the results of the simulation. In a very simple example like the one above the answer is obvious and we get a correlation of .998 % between the cost of material A and Total Project Cost. The cost of material B, even though it is much higher, only has a correlation of .05 %. So if we want to improve cost surety, we should focus on minimizing the variance in material A. A possible management strategy would be to purchase all materials in advance for a slightly higher guaranteed price.

SCENARIO ANALYSIS

Scenario analysis is a way of predicting future values based on certain potential events. Experts use scenario analysis to predict what might happen to an investment portfolio, for example, if specific events occur or don't occur. Economists and statisticians use scenario analysis to analyze and predict possible future events by considering *alternative worlds* – alternative possible outcomes.

Analysts, economists, company managers and directors, statisticians, and other professionals use scenario analysis – also known as *total return analysis* or *horizon analysis* – to test their plans against a number of possible scenarios to see what could happen if things do not go according to plan.

It is an important technique used by risk management professionals to help companies make sure they do not carry too much risk.

The risk manager presents the company with the results of his or her scenario analysis – he or she is not usually expected to put forward a scenario the company should take.

Purpose of Scenario Analysis

Scenario analysis can be done for many reasons such as:

- Through scenario analysis, investors & business managers can determine the amount of risk they are taking before making the investment or starting a new project.

- It is a way of structured thinking about the future. As scenario analysis helps identify potential future problems, we can take necessary precautions to eliminate the problems or reduce the impact of these problems.

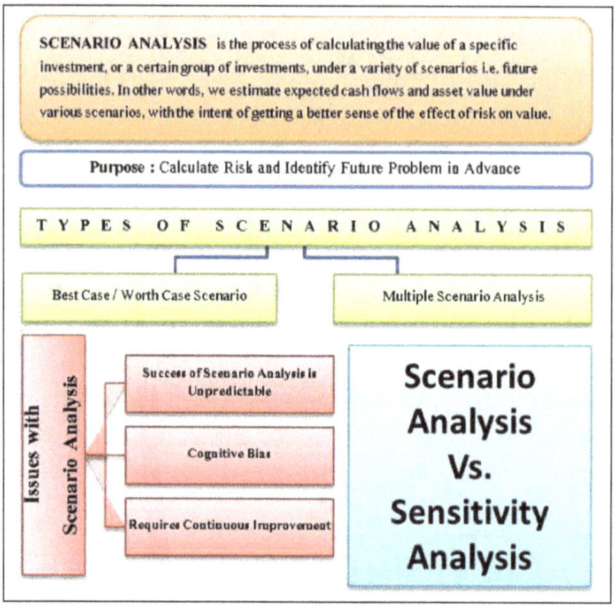

Types of Scenarios

There are mainly two types of scenario analysis that are widespread & used by most executives, managers, and investors. Following are the two types:

Best Case/ Worst Case Scenario

Many times we realize that the actual outcome of an investment is much different than the one we have assumed. This is because we make assumptions and predict the outcomes based on our assumptions. But we never question whether our assumptions are right or wrong? Are there any other possibilities?

When we do best case/ worst case scenario analysis, we consider multiple assumptions. In the best case scenario, each input value is set to the best. For example, the economy & industry will grow at 6% (best growth rate), we assume best projections and so on. Then we determine an outcome. This brings us to the situation where we say "if every factor works out to the best, we will have X amount of returns".

On the other hand, when we take worst case scenario, each input value is set to the worse and we can conclude that "if every factor works out to the worse, we will have Y amount of returns".

The best case/ worst case scenario gives out a range to the decision maker. For example, if we are doing a best case/ worst case scenario analysis for the stock price of Company A, we might get a result such as – In the best case, we will get a return of 12%, and in the worst case, we will get a return of 8%. So the investor will know for sure that his returns will be between 8% and 12%. This will help him make better decisions.

Multiple Scenario Analysis

Scenario analysis does not have to be restricted to the best and worst cases. In fact, most of the time the value of a particular investment is predicted taking multiple scenarios into questions. For example if Apple Inc. wants to predict its future sales, then it can take multiple scenarios such as if cell phone industry increases by 10% P.A., we will have X sales, if it increases by 15% P.A. we will have Y sales and if it increases by 20% P.A. we will have Z sales. This way they can predict multiple future outcomes and be more prepared.

Issues in Scenario Analysis

Success of Scenario Analysis is Unpredictable

We might do a proper detailed scenario analysis, get facts right, make clear assumptions about all the scenarios, but we can never know if the scenario will play out exactly as we expect it to. For example, suppose a manager of a chocolate manufacturing company might assume that in the year 2017 if world chocolate consumers increase by 20% then his sale would rise by 10%. He came to this conclusion after following step by step structured approach to scenario analysis. But when the year ended he realized that the world chocolate consumers increased by 22% but his sales increased only by 5%. After further investigation, he found that the increased consumers preferred white chocolate, while he manufactured milk chocolate. By this example, we can conclude that while making a scenario we may consider some factors, but we can't possibly consider all factors as thousands of factors affect a situation.

Cognitive Bias

There are times when decision-makers take multiple scenarios – say best, average & worst. This is a dangerous situation because as human nature we consider that occurrence of average scenario is the most likely. Thus we are biased to make decisions based on average scenarios. The human brain is wired in a certain way & its perceptions affect all decision making.

Requires Continuous Improvement

Scenarios require continuous revision, refinement & control by an expert or a specialized team. In this fast growing times, a scenario considered today may take a very form in next 3-month period. One must periodically update the scenario analysis & make wise decisions to get maximum benefit out of scenario analysis.

Working of Scenario Analysis

As a technique, scenario analysis involves computing different reinvestment rates for expected returns that are reinvested within the investment horizon. Based on mathematical and statistical principles, scenario analysis provides a process to estimate shifts in the value of a portfolio, based on the occurrence of different situations, referred to as scenarios, following the principles of "what if" analysis.

These assessments can be used to examine the amount of risk present within a given investment as related to a variety of potential events, ranging from highly probable to highly improbable. Depending on the results of the analysis, an investor can determine if the level of risk present falls within his comfort zone.

One type of scenario analysis that looks specifically at worst-case scenarios is stress testing. Stress testing is often employed using a computer simulation technique to test the resilience of institutions and investment portfolios against possible future critical situations. Such testing is customarily used by the financial industry to help gauge investment risk and the adequacy of assets, as well as to help evaluate internal processes and controls. In recent years, regulators have also required financial institutions to carry out stress tests to ensure their capital holdings and other assets are adequate.

Scenario Analysis and Investment Strategy

There are many different ways to approach scenario analysis. A common method is to determine the standard deviation of daily or monthly security returns and then compute what value is expected for the portfolio if each security generates returns that are two or three standard deviations above and below the average return. This way, an analyst can have a reasonable amount of certainty regarding the change in the value of a portfolio during a given time period, by simulating these extremes.

Scenarios being considered can relate to a single variable, such as the relative success or failure of a new product launch, or a combination of factors, such as the results of the product launch combined with possible changes in the activities of competitor businesses. The goal is to analyze the results of the more extreme outcomes to determine investment strategy.

Scenario Analysis in Personal and Corporate Finance

The same process used for examining potential investment scenarios can be applied to various other financial situations in order to examine value shifts based on theoretical scenarios. On the consumer side, a person can use scenario analysis to examine the different financial outcomes of purchasing an item on credit, as opposed to saving the funds for a cash purchase. Additionally, a person can look at the various financial changes that may occur when deciding whether to accept a new job offer.

Businesses can use scenario analysis to analyze the potential financial outcomes of certain decisions, such as selecting one of two facilities or storefronts from which the business could operate. This could include considerations such as the difference in rent, utility charges, and insurance, or any benefit that may exist in one location but not the other.

Benefits of Performing Scenario Analysis

There are many reasons why managers and investors perform the analysis. Predicting the future is an inherently risky business, so it's prudent to explore as many different cases of what could happen as is reasonably possible.

Key benefits include:

- Future planning: Gives investors a peek into the expected returns and risks involved when planning for future investments. The goal of any business venture is to increase revenue over time, and it is best to use informed calculations when deciding to include the investment in the portfolio.
- Proactive: Companies can avoid or decrease potential losses that result from uncontrollable factors by being aggressively preventive during worst-case scenarios by analyzing events and situations that may lead to unfavorable outcomes. As the saying goes, it is better to be proactive than reactive when a problem arises.
- Avoiding risk and failure: To avoid poor investment decisions, scenario analysis allows businesses or investors to assess investment prospects. It takes the best and worst probabilities into account so that investors can make an informed decision.
- Projecting investment returns or losses: The analysis makes use of tools to calculate the values or figures of potential gains or losses of an investment. This gives concrete, measurable data that investors can base the approaches they take for a better outcome.

Drawbacks of Scenario Analysis

Scenario analysis tends to be a demanding and time-consuming process that requires high-level skills and expertise. Due to the difficulty in forecasting exactly what takes place in the future, the actual outcome may be fully unexpected and not foreseen in the financial modeling.

It may be very difficult to envision all possible scenarios and assign probabilities to them. Investors must understand that there are risk factors associated with the outcomes and they must consider certain risk tolerance to be able to pursue a goal.

Sensitivity vs. Scenario Analysis

In finance, a sensitivity analysis is created to understand the impact a range of variables have on a given outcome. It is important to note that a sensitivity analysis is not the same as a scenario analysis. As an example, assume an equity analyst wants to do a sensitivity analysis and a scenario analysis around the impact of earnings per share (EPS) on a company's relative valuation by using the price-to-earnings (P/E) multiple.

The sensitivity analysis is based on the variables that affect valuation, which a financial model can depict using the variables' price and EPS. The sensitivity analysis isolates these variables and then records the range of possible outcomes. On the other hand, for a scenario analysis, the analyst determines a certain scenario such as a stock market crash or change in industry regulation. He then changes the variables within the model to align with that scenario. Put together, the analyst has a comprehensive picture. He now knows the full range of outcomes, given all extremes, and has an understanding of what the outcomes would be, given a specific set of variables defined by real-life scenarios.

BREAK-EVEN ANALYSIS

A break-even analysis is a useful tool for determining at what point your company, or a new product or service, will be profitable. Put another way, it's a financial calculation used to determine the number of products or services you need to sell to at least cover your costs. When you've broken even, you are neither losing money nor making money, but all your costs have been covered.

For example, a break-even analysis could help you determine how many cell phone cases you need to sell to cover your warehousing costs. Or how many hours of service you need to sell to pay for your office space. Anything you sell beyond your break-even point will add profit.

There are a few definitions you need to know in order to understand break-even analysis:

- Fixed Costs: Expenses that stay the same no matter how much you sell.
- Variable Costs: Expenses that fluctuate up and down with sales.

Importance of Break-even Analysis

There are many benefits to doing a break-even analysis.

Price Smarter: Finding your break-even point will help you price your products better. A lot of psychologygoes into effective pricing, but knowing how it will affect your profitability is just as important. You need to make sure you can pay all your bills.

Cover fixed costs: When most people think about pricing, they think about how much their product costs to create. Those are considered variable costs. You still need to cover your fixed costs like insurance or web development fees. Doing a break-even analysis helps you do that.

Catch missing expenses: It's easy to forget about expenses when you're thinking through a small business idea. When you do a break-even analysis you have to lay out all your financial commitments to figure out your break-even point. This will limit the number of surprises down the road.

Set revenue targets: After completing a break-even analysis, you know exactly how much you need to sell to be profitable. This will help you set more concrete sales goals for you and your team. When you have a clear number in mind, it will be much easier to follow through.

Make smarter decisions: Entrepreneurs often make business decisions based on emotion. If they feel good about a new venture, they go for it. How you feel is important, but it's not enough. Successful entrepreneurs make their decisions based on facts. It will be a lot easier to decide when you've put in the work and have useful data in front of you.

Limit financial strain: Doing a break-even analysis helps mitigate risk by showing you when to avoid a business idea. It will help you avoid failures and limit the financial toll that bad decisions can have on your business. Instead, you can be realistic about the potential outcomes.

Fund your business: A break-even analysis is a key component of any business plan . It's usually a requirement if you want to take on investors or other debt to fund your business. You have to prove your plan is viable. More than that, if the analysis looks good, you will be more comfortable taking on the burden of financing.

Using break-even Analysis

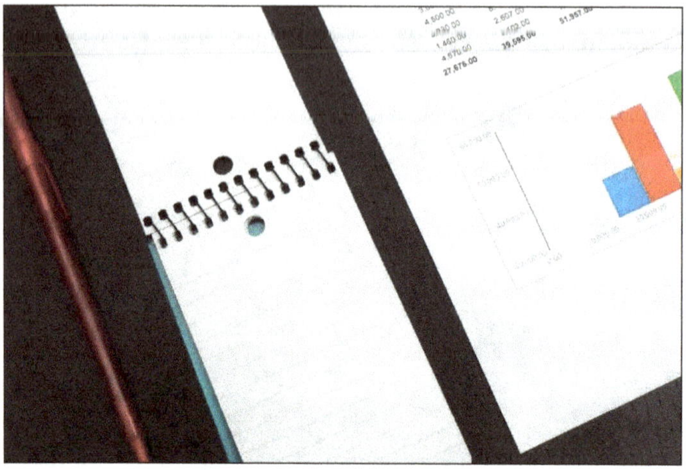

There are four common scenarios when it helps to do a break-even analysis.

Starting a New Business

If you're thinking about starting a new business, a break-even analysis is a must. Not only will it help you decide if your business idea is viable, but it will force you to do research and be realistic about costs, as well as think through your pricing strategy.

Creating a New Product

If you already have a business, you should still do a break-even analysis before committing to a new product—especially if that product is going to add significant expense. Even if your fixed costs, like an office lease, stay the same, you'll need to work out the variable costs related to your new product and set prices before you start selling.

Adding a New Sales Channel

Any time you add a new sales channel, your costs will change—even if your prices don't. For example, if you've been selling online and you're thinking about doing a pop-up shop , you'll want to make sure you at least break even. Otherwise, the financial strain could put the rest of your business at risk.

This applies equally to adding new online sales channels, like shoppable posts on Instagram. Will you be planning any additional costs to promote the channel, like Instagram ads? Those costs need to be part of your break-even analysis.

Changing the Business Model

If you're thinking about changing your business model, for example, switching from dropshipping products to carrying inventory, you should do a break-even analysis. Your costs could change significantly and this will help you figure out if your prices need to change too.

Break-even Analysis Formula

Before we start calculating break-even points, let's break down how the formula works.

Your break-even point is equal to your fixed costs, divided by your average price, minus variable costs.

Break-Even Point = Fixed Costs/(Average Price — Variable Costs).

Basically, you need to figure out what your net profit per unit sold is and divide your fixed costs by that number. This will tell you how many units you need to sell before you start earning a profit.

As you now know, your product sales need to pay for more than just the costs of producing them. The remaining profit is known as the contribution margin because it contributes cash to the fixed costs.

Now that you know what it is, how it works, and why it matters, let's break down how to calculate your break-even point.

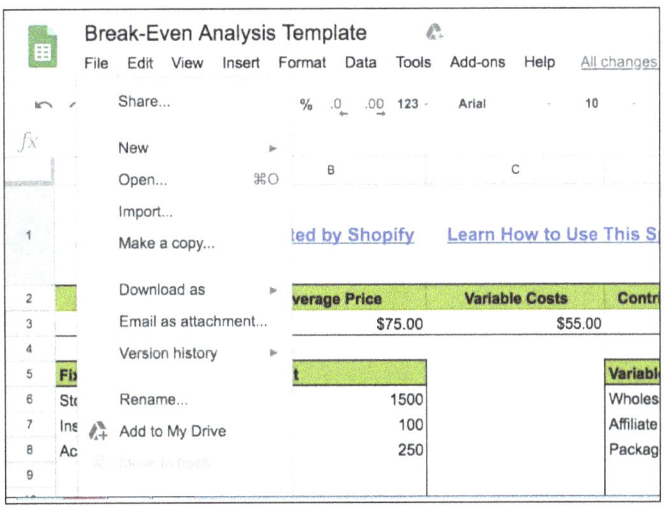

Step 1 - Gather your data: The first step is to list all the costs of doing business. Everything from the cost of your product, to rent, to bank fees. Think through everything you have to pay for and write it down.

The next step is to divide them into fixed costs, and variable costs.

Fixed costs: Fixed costs are any costs that stay the same, regardless of how much product you sell. This could include things like rent, software subscriptions, insurance, and labour.

Make a list of everything you have to pay for no matter what. In most cases, you can list the expenses as monthly amounts unless you're considering an event with a shorter time frame, such as a three-day festival. Add everything up. If you're using the break-even analysis spreadsheet, it will do the math for you automatically.

Fixed Costs	Amount
Storage	1500
Insurance	100
Accountant	250
Total	**1850**

Variable costs: Variable costs are costs that fluctuate based on the amount of product you sell. This could include things like materials, commissions, payment processing, and also labour.

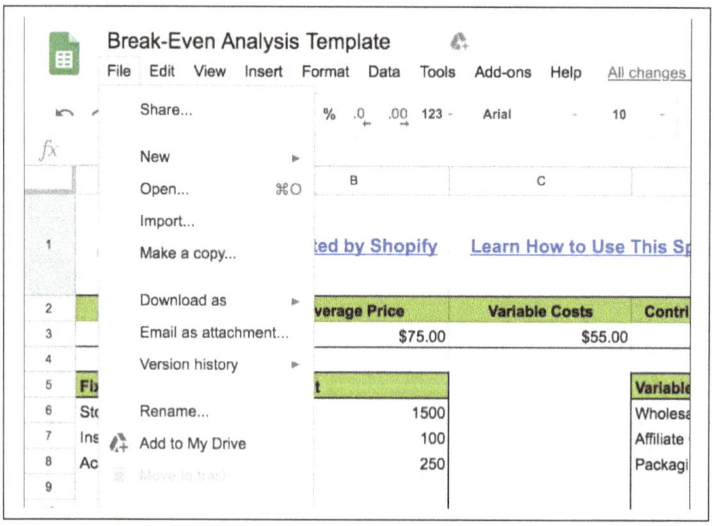

Some costs could go in either category, depending on your business. If you have salaried staff, they will go under fixed costs. But if you pay part-time hourly employees who only work when it's busy, they will be considered variable costs.

Make a list of all your costs that fluctuate depending on how much you sell. List the price per unit sold and add up all the costs, or use the spreadsheet which will add them up automatically.

Finally, decide on a price. Don't worry if you're not ready to commit to a final price yet, you can change this later. Keep in mind, this is the average price. If you offer some customers bulk discounts, it will lower the average price.

Step 2 - Plug in your data: Now it's time to plug in your data. The spreadsheet will pull your fixed cost total and variable cost total up into the break-even calculation. All you need to is to fill in is your average price in the appropriate cell. After that, the math will happen automatically. The number that gets calculated in the top right cell under break-even units is the number of units you need to sell to break even.

Fixed Costs	Average Price	Variable Costs	Contribution Margin	Break-Even Units
$1,850.00	$75.00	$55.00	$20.00	92.50

Fixed Costs	Amount
Storage	1500
Insurance	100
Accountant	250
Total	1850

Variable Costs	Per Unit Amount
Wholesale product	30
Affiliate Comission	20
Packaging	5
Total	55

In the break-even analysis example above, the break-even point is 92.5 units.

Step 3 - Make adjustments: Feel free to experiment with different numbers. See what happens if you lower your fixed or variable costs, or try changing the price. You may not get it right the first time, so make adjustments as you go.

Don't forget any expenses: The most common pitfall of break-even analysis is forgetting things—especially variable costs. Break-even analyses are an important step towards making important business decisions. That's why you need to make sure your data is as accurate as possible.

To make sure you don't miss any costs, think through your entire operations from start to finish. If you think through your unboxing experience, you might remember that you need to order branded tissue paper, and that one order lasts you 200 shipments. If you're thinking through your festival setup, you might remember that you'll need to provide napkins along with the food you're selling. These are variable costs that need to be included.

Limitations of Break-even Analysis

Break-even analysis plays an important role in making business decisions, but it's limited in the type of information it can provide.

Not a predictor of demand: It's important to note that a break-even analysis is not a predictor of demand. It won't tell you what your sales are going to be, or how many people will want what you're selling. It will only tell you how many units you need to sell in order to break even. It's also important to note that demand isn't stable. As you change your price, the number of people willing to buy your product will change as well.

Dependent on Reliable Data

Sometimes costs fall into both fixed and variable categories. This can make calculations complicated and you'll likely need to wedge them into one or the other. For example, you may have a baseline labour cost no matter what, as well as an additional labour cost top that could fluctuate based on how much product you sell.

The accuracy of your break-even point depends on accurate data. If you don't feed good data into the formula, you won't get a reliable result.

Simplistic

The break-even point formula is simplistic. Many businesses have multiple products with multiple prices. It won't be able to pick up that nuance. You'll likely need to work with one product at a time or estimate an average price based on all the products you might sell. If this is the case, it's best to run a few different scenarios to be better prepared.

As prices fluctuate, so do costs. This model assumes that only one thing changes at a time. Instead, if you lower your price and sell more, your variable costs might decrease because you have more buying power or are able to work more efficiently. Ultimately it's only an estimate.

Ignores Time

The break-even analysis ignores fluctuations over time. The time frame will be dependent on the period you use to calculate fixed costs (monthly is most common). Although you'll see how many units you need to sell over the course of the month, you won't see how things change if your sales fluctuate week to week, or seasonally over the course of a year. For this, you'll need to rely on good cash flow management, and possibly a solid sales forecast.

It also doesn't take the future into account. Break-even analysis only looks at here and now. If your raw materials cost doubles next year, your break-even point will be a lot of higher unless you raise your prices. If you raise your prices, you could lose customers. This delicate balance is always in flux.

Ignores Competitors

As a new entrant to the market, you're going to affect competitors and vice versa. They could change their prices, which could affect demand for your product, causing you to change your prices too. If they grow quickly and a raw material you both use becomes more scarce, the cost could go up.

Ultimately, break-even analysis will give you a very solid understanding of the baseline conditions for being successful. It is a must. But it's not the only research you need to do before you starting or making changes to a business.

Strategies to Lower your Break-even Point

What if you complete your break-even analysis and find out that the number of units you need to sell is too high? If the number seems unrealistic or unattainable, don't panic. You may be able to make some adjustments to lower your break-even point.

Lower Fixed Costs

See if there's an opportunity to lower your fixed costs. The lower you can get them, the fewer units you'll need to sell in order to break-even. For example, if you're thinking about opening a retail store and numbers aren't working out, consider selling online instead. How does that affect your fixed costs?

Raise your Prices

If you raise your prices, you won't need to sell as many units to break even. The marginal contribution per unit sold will be higher. When thinking about raising your prices, be mindful of what the market is willing to pay, and expectations that come with a price. You won't need to sell as many units, but you'll still need to sell enough—and if you charge more, buyers may expect a better product or better customer service.

Lower Variable Costs

Lowering your variable costs is often the most difficult option, especially if you're just going into business. But the more you scale, the easier it will be to reduce variable costs. It's worth trying to lower your costs by negotiating with your suppliers, changing suppliers, or changing your process. For example, maybe you'll find that packing peanuts are cheaper than bubble wrap for shipping fragile products.

Example of Break Even Analysis

Colin is the managerial accountant in charge of Company A, which sells water bottles. He previously determined that the fixed costs of Company A consist of property taxes, a lease, and executive salaries, which add up to $100,000. The variable costs associated with producing one water bottle is $2 per unit. The water bottle is sold at a premium price of $12. To determine the break even point of Company A's premium water bottle:

Break even quantity = $100,000 / ($12 – $2) = 10,000.

Therefore, given the fixed costs, variable costs, and selling price of the water bottles, Company A would need to sell 10,000 units of water bottles to break even.

Graphically Representing the Break Even Point

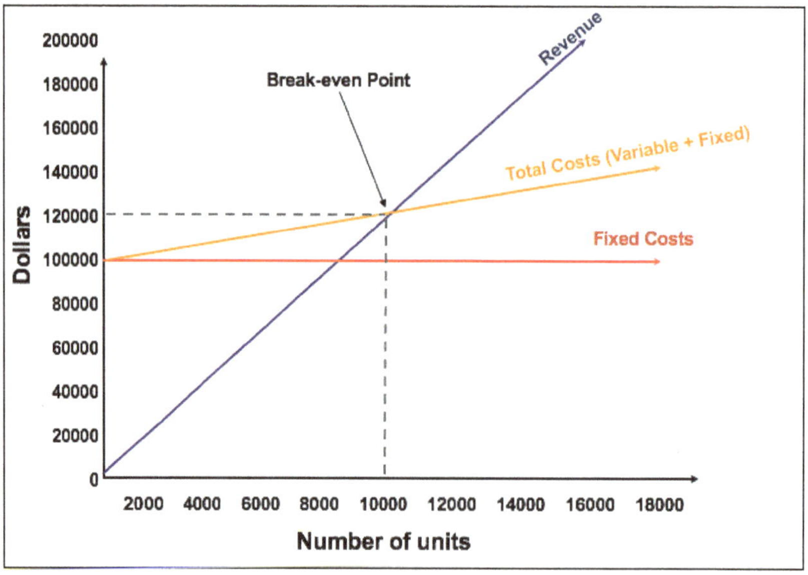

The graphical representation of unit sales and dollar sales needed to break even is referred to as the break even chart or Cost Volume Profit (CVP) graph. Below is the CVP graph of the example above:

- The number of units is on the X-axis (horizontal) and the dollar amount is on the Y-axis (vertical).

- The red line represents the total fixed costs of $100,000.
- The blue line represents revenue per unit sold. For example, selling 10,000 units would generate 10,000 x $12 = $120,000 in revenue.
- The yellow line represents total costs (fixed and variable costs). For example, if the company sells 0 units, the company would incur $0 in variable costs but $100,000 in fixed costs for total costs of $100,000. If the company sells 10,000 units, the company would incur 10,000 x $2 = $20,000 in variable costs and $100,000 in fixed costs for total costs of $120,000.
- The break even point is at 10,000 units. At this point, revenue would be 10,000 x $12 = $120,000 and costs would be 10,000 x 2 = $20,000 in variable costs and $100,000 in fixed costs.
- When the number of units exceeds 10,000, the company would be making a profit on the units sold. Note that the blue revenue line is greater than the yellow total costs line after 10,000 units are produced. Likewise, if the number of units is below 10,000, the company would be making a loss. From 0-9,999 units, the total costs line is above the revenue line.

HILLIER MODEL

According to the Hillier model, the risk associated with the project can be assessed through the standard deviation of expected cash flows. In other words, determining the viability of the project through calculating the deviations in the cash flows from the mean of expected cash flows.

Thus, Hillier model asserts that the computation of standard deviations of several ranges of cash flows enables a firm to determine the uncertainty involved in the future projects.

This model was proposed by F.S. Hillier and according to him, the expected Net Present Value and the standard deviation of the Net present value of the project can be determined through analytical derivations. Under this model, there are two cases of analysis:

- When there is no correlation among the cash flows.
- When there is a perfect correlation among the cash flows.

When the cash flows of different years are uncorrelated, then the cash flow in the year "t" is independent of the cash flow in the year "t-n". Whereas, if the cash flows of different years are perfectly correlated, then the cash flows in each period will be alike.

The formula to compute the Net present Value and the standard deviation under both the cases is given.

Uncorrelated Cash Flows

$$NPV = {}^{n}\sum_{t=1} [C_t / (1+i)^t] - I$$

$$\partial\ (NPV) = {}^{n}\sum_{t=1} [\partial_t^2 / (1+i)^{2t}]^{1/2}$$

Correlated Cash Flows

$$NPV = {}^{n}\sum_{t=1} [C_t / (1+i)^t] - I$$

$$\partial(NPV) = {}^{n}\sum_{t=1} [\ \partial_t / (1+t)^t]$$

Where, $C_{t\ =}$ Expected cash flow of the year "t".

∂_t= standard deviation of cash flow for the year "t".

i = risk free rate.

I = initial investment.

VALUE TREE ANALYSIS

Value tree analysis is a multi-criteria decision-making (MCDM) implement by which the decision-making attributes for each choice to come out with a preference for the decision makes are weighted. Usually, choices' attribute-specific values are aggregated into a complete method. Decision analysts (DAs) distinguished two types of utility. The preferences of value are made among alternatives when there is no uncertainty. Risk preferences solves the attitude of DM to risk taking under uncertainty. This learning package focuses on deterministic choices, namely value theory, and in particular a decision analysis tool called a value tree.

The concept of utility was used by Daniel Bernoulli (1738) first in 1730s while explaining the evaluation of St Petersburg paradox, a specific uncertain gable. He explained that money was not enough to measure how much value is. For an individual, however, the worth of money was a non-linear function. This discovery led to the emergence of utility theory, which is a numerical measure that indicates how much value alternative choices have. With the development of decision analysis, utility played an important role in the explanation of economics behavior. Some utilitarian philosophers like Bentham and Mill took advantage of it as an implement to build a certain kind of ethics theory either. Nevertheless, there was no possibility of measuring one's utility function. Moreover, the theory was not so important as in practice. With the time past, the utility theory gradually based on a solid theoretical foundation. People started to use theory of games to explain the behavior of those who are rational and calm when engaging with others with conflict happening. In 1944 John von Neumann and Oskar Morgenstern's

Theory of Games and Economic Behavior was published. Afterwards, it emerged since it has become of the key implement researchers and practitioners from statistics and operations research use to give a helping hand to decision makers when it was hard to make a decision. Decision analysts can be separated into two sorts of utility. The attitude of decision makers towards uncertain risk are solved by risk preference.

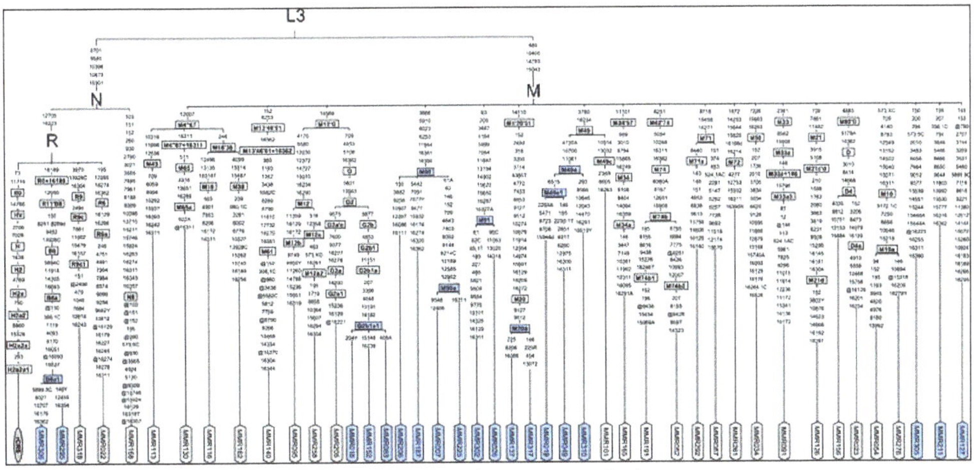

instance for Value Tree Analysis.

Process

The goal of the value tree analysis process is to offer a well-organized way to think and discuss about alternatives and support subjective judgements which are critical for correct or excellent decisions. The phases of process of the value tree analysis is shown as below:

- Problem structuring:
    - Defining the decision context.
    - Identifying the objectives.
    - Generating and identifying decision alternatives.
    - Creating a hierarchical model of the objectives.
    - Specifying the attributes.
- Preference elicitation.
- Recommended decision.
- Sentitvity analysis.

These processes are usually large and iterative. For example, problem structure, collection of related information, and modeling of DM preferences often require a lot of work. DM's perception of the problem and preferences for results not previously considered may change and evolve during this process.

Methodology

Value tree was built to be an effective and essential technique for improving and enhancing goals and values by several aspects. The tree analysis displays a visual mode to problems that used to be only available in a verbal mode. Plus separate aspects, thoughts and opinions are united to a single visual representation, which gives birth to great clarity, stimulation of creative thinking, and constructive communication.

We take the steps below to create a value tree analysis with an example to help illustrate the steps:

Step1: Initial Pool

Using a free brainstorming of all the values as a beginning, by which we mean all the problems which are related to the decision: the goals and criteria, the demands, etc.—all the things which have relevance to decision making. Write down what each value is on a piece of paper.

Begin the process with several things:

- Essences in your decision.
- The things that matter.
- The thing that you are looking for.
- The thing you want.
- Your passions, intentions, joys, ambition.
- The things which joy you.
- The things that you are fierce of.

Once you've exhausted your thoughts after this very open phase, consider the following topics to help you come up with comprehensive values, interests, and concerns related to your decision:

- Stakeholders.

Consider who is affected by the decision and what their values might be. Stakeholders may be family, friends, neighbors, society, offspring or other species, but they can be anyone who might be affected by your decision, whether intentional or not.

- Basic human needs:
    - Physiological value: Health and nutrition.
    - Safety value: Feel safe.

  - Social values: Be loved and respected.
  - Self-realizing value: Doing and becoming "fit".
  - Cognitive value: Eager to satisfy curiosity, know, explain and understand.
  - Aesthetic value: Experience beauty.
- Intangible consequences. We are most inclined to ignore intangible consequences, such as:
  - If you make this choice, how would you feel about yourself?
  - How do others see you making this choice?

The lack of awareness of this intangible consequence can easily lead to our regretful decision. Moreover, if there is a disagreement between our intuitive and thorough analysis of decision-making, we are usually not aware of the underlying intangible consequences.

- The pros and cons of the options you have seen:
  - For each option you can think of, what are the best and worst aspects of yourself? These will be values.
  - Special consideration of costs and risks. We tend to start our plan by thinking about the positive goals we hope to achieve. Considering costs and risks requires extra effort, but considering them is the first step to avoid them.
- Future values:
  - Consider future impacts and current impacts. People tend to ignore or mitigate future consequences.
  - Imagine your own future, perhaps in your death bed, reviewing this decision. What is important to you?

Step2: Clustering

When lacking of ideas, clustering the ideas is an efficient way to move the paper around until similar ideas are gathered together.

Step3: Labeling

Mark each group with a higher level value that holds them together to make each element clearer.

Example: As a simplified example, let us assume that some of the initial values we propose are self-determined, family, safe, friend and healthy. Health, safety and self-realization can be grouped together and labeled as "self", where families and friends can be grouped together and labeled as "other".

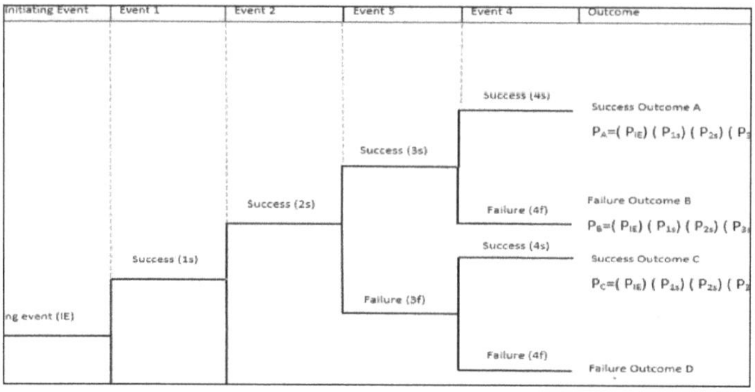

Step4: Moving up the Tree

Seeing whether these groups can be grouped into still larger groups

Example: SELF and OTHERS group into OVERALL VALUE.

Step5: Moving down the Tree

Also seeing if these groups can be divided into still smaller sub-groups.

Example: SELF-ACTUALIZATION could be divided into WORK and RECREATION.

Step6: Moving across the Tree

Asking themselves is another valid way to bring new ideas to a tree, whether any additional thoughts at that level can come out(moving across the tree).

Example: In addition to FAMILY and FRIENDS, we could add SOCIETY.

The diagram shows the final result of the (still simplified) example. Bold, italic indicates the basic values that were not originally written by us, but were thought of when we tried to fill in the tree.

Tool

PRIME Decisions

PRIME Decisions is a decision helping implement which use PRIME method to analyze incomplete preference information. Novel features are also offered by PRIME Decisions, which gives support to interactive decision process which includes an elicitation tour. PRIME Decisions are seen as an essential catalyst for further applied work due to its practitioners benefit from M. Köksalan et al. (eds.), Multiple Criteria Decision Making in the New Millennium the explicit recognition of incomplete information.

Web-HIPRE

Web-HIPRE, a Java applet, provides help to multiple criteria decision analysis. Moreover, a normal platform is provided for individual and group decision making. People can process the model at the same time at anytime. Plus, they can easily have access to the model. It is possible to define links to other websites. All other sorts of information like geography, media files describing the criteria or alternatives can be referred to this link, which help make a better quality of decision support significantly.

Application

Some indicators obtained by process analysis are of great help to the value tree analysis. Especially in the value decomposition of internal operation indicators, the driving indicators of a first-level process indicator are usually the secondary sub-process indicators. For instance, the new product launch cycle (in terms of R&D project to production) is actually driven by two processes: R&D and testing in the company. The standardized R&D and testing process is a key success factor for improving the speed of innovation. To this end, the two process indicators development cycle, test cycle, sample acceptance and other indicators are the vital elements which drive the new product launch cycle indicators. Therefore, combining process analysis is of great significance for the decomposition of indicator value, especially for the decomposition of internal operational indicators. The instances of the main application areas are shown as below.

Application on Business, Production and Services

Budget Allocation

Allocating the engineering budget for products and projects annually is always a challenge. With value tree analysis aspects, such as strategic fit, which have no natural evaluation measure, but may have a significant role in decision-making can be included into the analysis. Furthermore, there is likelihood of communication being increased by explicit modelling of the relevant facts and a base for justified decisions is also provided.

Selection of R&D programs

As it is known to all that the risk in high in many R&D programs sometimes, thus the role of a good reason may be as essential as the decision itself. Value tree analysis offers a tool to give support to the reasoning of the selection of the R&D programme and modelling the facts affecting the decision.

Developing and Deciding on Marketing Strategies

For instance, the analysis of new strategies for merchandising gasoline and other products through full-facility service stations.

Application on Public Policy Problems

Analysis of Responses to Environmental Risks

For instance, organization of negotiations between several parties in order to identify compromise regulations for acid rain and identify the objectives of the regulations.

Negotiation for Oil and Gas Leases

Carry out an evaluation report of subcontractors and analyze the criteria which should be used.

Comparisons between Alternative Energy Sources

For instance, organizing a debate about nuclear power, aiding the decision process, and studying value differences between the decision-makers.

Application on Medicine

- Deciding on the optimal usage and inventory of blood in a blood bank.
- Helping individuals to understand the risks of different treatments.
- In addition to the decision-making problems value tree analysis serves also other purposes.
- Identifying and reformulating options.

Definition of Objectives

- Providing a common language for communication.
- Quantification of subjective variables.
- For instance, a scale which measures the worth of military targets.
- Development of value-relevant indices.

Application on Empirical Pilot Study Variable Selection

As value tree analysis is an approach that costs and computes little, it is one the best choices for time-sensitive variable selection in empirical pilot healthcare studies. Moreover, value tree analysis offers a well-structured and strategic process for decision-making so that pilot study and patient data constraints can be accounted for and value for study stakeholders can be maximized.

Application on Coaching

Value tree analysis help creative and critical thinking and organize the thoughts in a logical way. Moreover, when a decision has come up, value tree analysis can also be an effective way to think about one's core goals and values. Afterwards, we can actively look for decision opportunities with the analysis done before.

EVENT TREE ANALYSIS

Event tree analysis (ETA) is a forward, top-down, logical modeling technique for both success and failure that explores responses through a single initiating event and lays a path for assessing probabilities of the outcomes and overall system analysis. This analysis technique is used to analyze the effects of functioning or failed systems given that an event has occurred. ETA is a powerful tool that will identify all consequences of a system that have a probability of occurring after an initiating event that can be applied to a wide range of systems including: nuclear power plants, spacecraft, and chemical plants. This technique may be applied to a system early in the design process to identify potential issues that may arise, rather than correcting the issues after they occur. With this forward logic process, use of ETA as a tool in risk assessment can help to prevent negative outcomes from occurring, by providing a risk assessor with the probability of occurrence. ETA uses a type of modeling technique called event tree, which branches events from one single event using Boolean logic.

The name Event Tree was first introduced during the WASH-1400 nuclear power plant safety study, where the WASH-1400 team needed an alternate method to fault tree analysis due to the fault trees being too large. Though not using the name event tree, the UKAEA first introduced ETA in its design offices in 1968, initially to try to use whole plant risk assessment to optimize the design of a 500MW Steam Generating Heavy Water Reactor. This study showed ETA condensed the analysis into a manageable form. ETA was not initially developed during WASH-1400, this was one of the first cases in which it was thoroughly used. The UKAEA study used the assumption that protective systems either worked or failed, with the probability of failure per demand being calculated using fault trees or similar analysis methods. ETA identifies all sequences which follow an initiating event. Many of these sequences can be eliminated from the analysis because their frequency or effect are too small to affect the overall result. A paper presented at a CREST symposium in Munich, Germany, in 1971 shows how this was done. The conclusions of the US EPA study of the Draft WASH-1400 acknowledges the role of Ref 1 and its criticism of the Maximum Credible Accident approach used by AEC. MCA sets the reliability target for the containment but those for all other safety systems are set by smaller but more frequent accidents and would be missed by MCA.

In 2009 a risk analysis was conducted on underwater tunnel excavation under the Han River in Korea using an earth pressure balance type tunnel boring machine. ETA was used to quantify risk, by providing the probability of occurrence of an event, in the preliminary design stages of the tunnel construction to prevent any injuries or fatalities because tunnel construction in Korea has the highest injury and fatality rates within the construction category.

Theory

Performing a probabilistic risk assessment starts with a set of initiating events that change the state or configuration of the system. An initiating event is an event that starts a reaction, such as the way a spark (initiating event) can start a fire that could lead to other events (intermediate events) such as a tree burning down, and then finally an outcome, for example, the burnt tree no longer provides apples for food. Each initiating event leads to another event and continuing through this path, where each intermediate event's probability of occurrence may be calculated by using fault tree analysis, until an end state is reached (the outcome of a tree no longer providing apples for food). Intermediate events are commonly split into a binary (success/failure or yes/no) but may be split into more than two as long as the events are mutually exclusive, meaning that they can not occur at the same time. If a spark is the initiating event there is a probability that the spark will start a fire or will not start a fire (binary yes or no) as well as the probability that the fire spreads to a tree or does not spread to a tree. End states are classified into groups that can be successes or severity of consequences. An example of a success would be that no fire started and the tree still provided apples for food while the severity of consequence would be that a fire did start and we lose apples as a source of food. Loss end states can be any state at the end of the pathway that is a negative outcome of the initiating event. The loss end state is highly dependent upon the system, for example if you were measuring a quality process in a factory a loss or end state would be that the product has to be reworked or thrown in the trash. Some common loss end states:

- Loss of Life or Injury/ Illness to personnel.
- Damage to or loss of equipment or property (including software).
- Unexpected or collateral damage as a result of tests.
- Failure of mission.
- Loss of system availability.
- Damage to the environment.

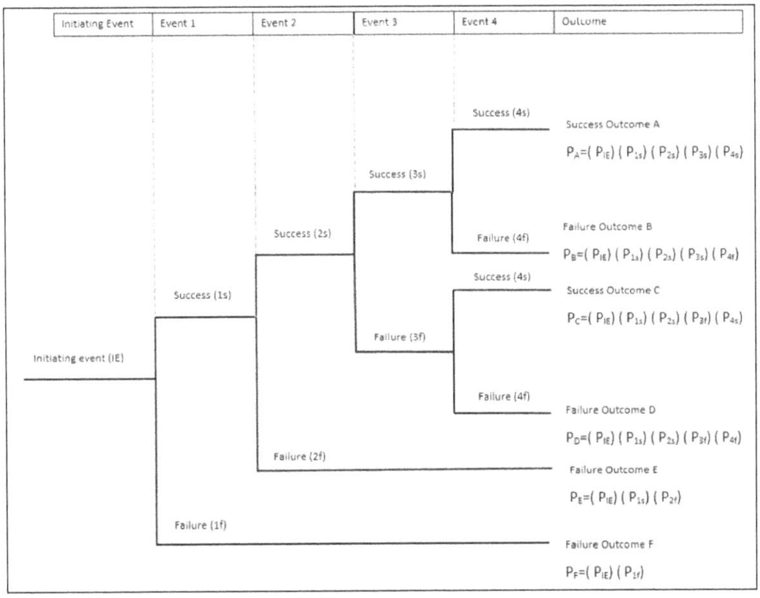

Event tree diagram example.

Methodology

The overall goal of event tree analysis is to determine the probability of possible negative outcomes that can cause harm and result from the chosen initiating event. It is necessary to use detailed information about a system to understand intermediate events, accident scenarios, and initiating events to construct the event tree diagram. The event tree begins with the initiating event where consequences of this event follow in a binary (success/failure) manner. Each event creates a path in which a series of successes or failures will occur where the overall probability of occurrence for that path can be calculated. The probabilities of failures for intermediate events can be calculated using fault tree analysis and the probability of success can be calculated from 1 = probability of success (ps) + probability of failure (pf). For example, in the equation 1 = (ps) + (pf) if we know that pf=.1 from fault tree analysis then through simple algebra we can solve for ps where ps = (1) - (pf) then we would have ps = (1) - (.1) and ps=.9.

The event tree diagram models all possible pathways from the initiating event. The initiating event starts at the left side as a horizontal line that branches vertically. the vertical branch is representative of the success/failure of the initiating event. At the end of the vertical branch a horizontal line is drawn on each the top and the bottom representing the success or failure of the first event where a description (usually success or failure) is written with a tag that represents the path such as 1s where s is a success and 1 is the event number similarly with 1f where 1 is the event number and f denotes a failure. This process continues until the end state is reached. When the event tree diagram has reached the end state for all pathways the outcome probability equation is written.

Steps to perform an event tree analysis:

- Define the system: Define what needs to be involved or where to draw the boundaries.
- Identify the accident scenarios: Perform a system assessment to find hazards or accident scenarios within the system design.
- Identify the initiating events: Use a hazard analysis to define initiating events.
- Identify intermediate events: Identify countermeasures associated with the specific scenario.
- Build the event tree diagram
- Obtain event failure probabilities: If the failure probability can not be obtained use fault tree analysis to calculate it.
- Identify the outcome risk: Calculate the overall probability of the event paths and determine the risk.
- Evaluate the outcome risk: Evaluate the risk of each path and determine its acceptability.
- Recommend corrective action: If the outcome risk of a path is not acceptable develop design changes that change the risk.
- Document the ETA: Document the entire process on the event tree diagrams and update for new information as needed.

Mathematical Concepts

1 = (probability of success) + (probability of failure).

The probability of success can be derived from the probability of failure.

Overall path probability = (probability of event 1) X (probability of event 2) X (probability of event n).

In Risk Analysis

Event tree analysis can be used in risk assessment by determining the probability that is used to determine the risk when multiplied by the hazard of the event. Event Tree Analysis is a tool that makes easy to see what pathway is creating the greatest probability of failure for a specific system. It is common to find single point failures that do not have any intervening events between the initiating event and a failure. With Event Tree Analysis single point failure can be targeted to include an intervening step that will reduce the overall probability of failure and thus reducing the risk of the system.

The idea of adding an intervening event can happen anywhere in the system for any pathway that generates too great of a risk, the added intermediate event can reduce the probability and thus reduce the risk.

Advantages

- Enables the assessment of multiple, co-existing faults and failures.
- Functions simultaneously in cases of failure and success.
- No need to anticipate end events.
- Areas of single point failure, system vulnerability, and low payoff countermeasures may be identified and assessed to deploy resources properly.
- paths in a system that lead to a failure can be identified and traced to display ineffective countermeasures.
- Work can be computerized.
- Can be performed on various levels of details.
- Visual cause and effect relationship.
- Relatively easy to learn and execute.
- Models complex systems into an understandable manner.
- Follows fault paths across system boundaries.
- Combines hardware, software, environment, and human interaction.
- Permits probability assessment.
- Commercial software is available.

Limitations

- Addresses only one initiating event at a time.
- The initiating challenge must be identified by the analyst.
- Pathways must be identified by the analyst.
- Level of loss for each pathway may not be distinguishable without further analysis.
- Success or failure probabilities are difficult to find.
- Can overlook subtle system differences.

- Partial successes/failures are not distinguishable.
- Requires an analyst with practical training and experience.

QUALITATIVE RISK ANALYSIS

Qualitative risk analysis is the process of assessing individual project risk characteristics - the probability of occurrence and the impact they would have on a project if happening - against a scale.

The concept of qualitative risk analysis is of fundamental importance when it comes to the need for the project management team and or the project management team leader to take the action at the onset or prior to the onset of the project to adequately and appropriately ascertain the approximate level of risk that so may exist in regards to the conduction of the given project and or series of projects. Specifically speaking, the concept of the qualitative risk analysis refers specifically to the project related process of performing a thorough and complete analysis of the overall effect of the complete and total set risks in the entirety of the predetermined list of project objectives that have been set forth by the project management team and or project management team leader. The qualitative risk analysis can be conducted at any point in a project life cycle, however at least once at the onset it should be conducted. The primary goal is to determine proportion of effect and theoretical response.

Perform Qualitative Risk Analysis

The perform qualitative risk analysis is a process that involves prioritizing risks for further action or analysis by assessing as well as combining the probability of occurrence. The benefit of this type of project management process is that it allows the project managersto minimize the level of uncertainty so that they can focus on the high priority risks.

To perform qualitative risk analysis, it is crucial to use different inputs like the risk management plan, risk register, scope baseline, enterprise environmental factors and organizational process assets. Using this process can result in the updates of the project documents.

This particular project management process is used in assessing the risks that are identified. The corresponding impact on the objectives should the risk occur is also calculated as well as other factors like the time frame of response, scope, schedule, constraints of cost and quality.

This particular project management process is cost effective. It is also a rapid method for establishing priorities for the Plan Risk Response process. Moreover, it also lays the base or foundation for the Perform Quantitative Risk Analysis.

QUANTITATIVE RISK ANALYSIS

Qualitative risk analysis is a numeric estimate of the overall effect of risk on the project objectives such as cost and schedule objectives. The results provide insight into the likelihood of project success and is used to develop contingency reserves.

Importance of Qualitative Risk Analysis

Better Overall Project Risk Analysis

Individual risks are evaluated in the qualitative risk analysis. But the quantitative analysis allows us to evaluate the overall project risk from the individual risks.

Better Business Decisions

Business decisions are rarely made with all the information or data we desire. For more critical decisions, quantitative risk analysis provides more objective information and data than the qualitative analysis. Keep in mind: While the quantitative analysis is more objective, it is still an estimate. Wise project managers consider other factors in the decision-making process.

Better Estimates

A project manager estimated a project's duration at eight months with a cost of $300,000. The project actually took twelve months and cost $380,000. What happened?

The project manager did a Work Breakdown Structure (WBS) and estimated the work. However, the project manager failed to consider the potential impact of the risks (good and bad) on the schedule and budget.

Performing Quantitative Risk Analysis

First, we identify risks. Then we can evaluate the risks qualitatively and quantitatively.

Consider using Quantitative Risk Analysis for:

- Projects that require a Contingency Reserve for the schedule and budget.
- Large, complex projects that require Go/No Go decisions (the Go/No Go decision may occur multiple times in a project).
- Projects where upper management wants more detail about the probability of completing the project on schedule and within budget.

Quantitative Risk Assessment Tools and Techniques

Quantitative Risk Analysis tools and techniques include but are not limited to:

- Three Point Estimate: A technique that uses the optimistic, most likely, and pessimistic values to determine the best estimate.
- Decision Tree Analysis: A diagram that shows the implications of choosing one or other alternatives.
- Expected Monetary Value (EMV) : A method used to establish the contingency reserves for a project budget and schedule.
- Monte Carlo Analysis: A technique that uses optimistic, most likely, and pessimistic estimates to determine the total project cost and project completion dates. For example, we could estimate the probability of completing a project at a cost of $20M. Or what is a company wanted to have an 80% probability of achieving its cost objectives. What is the cost to achieve 80%?
- Sensitivity Analysis: A technique used to determine which risks have the greatest impact on a project.
- Fault Tree Analysis (FMEA): The analysis of a structured diagram which identifies elements that can cause system failure.

Quantitative Risk Analysis Example

Let's look at a simple Expected Monetary Value (EMV) example:

Keep in mind that risks include both threats and opportunities. Threats have adverse impacts on cost. Opportunities are benefits that reduce cost. Expected Monetary Value = Probability x Impact.

Risk	Probability	Cost Impact	EMV
A (Threat)	20%	$100,000	$20,000
B (Opportunity)	40%	($10,000)	($4,000)
C (Threat)	30%	$50,000	$15,000
Total EMV			$31,000

Notice we subtracted the benefit of the Opportunity from the EMV. The Total EVM represents the project risk exposure and the amount of our Contingency Reserve.

Perform Quantitative Risk Analysis

The Perform Quantitative Risk Analysis is a project management process that numerically analyzes the effects of identified risks on the entire project objectives. The benefit of this process is that it creates information of the quantitative risks to support the decision-making of project managers to minimize the uncertainty of the projects.

To do this particular process, inputs are necessary. The inputs include the risk management plan, risk register, enterprise environmental factors, cost management plan, and organizational assets are used to produce the project document updates.

This particular project management process is used on the risks that have been identified and prioritized by the Perform Qualitative Risk Analysis process that can substantially impact the competing demands of the project. Thus, this particular process is used to analyze the effect of the risk on the project objectives. It is used in evaluating the aggregate effects of the risks that affect the project. It is important to take note that the process is used to provide numerical priority rating to the individual risks. However, this process might not be executed due to the lack of insufficient data.

References

- Risk-analysis-16522: techopedia.com, Retrieved 18 May, 2019
- Sensitivity-analysis-for-project-management: intaver.com, Retrieved 10 July, 2019
- Scenario-analysis-definition-meaning, financial-glossary: marketbusinessnews.com, Retrieved 25 August, 2019
- Scenario-analysis, financial-analysis: efinancemanagement.com, Retrieved 15 February, 2019
- Scenario-analysis, resources-knowledge-modelling: corporatefinanceinstitute.com, Retrieved 19 July, 2019
- Break-even-analysis: shopify.in, Retrieved 29 March, 2019
- Evaluating-risks-using-quantitative-risk-analysis: projectriskcoach.com, Retrieved 20 April, 2019

Market Risk

CHAPTER 4

The risk of losses arising due to fluctuations in market prices is referred to as market risk. Equity risk, credit risk, foreign exchange risk, liquidity risk, commodity risk, etc. are some common forms of the market risks. This chapter has been carefully written to provide an easy understanding of these market risks.

Market risk is the possibility of an investor experiencing losses due to factors that affect the overall performance of the financial markets in which he or she is involved. Market risk, also called "systematic risk," *cannot* be eliminated through diversification, though it can be hedged against in other ways. Sources of market risk include recessions, political turmoil, changes in interest rates, natural disasters and terrorist attacks. Systematic, or market risk tends to influence the entire market at the same time.

This can be contrasted with unsystematic risk, which is unique to a specific company or industry. Also known as "nonsystematic risk," "specific risk," "diversifiable risk" or "residual risk," in the context of an investment portfolio, unsystematic risk can be reduced through diversification.

Market (systematic) risk and specific risk (unsystematic) make up the two major categories of investment risk. The most common types of market risks include interest rate risk, equity risk, currency risk and commodity risk.

Publicly traded companies in the United States are required by the Securities and Exchange Commission (SEC) to disclose how their productivity and results may be linked to the performance of the financial markets. This requirement is meant to detail a company's exposure to financial risk. For example, a company providing derivative investments or foreign exchange futures may be more exposed to financial risk than companies that do not provide these types of investments. This information helps investors and traders make decisions based on their own risk management rules.

In contrast to market risk, specific risk or "unsystematic risk" is tied directly to the performance of a particular security and can be protected against through investment diversification. One example of unsystematic risk is a company declaring bankruptcy, thereby making its stock worthless to investors.

Main Types of Market Risk

Interest rate risk covers the volatility that may accompany interest rate fluctuations due to fundamental factors, such as central bank announcements related to changes in monetary policy. This risk is most relevant to investments in fixed-income securities, such as bonds.

Equity risk is the risk involved in the changing prices of stock investments, and commodity risk covers the changing prices of commodities such as crude oil and corn.

Currency risk, or exchange-rate risk, arises from the change in the price of one currency in relation to another; investors or firms holding assets in another country are subject to currency risk.

Volatility and Hedging Market Risk

Market risk exists because of price changes. The standard deviation of changes in the prices of stocks, currencies or commodities is referred to as price volatility. Volatility is rated in annualized terms and may be expressed as an absolute number, such as $10, or a percentage of the initial value, such as 10%.

Investors can utilize hedging strategies to protect against volatility and market risk. Targeting specific securities, investors can buy put options to protect against a downside move, and investors who want to hedge a large portfolio of stocks can utilize index options.

Measuring Market Risk

To measure market risk, investors and analysts use the value-at-risk (VaR) method. VaR modeling is a statistical risk management method that quantifies a stock or portfolio's potential loss as well as the probability of that potential loss occurring. While well-known and widely utilized, the VaR method requires certain assumptions that limit its precision. For example, it assumes that the makeup and content of the portfolio being measured is unchanged over a specified period. Though this may be acceptable for short-term horizons, it may provide less accurate measurements for long-term investments.

Beta is another relevant risk metric, as it measures the volatility or market risk of a security or portfolio in comparison to the market as a whole; it is used in the capital asset pricing model (CAPM) to calculate the expected return of an asset.

Market risk is the risk that an investor faces due to the decrease in the market value of a financial product arising out of the factors that affect the whole market and is not limited to a particular financial commodity. Often called a systematic risk, market risk arises because of uncertainties in the economy, political environment, natural or man-made disasters or recession and can only be hedged, however, cannot eliminate by diversification.

Types of Market Risk

There are four major types of market risk:

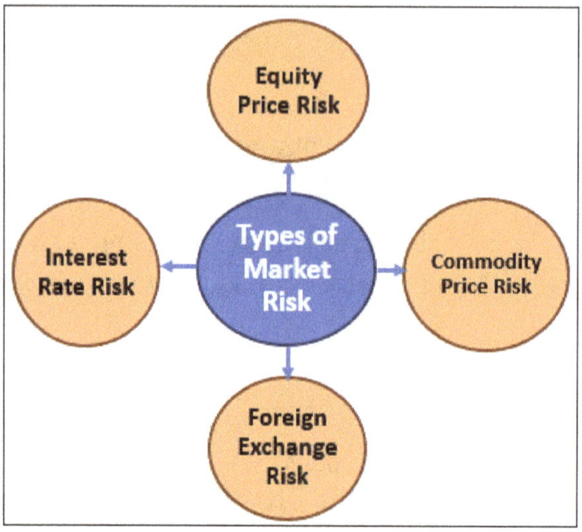

Interest Rate Risk

Interest rate risk arises when the value of security might fall because of the increase and a decrease in the prevailing and long-term interest rates. It is a broader term and comprises multiple components like basis risk, yield curve risk, options risk, and repricing risk.

Foreign Exchange Risk

Foreign exchange risk arises because of the fluctuations in the exchange rates between the domestic currency and the foreign currency. The most affected by this risk is the MNCs that operate across geographies and have their payments coming in different currencies.

Commodity Price Risk

Like foreign exchange risk, commodity price risk arises because of fluctuations in the prices of commodities like crude, gold, silver, etc. However, unlike foreign exchange risk, commodity risks not only affect the multinational companies but also the common people like farmers, small business enterprises, commercial traders, exporters, and governments.

Equity Price Risk

The last component of market risk is the equity price risk which refers to the change in the stock prices in the financial products. As equity is most sensitive to any change in the economy, equity price risk is one of the biggest parts of the market risk.

Market Risk Premium Formula

One factor used to calculate gauge market risk is the calculation of market risk premium. Simply put market risk premium is the difference between the expected rate of return and the prevailing risk-free rate of return.

Mathematically market risk premium formula is as follows:

Market Risk Premium = Expected Return–Risk-Free Rate.

The market risk premium has two major aspects–required marked risk premium and historical premium. It is based on the expectations that the investor community has in the future or based on historical patterns.

The risk-free rate is defined as the expected return without taking any risk. Most often US treasury rate as US sovereign risk is almost zero is referred to as risk-free rate.

Example of Market Risk

Let's consider the example of an IT major firm–HP. An investor wants to calculate the market risk premium associated with the stock price which is currently quoting at $1000. Let's assume the investor expects the stock price to hot $1100 because of expected growth. The following is the calculation in Excel.

Calculation of Risk Premium will be:

B10 =B7-B8

	A	B
2	Particulars	Value
3	Current Stock Price	1000
4	Expected Stock Price	1100
5	Time (in months)	8
6	Expected Rate of Return	10%
7	Annualized Return	15%
8	US Treasury Bills	4%
9	Inflation	3.50%
10	Market Risk Premium	11%
11		

Market Risk Premium = Expected Return – Risk-Free Rate

Market Risk Premium = 11%.

Advantages

Some advantages are as follows:

- Most often than not, financial products are sold to the investor community by aggressive marketing and by presenting only the growth part while completely ignoring the risks and downfalls. This is the reason we see such products being bought more in the economic expansion cycles while in the recession, investors especially the retail ones are trapped. Had the investor known of the concept of market risk and its calculations, they can understand the financial products in a much better way and decide if it suits them for such volatilities.

- Market risk premium, as explained in the example above, helps an investor to calculate the real rate of return. Even though the financial product might enjoy presenting a lucrative return, the investor should gauge the investment in terms of the real rate it provides. This can be calculated by taking into account the prevailing risk-free interest rate and inflation rate.

Disadvantages

Some disadvantages are as follows:

- We cannot completely ignore them. It can only be hedged which comes with cost and intensive calculations. An investor has to be apt to understand what data to analyze and what data it should filter out.
- It is very prone to recession or cyclic changes in the economy. Ans since it affects the whole market simultaneously, it is even more difficult to manage as diversification will not help. Unlike credit risk, which is very much counterparty specific, market risk affects all asset classes.

EQUITY RISK

Equity risk is "the financial risk involved in holding equity in a particular investment". Equity risk often refers to equity in companies through the purchase of stocks, and does not commonly refer to the risk in paying into real estate or building equity in properties.

The measure of risk used in the equity markets is typically the standard deviation of a security's price over a number of periods. The standard deviation will delineate the normal fluctuations one can expect in that particular security above and below the mean, or average. However, since most investors would not consider fluctuations above the average return as "risk", some economists prefer other means of measuring it.

Equity risk premium is defined as "excess return that an individual stock or the overall stock market provides over a risk-free rate". This excess compensates investors for taking on the relatively higher risk of the equity market. The size of the premium can vary as the risk in the stock, or just the stock market in general, increases. For example, higher risks have a higher premium. The concept of this is to entice investors to take on riskier investments. A key component in this is the risk-free rate, which is quoted as "the rate on longer-term government bonds". These are considered risk free because there is a low chance that the government will default on its loans. However, the investment in stocks isn't guaranteed, because businesses often suffer downturns or go out of business.

To calculate the equity-risk premium, subtract the risk free rate from the return of a stock over a period of time. For example, if the return on a stock is 17% and the risk-free rate over the same period of time is 9%, then the equity-risk premium would be 8% for the stock over that period of time.

CREDIT RISK

A credit risk is the risk of default on a debt that may arise from a borrower failing to make required payments. In the first resort, the risk is that of the lender and includes lost principal and interest, disruption to cash flows, and increased collection costs. The loss may be complete or partial. In an efficient market, higher levels of credit risk will be associated with higher borrowing costs. Because of this, measures of borrowing costs such as yield spreads can be used to infer credit risk levels based on assessments by market participants.

Losses can arise in a number of circumstances, for example:

- A consumer may fail to make a payment due on a mortgage loan, credit card, line of credit, or other loan.
- A company is unable to repay asset-secured fixed or floating charge debt.
- A business or consumer does not pay a trade invoice when due.
- A business does not pay an employee's earned wages when due.
- A business or government bond issuer does not make a payment on a coupon or principal payment when due.
- An insolvent insurance company does not pay a policy obligation.
- An insolvent bank won't return funds to a depositor.
- A government grants bankruptcy protection to an insolvent consumer or business.

To reduce the lender's credit risk, the lender may perform a credit check on the prospective borrower, may require the borrower to take out appropriate insurance, such as mortgage insurance, or seek security over some assets of the borrower or a guarantee from a third party. The lender can also take out insurance against the risk or on-sell the debt to another company. In general, the higher the risk, the higher will be the interest rate that the debtor will be asked to pay on the debt. Credit risk mainly arises when borrowers are unable to pay due willingly or unwillingly.

A credit risk can be of the following types:

- Credit default risk: The risk of loss arising from a debtor being unlikely to pay its loan obligations in full or the debtor is more than 90 days past due on any material credit obligation; default risk may impact all credit-sensitive transactions, including loans, securities and derivatives.
- Concentration risk: The risk associated with any single exposure or group of exposures with the potential to produce large enough losses to threaten a bank's core operations. It may arise in the form of single-name concentration or industry concentration.
- Country risk: The risk of loss arising from a sovereign state freezing foreign currency payments (transfer/conversion risk) or when it defaults on its obligations (sovereign risk); this type of risk is prominently associated with the country's macroeconomic performance and its political stability.

Assessment

Significant resources and sophisticated programs are used to analyze and manage risk. Some companies run a credit risk department whose job is to assess the financial health of their customers, and extend credit (or not) accordingly. They may use in-house programs to advise on avoiding, reducing and transferring risk. They also use the third party provided intelligence. Companies like Standard & Poor's, Moody's, Fitch Ratings, DBRS, Dun and Bradstreet, Bureau van Dijk and Rapid Ratings International provide such information for a fee.

For large companies with liquidly traded corporate bonds or Credit Default Swaps, bond yield spreads and credit default swap spreads indicate market participants assessments of credit risk and may be used as a reference point to price loans or trigger collateral calls.

Most lenders employ their models (credit scorecards) to rank potential and existing customers according to risk, and then apply appropriate strategies. With products such as unsecured personal loans or mortgages, lenders charge a higher price for higher-risk customers and vice versa. With revolving products such as credit cards and overdrafts, the risk is controlled through the setting of credit limits. Some products also require collateral, usually an asset that is pledged to secure the repayment of the loan.

Credit scoring models also form part of the framework used by banks or lending institutions to grant credit to clients. For corporate and commercial borrowers, these models generally have qualitative and quantitative sections outlining various aspects of the risk including, but not limited to, operating experience, management expertise, asset quality, and leverage and liquidity ratios, respectively. Once this information has been fully reviewed by credit officers and credit committees, the lender provides the funds subject to the terms and conditions presented within the contract.

Sovereign Risk

Sovereign credit risk is the risk of a government being unwilling or unable to meet its loan obligations, or reneging on loans it guarantees. Many countries have faced sovereign risk in the late-2000s global recession. The existence of such risk means that creditors should take a two-stage decision process when deciding to lend to a firm based in a foreign country. Firstly one should consider the sovereign risk quality of the country and then consider the firm's credit quality.

Five macroeconomic variables that affect the probability of sovereign debt rescheduling are:

- Debt service ratio.
- Import ratio.
- Investment ratio.
- Variance of export revenue.
- Domestic money supply growth.

The probability of rescheduling is an increasing function of debt service ratio, import ratio, the variance of export revenue and domestic money supply growth. The likelihood of rescheduling is a decreasing function of investment ratio due to future economic productivity gains. Debt rescheduling likelihood can increase if the investment ratio rises as the foreign country could become less dependent on its external creditors and so be less concerned about receiving credit from these countries/investors.

Counterparty Risk

A counterparty risk, also known as a default risk or counterparty credit risk (CCR), is a risk that a counterparty will not pay as obligated on a bond, derivative, insurance policy, or other contract. Financial institutions or other transaction counterparties may hedge or take out credit insurance or, particularly in the context of derivatives, require the posting of collateral. Offsetting counterparty risk is not always possible, e.g. because of temporary liquidity issues or longer-term systemic reasons. Further, counterparty risk increases due to positively correlated risk factors; accounting for this correlation between portfolio risk factors and counterparty default in risk management methodology is not trivial.

In March 2014, the Basel Committee published SA-CCR, its standardised approach for measuring counterparty credit risk exposures.

SA-CCR calculates the exposure at default of derivatives and long-settlement transactions exposed to counterparty credit risk. It builds EAD as (i) a "Replacement Cost", were the counterparty to default today, combined with (ii) an "Add On" with its appropriate multiplier, essentially potential future exposure. (For the former: exposure is aggregated by counterparty, and then netted-off with haircutted-collateral. For the latter: per asset class, trade exposures - as reduced by hedging - are aggregated to "hedging sets"; these are then combined to "netting sets", and offset by the counterparty's collateral.)

The SA-CCR EAD is an input to the bank's regulatory capital calculation where it is combined with the counterparty's PD and LGD to derive RWA; (some) banks thus incorporate SA-CCR into their KVA calculations.

The framework replaced both non-internal model approaches: the current exposure method (CEM) and the standardised method (SM). It was intended to be a "risk-sensitive methodology", i.e. conscious of asset class and hedging, that differentiates between margined and non-margined trades and recognizes netting benefits; issues insufficiently addressed under the preceding frameworks.

Mitigation

Lenders mitigate credit risk in a number of ways, including:

- Risk-based pricing – Lenders may charge a higher interest rate to borrowers who are more likely to default, a practice called risk-based pricing. Lenders consider factors relating to the loan such as loan purpose, credit rating, and loan-to-value ratio and estimates the effect on yield (credit spread).
- Covenants – Lenders may write stipulations on the borrower, called covenants, into loan agreements, such as:
    - Periodically report its financial condition.
    - Refrain from paying dividends, repurchasing shares, borrowing further, or other specific, voluntary actions that negatively affect the company's financial position.
    - Repay the loan in full, at the lender's request, in certain events such as changes in the borrower's debt-to-equity ratio or interest coverage ratio.
- Credit insurance and credit derivatives – Lenders and bond holders may hedge their credit risk by purchasing credit insurance or credit derivatives. These contracts transfer the risk from the lender to the seller (insurer) in exchange for payment. The most common credit derivative is the credit default swap.

- Tightening – Lenders can reduce credit risk by reducing the amount of credit extended, either in total or to certain borrowers. For example, a distributor selling its products to a troubled retailer may attempt to lessen credit risk by reducing payment terms from *net 30* to *net 15*.
- Diversification – Lenders to a small number of borrowers (or kinds of borrower) face a high degree of unsystematic credit risk, called concentration risk. Lenders reduce this risk by diversifying the borrower pool.
- Deposit insurance – Governments may establish deposit insurance to guarantee bank deposits in the event of insolvency and to encourage consumers to hold their savings in the banking system instead of in cash.

FOREIGN EXCHANGE RISK

Foreign exchange risk (also known as FX risk, exchange rate risk or currency risk) is a financial risk that exists when a financial transaction is denominated in a currency other than the domestic currency of the company. The exchange risk arises when there is a risk of significant appreciation of the domestic currency in relation to the denominated currency before the date when the transaction is completed.

Foreign exchange risk also exists when the foreign subsidiary of a firm maintains financial statements in a currency other than the domestic currency of the consolidated entity.

Investors and businesses exporting or importing goods and services, or making foreign investments, have an exchange-rate risk but can take steps to manage (i.e. reduce) the risk.

Types of Foreign Exchange Risk

Economic Risk

A firm has *economic risk* (also known as *forecast risk*) to the degree that its market value is influenced by unexpected exchange-rate fluctuations, which can severely affect the firm's market share with regard to its competitors, the firm's future cash flows, and ultimately the firm's value. Economic risk can affect the present value of future cash flows. An example of an economic risk would be a shift in exchange rates that influences the demand for a good sold in a foreign country.

Another example of an economic risk is the possibility that macroeconomic conditions will influence an investment in a foreign country. Macroeconomic conditions include exchange rates, government regulations, and political stability. When financing an investment or a project, a company's operating costs, debt obligations, and the ability to predict economically unsustainable circumstances should be thoroughly calculated in order to produce adequate revenues in covering those economic risks. For instance, when an American company invests money in a manufacturing plant in Spain, the Spanish government might institute changes that negatively impact the American company's ability to operate the plant, such as changing laws or even seizing the plant, or to otherwise make it difficult for the American company to move its profits out of Spain. As a result, all possible risks that outweigh an investment's profits and outcomes need to be closely scrutinized and strategically planned before initiating the investment. Other examples of potential economic risk are steep market downturns, unexpected cost overruns, and low demand for goods.

International investments are associated with significantly higher economic risk levels as compared to domestic investments. In international firms, economic risk heavily affects not only investors but also bondholders and shareholders, especially when dealing with the sale and purchase of foreign government bonds. However, economic risk can also create opportunities and profits for investors globally. When investing in foreign bonds, investors can profit from the fluctuation of the foreign-exchange markets and interest rates in different countries. Investors should always be aware of possible changes by the foreign regulatory authorities. Changing laws and regulations regarding sizes, types, timing, credit quality, and disclosures of bonds will immediately and directly affect investments in foreign countries. For example, if a central bank in a foreign country raises interest rates or the legislature increases taxes, the return on investment will be significantly impacted. As a result, economic risk can be reduced by utilizing various analytical and predictive tools that consider the diversification of time, exchange rates, and economic development in multiple countries, which offer different currencies, instruments, and industries.

When making a comprehensive economic forecast, several risk factors should be noted. One of the most effective strategies is to develop a set of positive and negative risks that associate with the standard economic metrics of an investment. In a macroeconomic model, major risks include changes in GDP, exchange-rate fluctuations, and commodity-price and stock-market fluctuations. It is equally critical to identify the stability of the economic system. Before initiating an investment, a firm should consider the stability of the investing sector that influences the exchange-rate changes. For instance, a service sector is less likely to have inventory swings and exchange-rate changes as compared to a large consumer sector.

Contingent Risk

A firm has *contingent risk* when bidding for foreign projects, negotiating other contracts, or handling direct foreign investments. Such a risk arises from the potential of a firm to suddenly face a transnational or economic foreign-exchange risk contingent on the outcome of some contract or negotiation. For example, a firm could be waiting for a project bid to be accepted by a foreign business or government that, if accepted, would result in an immediate receivable. While waiting, the firm faces a contingent risk from the uncertainty as to whether or not that receivable will accrue.

Transaction Risk

Companies will often participate in a transaction involving more than one currency. In order to meet the legal and accounting standards of processing these transactions, companies have to translate foreign currencies involved into their domestic currency. A firm has *transaction risk* whenever it has contractual cash flows (receivables and payables) whose values are subject to unanticipated changes in exchange rates due to a contract being denominated in a foreign currency. To realize the domestic value of its foreign-denominated cash flows, the firm must exchange, or translate, the foreign currency for domestic.

When firms negotiate contracts with set prices and delivery dates in the face of a volatile foreign exchange market, with rates constantly fluctuating between initiating a transaction and its settlement, or payment, those firms face the risk of significant loss. Businesses have the goal of making all monetary transactions profitable ones, and the currency markets must thus be carefully observed.

Applying public accounting rules causes firms with transnational risks to be impacted by a process known as "re-measurement". The current value of contractual cash flows are remeasured on each balance sheet.

Translation Risk

A firm's *translation risk* is the extent to which its financial reporting is affected by exchange-rate movements. As all firms generally must prepare consolidated financial statements for reporting purposes, the consolidation process for multinationals entails translating foreign assets and liabilities, or the financial statements of foreign subsidiaries, from foreign to domestic currency. While translation risk may not affect a firm's cash flows, it could have a significant impact on a firm's reported earnings and therefore its stock price.

Translation risk deals with the risk to a company's equities, assets, liabilities, or income, any of which can change in value due to fluctuating foreign exchange rates when a portion is denominated in a foreign currency. A company doing business in a foreign country will eventually have to exchange its host country's currency back into their domestic currency. When exchange rates appreciate or depreciate, significant, difficult-to-predict changes in the value of the foreign currency can occur. For example, U.S. companies must translate Euro, Pound, Yen, etc., statements into U.S. dollars. A foreign subsidiary's income statement and balance sheet are the two financial statements that must be translated. A subsidiary doing business in the host country usually follows that country's prescribed translation method, which may vary, depending on the subsidiary's business operations.

Subsidiaries can be characterized as either an integrated or a self-sustaining foreign entity. An integrated foreign entity operates as an extension of the parent company, with cash flows and business operations that are highly interrelated with those of the parent. A self-sustaining foreign entity operates in its local economic environment, independent of the parent company. Both integrated and self-sustaining foreign entities operate use functional currency, which is the currency of the primary economic environment in which the subsidiary operates and in which day-to-day operations are transacted. Management must evaluate the nature of its foreign subsidiaries to determine the appropriate functional currency for each.

There are three translation methods: current-rate method, temporal method, and U.S. translation procedures. Under the current-rate method, all financial statement line items are translated at the "current" exchange rate. Under the temporal method, specific assets and liabilities are translated at exchange rates consistent with the timing of the item's creation. The U.S. translation procedures differentiate foreign subsidiaries by functional currency, not subsidiary characterization. If a firm translates by the temporal method, a zero net exposed position is called fiscal balance. The temporal method cannot be achieved by the current-rate method because total assets will have to be matched by an equal amount of debt, but the equity section of the balance sheet must be translated at historical exchange rates.

Measuring Risk

If foreign-exchange markets are efficient—such that purchasing power parity, interest rate parity, and the international Fisher effect hold true—a firm or investor needn't concern itself with foreign exchange risk. A deviation from one or more of the three international parity conditions generally needs to occur for there to be a significant exposure to foreign-exchange risk.

Financial risk is most commonly measured in terms of the variance or standard deviation of a quantity such as percentage returns or rates of change. In foreign exchange, a relevant factor would be the rate of change of the foreign currency spot exchange rate. A variance, or spread, in exchange rates indicates enhanced risk, whereas standard deviation represents exchange-rate risk by the amount exchange rates deviate, on average, from the mean exchange rate in a probabilistic distribution. A higher standard deviation would signal a greater currency risk. Because of its uniform treatment of deviations and for the automatically squaring of deviation values, economists have criticized the accuracy of standard deviation as a risk indicator. Alternatives such as average absolute deviation and semivariance have been advanced for measuring financial risk.

Value at Risk

Practitioners have advanced, and regulators have accepted, a financial risk management technique called value at risk (VaR), which examines the tail end of a distribution of returns for changes in exchange rates, to highlight the outcomes with the worst returns. Banks in Europe have been authorized by the Bank for International Settlements to employ VaR models of their own design in establishing capital requirements for given levels of market risk. Using the VaR model helps risk managers determine the amount that could be lost on an investment portfolio over a certain period of time with a given probability of changes in exchange rates.

Managing Risk

Transaction Hedging

Firms with exposure to foreign-exchange risk may use a number of hedging strategies to reduce that risk. Transaction exposure can be reduced either with the use of money markets, foreign exchange derivatives—such as forward contracts, options, futures contracts, and swaps—or with operational techniques such as currency invoicing, leading and lagging of receipts and payments, and exposure netting. Each hedging strategy comes with its own benefits that may make it more suitable than another, based on the nature of the business and risks it may encounter.

Forward and futures contracts serve similar purposes: they both allow transactions that take place in the future—for a specified price at a specified rate—that offset otherwise adverse exchange fluctuations. Forward contracts are more flexible, to an extent, because they can be customized to specific transactions, whereas futures come in standard amounts and are based on certain commodities or assets, such as other currencies. Because futures are only available for certain currencies and time periods, they cannot entirely mitigate risk, because there is always the chance that exchange rates will move in your favor. However, the standardization of futures can be a part of what makes them attractive to some: they are well-regulated and are traded only on exchanges.

Two popular and inexpensive methods companies can use to minimize potential losses is hedging with options and forward contracts. If a company decides to purchase an option, it is able to set a rate that is "at-worst" for the transaction. If the option expires and it's out-of-the-money, the company is able to execute the transaction in the open market at a favorable rate. If a company decides to take out a forward contract, it will set a specific currency rate for a set date in the future.

Currency invoicing refers to the practice of invoicing transactions in the currency that benefits the firm. It is important to note that this does not necessarily eliminate foreign exchange risk, but rather moves its burden from one party to another. A firm can invoice its imports from another country in its home currency, which would move the risk to the exporter and away from itself. This technique may not be as simple as it sounds; if the exporter's currency is more volatile than that of the importer, the firm would want to avoid invoicing in that currency. If both the importer and exporter want to avoid using their own currencies, it is also fairly common to conduct the exchange using a third, more stable currency.

If a firm looks to leading and lagging as a hedge, it must exercise extreme caution. Leading and lagging refer to the movement of cash inflows or outflows either forward or backward in time. For example, if a firm must pay a large sum in three months but is also set to receive a similar amount from another order, it might move the date of receipt of the sum to coincide with the payment. This delay would be termed lagging. If the receipt date were moved sooner, this would be termed leading the payment.

Another method to reduce exposure transaction risk is natural hedging (or netting foreign-exchange exposures), which is an efficient form of hedging because it will reduce the margin that is taken by banks when businesses exchange currencies; and it is a form of hedging that is easy to understand. To enforce the netting, there will be a systematic-approach requirement, as well as a real-time look at exposure and a platform for initiating the process, which, along with the foreign cash flow uncertainty, can make the procedure seem more difficult. Having a back-up plan, such as foreign-currency accounts, will be helpful in this process. The companies that deal with inflows and outflows in the same currency will experience efficiencies and a reduction in risk by calculating the net of the inflows and outflows, and using foreign-currency account balances that will pay in part for some or all of the exposure.

Translation Hedging

Translation exposure is largely dependent on the translation methods required by accounting standards of the home country. For example, the United States Federal Accounting Standards Board specifies when and where to use certain methods. Firms can manage translation exposure by performing a balance sheet hedge, since translation exposure arises from discrepancies between net assets and net liabilities solely from exchange rate differences. Following this logic, a firm could acquire an appropriate amount of exposed assets or liabilities to balance any outstanding discrepancy. Foreign exchange derivatives may also be used to hedge against translation exposure.

A common technique to hedge translation risk is called balance-sheet hedging, which involves speculating on the forward market in hopes that a cash profit will be realized to offset a non-cash loss from translation. This requires an equal amount of exposed foreign currency assets and liabilities on the firm's consolidated balance sheet. If this is achieved for each foreign currency, the net translation exposure will be zero. A change in the exchange rates will change the value of exposed liabilities to an equal degree but opposite to the change in the value of exposed assets.

Companies can also attempt to hedge translation risk by purchasing currency swaps or futures contracts. Companies can also request clients to pay in the company's domestic currency, whereby the risk is transferred to the client.

Strategies other than Financial Hedging

Firms may adopt strategies other than financial hedging for managing their economic or operating exposure, by carefully selecting production sites with a mind for lowering costs, using a policy of flexible sourcing in its supply chain management, diversifying its export market across a greater number of countries, or by implementing strong research and development activities and differentiating its products in pursuit of less foreign-exchange risk exposure.

By putting more effort into researching alternative methods for production and development, it is possible that a firm may discover more ways to produce their outputs locally rather than relying on export sources that would expose them to the foreign exchange risk. By paying attention to currency fluctuations around the world, firms can advantageously relocate their production to other countries. For this strategy to be effective, the new site must have lower production costs. There are many factors a firm must consider before relocating, such as a foreign nation's political and economic stability.

HOLDING PERIOD RISK

Holding period risk refers to the risk, whilst holding a bond, that a better opportunity will come around that you may be unable to act upon. The longer a bond's term, the more likely that a more attractive investment opportunity may arise.

You may have come across this term after investing in a security that you don't intend to sell on for a while. Generally, a holding period is considered long term when the investment is held for longer than one year.

An example of a holding period risk is a firm giving a potential retail client a sales quote that is active for a certain time. With the potential client having a certain time period in which to sign the offer for the commodity, the offering firm puts itself at a financial disadvantage since the market's price on the wholesale market may change. This financial risk is usually reduced by the offering firm placing a risk premium onto the wholesale price of a commodity.

LIQUIDITY RISK

Liquidity risk is a financial risk that for a certain period of time a given financial asset, security or commodity cannot be traded quickly enough in the market without impacting the market price.

Types

Market liquidity – An asset cannot be sold due to lack of liquidity in the market essentially a sub-set of market risk. This can be accounted for by:

- Widening bid/offer spread.
- Making explicit liquidity reserves.
- Lengthening holding period for VaR calculations.

Funding liquidity – Risk that liabilities:

- Cannot be met when they fall due.
- Can only be met at an uneconomic price.
- Can be name-specific or systemic.

Causes

Liquidity risk arises from situations in which a party interested in trading an asset cannot do it because nobody in the market wants to trade for that asset. Liquidity risk becomes particularly important to parties who are about to hold or currently hold an asset, since it affects their ability to trade.

Manifestation of liquidity risk is very different from a drop of price to zero. In case of a drop of an asset's price to zero, the market is saying that the asset is worthless. However, if one party cannot find another party interested in trading the asset, this can potentially be only a problem of the market participants with finding each other. This is why liquidity risk is usually found to be higher in emerging markets or low-volume markets.

Liquidity risk is financial risk due to uncertain liquidity. An institution might lose liquidity if its credit rating falls, it experiences sudden unexpected cash outflows, or some other event causes counterparties to avoid trading with or lending to the institution. A firm is also exposed to liquidity risk if markets on which it depends are subject to loss of liquidity.

Market and funding liquidity risks compound each other as it is difficult to sell when other investors face funding problems and it is difficult to get funding when the collateral is hard to sell. Liquidity risk also tends to compound other risks. If a trading organization has a position in an illiquid asset, its limited ability to liquidate that position at short notice will compound its market risk. Suppose a firm has offsetting cash flows with two different counterparties on a given day. If the counterparty that owes it a payment defaults, the firm will have to raise cash from other sources to make its payment. Should it be unable to do so, it too will default. Here, liquidity risk is compounding credit risk.

A position can be hedged against market risk but still entail liquidity risk. This is true in the above credit risk example—the two payments are offsetting, so they entail credit risk but not market risk. Another example is the 1993 *Metallgesellschaft* debacle. Futures contracts were used to hedge an over-the-counter finance (OTC) obligation. It is debatable whether the hedge was effective from a market risk standpoint, but it was the liquidity crisis caused by staggering margin calls on the futures that forced Metallgesellschaft to unwind the positions.

Accordingly, liquidity risk has to be managed in addition to market, credit and other risks. Because of its tendency to compound other risks, it is difficult or impossible to isolate liquidity risk. In all but the most simple of circumstances, comprehensive metrics of liquidity risk do not exist. Certain techniques of asset liability management can be applied to assessing liquidity risk. A simple test for liquidity risk is to look at future net cash flows on a day-by-day basis. Any day that has a sizeable negative net cash flow is of concern. Such an analysis can be supplemented with stress testing. Look at net cash flows on a day-to-day basis assuming that an important counterparty defaults.

Analyses such as these cannot easily take into account contingent cash flows, such as cash flows from derivatives or mortgage-backed securities. If an organization's cash flows are largely contingent, liquidity risk may be assessed using some form of scenario analysis. A general approach using scenario analysis might entail the following high-level steps:

- Construct multiple scenarios for market movements and defaults over a given period of time.
- Assess day-to-day cash flows under each scenario.

Because balance sheets differ so significantly from one organization to the next, there is little standardization in how such analyses are implemented.

Regulators are primarily concerned about systemic implications of liquidity risk.

Pricing

Risk-averse investors naturally require higher expected return as compensation for liquidity risk. The liquidity-adjusted CAPM pricing model therefore states that, the higher an asset's market-liquidity risk, the higher its required return.

A common method for estimating the upper bound for a security illiquidity discount is by using a Lookback option, where the premia is equal to the difference between the maximum value of a security during a restricted trading period and its value at the end of the period. When the method is extended for corporate debt it is shown that liquidity risk increases with a bond credit risk.

Measures of Liquidity Risk

Liquidity Gap

Culp defines the liquidity gap as the net liquid assets of a firm. The excess value of the firm's liquid assets over its volatile liabilities. A company with a negative liquidity gap should focus on their cash balances and possible unexpected changes in their values.

As a static measure of liquidity risk it gives no indication of how the gap would change with an increase in the firm's marginal funding cost.

Elasticity

Culp denotes the change of net of assets over funded liabilities that occurs when the liquidity premium on the bank's marginal funding cost rises by a small amount as the liquidity risk elasticity. For banks this would be measured as a spread over libor, for nonfinancials the LRE would be measured as a spread over commercial paper rates.

Problems with the use of liquidity risk elasticity are that it assumes parallel changes in funding spread across all maturities and that it is only accurate for small changes in funding spreads.

Measures of Asset Liquidity

Bid-offer Spread

The bid-offer spread is used by market participants as an asset liquidity measure. To compare different products the ratio of the spread to the product's bid price can be used. The smaller the ratio the more liquid the asset is.

This spread is composed of operational, administrative, and processing costs as well as the compensation required for the possibility of trading with a more informed trader.

Market Depth

Hachmeister refers to market depth as the amount of an asset that can be bought and sold at various bid-ask spreads. Slippage is related to the concept of market depth. Knight and Satchell mention a flow trader needs to consider the effect of executing a large order on the market and to adjust the bid-ask spread accordingly. They calculate the liquidity cost as the difference of the execution price and the initial execution price.

Immediacy

Immediacy refers to the time needed to successfully trade a certain amount of an asset at a prescribed cost.

Resilience

Hachmeister identifies the fourth dimension of liquidity as the speed with which prices return to former levels after a large transaction. Unlike the other measures, resilience can only be determined over a period of time, i.e., resilience is the capacity to recover.

Management

Liquidity-adjusted Value at Risk

Liquidity-adjusted VAR incorporates exogenous liquidity risk into Value at Risk. It can be defined at VAR + ELC (Exogenous Liquidity Cost). The ELC is the worst expected half-spread at a particular confidence level.

Another adjustment, introduced in the 1970s with a regulatory precursor to today's VAR measures, is to consider VAR over the period of time needed to liquidate the portfolio. VAR can be calculated over this time period. The BIS mentions "a number of institutions are exploring the use of liquidity adjusted-VAR, in which the holding periods in the risk assessment are adjusted by the length of time required to unwind positions".

Liquidity at Risk

Alan Greenspan (1999) discusses management of foreign exchange reserves and suggested a measure called Liquidity at risk. A country's liquidity position under a range of possible outcomes for relevant financial variables (exchange rates, commodity prices, credit spreads, etc.) is considered. It might be possible to express a standard in terms of the probabilities of different outcomes. For example, an acceptable debt structure could have an average maturity—averaged over estimated distributions for relevant financial variables—in excess of a certain limit. In addition, countries could be expected to hold sufficient liquid reserves to ensure that they could avoid new borrowing for one year with a certain ex ante probability, such as 95 percent of the time.

Scenario Analysis-based Contingency Plans

The FDIC discuss liquidity risk management and write "Contingency funding plans should incorporate events that could rapidly affect an institution's liquidity, including a sudden inability to securitize assets, tightening of collateral requirements or other restrictive terms associated with secured borrowings, or the loss of a large depositor or counterparty." Greenspan's liquidity at risk concept is an example of scenario based liquidity risk management.

Diversification of Liquidity Providers

If several liquidity providers are on call then if any of those providers increases its costs of supplying liquidity, the impact of this is reduced. The American Academy of Actuaries wrote "While a company is in good financial shape, it may wish to establish durable, ever-green (i.e., always available) liquidity lines of credit. The credit issuer should have an appropriately high credit rating to increase the chances that the resources will be there when needed."

Derivatives

Bhaduri, Meissner and Youn discuss five derivatives created specifically for hedging liquidity risk:

- Withdrawal option: A put of the illiquid underlying at the market price.
- Bermudan-style return put option: Right to put the option at a specified strike.
- Return swap: Swap the underlying's return for LIBOR paid periodicially.
- Return swaption: Option to enter into the return swap.
- Liquidity option: "Knock-in" barrier option, where the barrier is a liquidity metric.

REINVESTMENT RISK

Reinvestment risk refers to the possibility that an investor will be unable to reinvest cash flows (e.g., coupon payments) at a rate comparable to their current rate of return. Zero-coupon bonds are the only fixed-income security to have no investment risk since they issue no coupon payments.

Reinvestment risk is the likelihood that an investment's cash flows will earn less in a new security. For example, an investor buys a 10-year $100,000 Treasury note with an interest rate of 6%. The investor expects to earn $6,000 per year from the security.

However, at the end of the term, interest rates are 4%. If the investor buys another 10-year $100,000 Treasury note, they will earn $4,000 annually rather than $6,000. Also, if interest rates subsequently increase and they sell the note before its maturity date, they lose part of the principal.

Callable bonds are especially vulnerable to reinvestment risk. This is because callable bonds are typically redeemed when interest rates begin to fall. Upon redeeming the bonds, the investor will receive the face value, and the issuer has a new opportunity to borrow at a lower rate. If they are willing to reinvest, the investor will do so receiving a lower rate of interest.

Another Related Risk

Reinvestment risk also occurs with callable bonds. "Callable" means that the issuer can pay off the bond before maturity. One of the primary reasons bonds are called is because interest rates have fallen since the bond's issuance, and the corporation or the government can now issue new bonds with lower rates, thus saving the difference between the higher rate and the new lower rate.

It makes sense for the issuer to do this and it's a part of the contract the investor agrees to when buying a callable bond, but, unfortunately, this also means that, once again, the investor will have to put the cash back to work at the lower prevailing rate.

Avoiding Reinvestment Risk

Investors can try to fight reinvestment risk by investing in longer-term securities since this decreases the frequency at which cash becomes available and needs to be reinvested. Unfortunately, this also exposes the portfolio to even greater interest rate risk.

What investors may sometimes do—and did so increasingly in the low-interest-rate environment that followed the collapse of financial markets in late 2007—is to try to make up the lost interest income by investing in high-yield bonds (otherwise known as junk bonds). This is an understandable, but dubious, strategy because it's also well-known that junk bonds fail at particularly high rates when the economy isn't doing well, which generally coincides with a low-interest-rate environment.

A better way of at least partially mitigating reinvestment risk is to create a "bond ladder," a portfolio holding bonds with widely varying maturity dates. Because the market is essentially cyclical, high interest rates fall too low and then rise again. Chances are that only some of your bonds will mature in a low-interest-rate environment and these can usually be offset by other bonds that mature when interest rates are high.

Investing in actively managed bond funds may reduce the impact of reinvestment risk because the fund manager can take similar steps to mitigate risk. Over time, however, the yields on bond funds do tend to rise and fall with the market, so actively managed bond funds provide only limited protection against reinvestment risk.

Another possible strategy is to reinvest in investments not directly affected by falling interest rates. One goal of investments generally is to make them as uncorrelated as possible. This strategy, if successfully executed, achieves that. But it also involves a degree of sophistication and investment experience that not many retail investors possess.

Example of Reinvestment Risk

For example, Company A issues callable bonds with an 8% interest rate. Interest rates subsequently drop to 4%, presenting the company with an opportunity to borrow at a much lower rate. As a result, the company calls the bonds, pays each investor their share of principal and a small call premium, and issues new callable bonds with a 4%

interest rate. Investors may reinvest at the lower rate or seek other securities with higher interest rates.

Investors may reduce reinvestment risk by investing in non-callable securities. Also, zero-coupon bonds may be purchased since they do not make regular interest payments. Investing in longer-term securities is also an option since cash becomes available less frequently and does not need to be reinvested often.

A bond ladder, a portfolio of fixed-income securities with varying maturity dates, may help mitigate reinvestment risk. Bonds maturing when interest rates are low may be offset by bonds maturing when rates are high.

Having a fund manager can help reduce reinvestment risk; therefore, some investors consider allocating money into actively managed bond funds. However, because bond yields fluctuatex with the market, reinvestment risk still exists.

COMMODITY RISK

Commodity risk refers to the uncertainties of future market values and of the size of the future income, caused by the fluctuation in the prices of commodities. These commodities may be grains, metals, gas, electricity etc. A commodity enterprise needs to deal with the following kinds of risks:

- Price risk is arising out of adverse movements in the world prices, exchange rates, basis between local and world prices. The related price area risk usually has a rather minor impact.
- Quantity or volume risk.
- Cost risk (Input price risk).
- Political risk.

Groups at Risk

There are broadly four categories of agents who face the commodities risk:

- Producers (farmers, plantation companies, and mining companies) face price risk, cost risk (on the prices of their inputs) and quantity risk.
- Buyers (cooperatives, commercial traders and trait ants) face price risk between

the time of up-country purchase buying and sale, typically at the port, to an exporter.

- Exporters face the same risk between purchase at the port and sale in the destination market; and may also face political risks with regard to export licenses or foreign exchange conversion.
- Governments face price and quantity risk with regard to tax revenues, particularly where tax rates rise as commodity prices rise (generally the case with metals and energy exports) or if support or other payments depend on the level of commodity prices.

VOLUME RISK

Volume risk is a commodity risk which refers to the fact that a player in the commodity market has uncertain quantities of consumption or sourcing, i.e. production of the respective commodity. Examples of other circumstances which can cause large deviations from a volume forecast are weather (e.g. temperature-changes for gas consumption), the plant-availability, the collective customer outrage, but also regulatory interventions.

Another relevant cause of volatility risk in volumes and (or) prices of commodities is the financial investment in options or future contracts related to a commodity, which is achieved with the purpose of speculating, rather than hedging in order to reduce the risk of adverse price movements in assets.

Example: An electricity retailer cannot accurately predict the demand of all house holds for a given time which is why the producer cannot forecast the precise time that a power plant will provide more electricity that consumed, even if the plant always delivers the same output of energy.

EXPECTED SHORTFALL

Expected shortfall (ES) is a risk measure—a concept used in the field of financial risk measurement to evaluate the market risk or credit risk of a portfolio. The "expected shortfall at q% level" is the expected return on the portfolio in the worst $q\%$ of cases. ES is an alternative to value at risk that is more sensitive to the shape of the tail of the loss distribution.

Expected shortfall is also called conditional value at risk (CVaR), average value at risk (AVaR), and expected tail loss (ETL).

ES estimates the risk of an investment in a conservative way, focusing on the less profitable outcomes. For high values of q it ignores the most profitable but unlikely possibilities, while for small values of q it focuses on the worst losses. On the other hand, unlike the discounted maximum loss, even for lower values of q the expected shortfall does not consider only the single most catastrophic outcome. A value of q often used in practice is 5%.

Expected shortfall is considered a more useful risk measure than VaR because it is a coherent, and moreover a spectral, measure of financial portfolio risk. It is calculated for a given quantile-level q, and is defined to be the mean loss of portfolio value given that a loss is occurring at or below the q-quantile.

If $X \in L^p(\mathcal{F})$ (an Lp space) is the payoff of a portfolio at some future time and $0 < \alpha < 1$ then we define the expected shortfall as:

$$\mathrm{ES}_\alpha = -\frac{1}{\alpha}\int_0^\alpha VaR_\gamma(X)d\gamma ,$$

where VaR_γ is the value at risk. This can be equivalently written as:

$$ES_\alpha = -\frac{1}{\alpha}\left(\mathrm{E}[X\,1_{\{X\le x_\alpha\}}] + x_\alpha(\alpha - P[X \le x_\alpha])\right),$$

where $x_\alpha = \inf\{x \in \mathbb{R} : P(X \le x) \ge \alpha\}$ is the lower α-quantile and $1_A(x) = \begin{cases} 1 & \text{if } x \in A \\ 0 & \text{else} \end{cases}$ is the indicator function. The dual representation is:

$$\mathrm{ES}_\alpha = \inf_{Q \in \mathcal{Q}_\alpha} E^Q[X],$$

where $\mathcal{Q}_\alpha$ is the set of probability measures which are absolutely continuous to the physical measure P such that $\frac{dQ}{dP} \le \alpha^{-1}$ almost surely. Note that $\frac{dQ}{dP}$ is the Radon–Nikodym derivative of Q with respect to P.

Expected shortfall can be generalized to a general class of coherent risk measures on L^p spaces (Lp space) with a corresponding dual characterization in the corresponding L^q dual space. The domain can be extended for more general Orlitz Hearts.

If the underlying distribution for X is a continuous distribution then the expected shortfall is equivalent to the tail conditional expectation defined by $\mathrm{TCE}_\alpha(\mathrm{X}) = \mathrm{E}[\mathrm{X} \mid \mathrm{X} \le \text{-}\mathrm{VaR}_\alpha(\mathrm{X})]$.

Informally, and non rigorously, this equation amounts to saying "in case of losses so severe that they occur only alpha percent of the time, what is our average loss".

Expected shortfall can also be written as a distortion risk measure given by the distortion function:

$$g(x) = \begin{cases} \dfrac{x}{1-\alpha} & \text{if } 0 \le x < 1-\alpha, \\ 1 & \text{if } 1-\alpha \le x \le 1. \end{cases}$$

Example: If we believe our average loss on the worst 5% of the possible outcomes for our portfolio is EUR 1000, then we could say our expected shortfall is EUR 1000 for the 5% tail.

Example: Consider a portfolio that will have the following possible values at the end of the period:

probability of event	ending value of the portfolio
10%	0
30%	80
40%	100
20%	150

Now assume that we paid 100 at the beginning of the period for this portfolio. Then the profit in each case is (*ending value*−100) or:

probability of event	profit
10%	−100
30%	−20
40%	0
20%	50

From this table let us calculate the expected shortfall ES_q for a few values of q:

q	expected shortfall ES_q
5%	100
10%	100
20%	60
30%	$46.\bar{6}$
40%	40
50%	32
60%	$26.\bar{6}$
80%	20
90%	$12.\bar{2}$
100%	6

To see how these values were calculated, consider the calculation of $ES_{0.05}$, the expectation in the worst 5% of cases. These cases belong to (are a subset of) row 1 in the profit table, which have a profit of −100 (total loss of the 100 invested). The expected profit for these cases is −100.

Now consider the calculation of $ES_{0.20}$, the expectation in the worst 20 out of 100 cases. These cases are as follows: 10 cases from row one, and 10 cases from row two (note that 10+10 equals the desired 20 cases). For row 1 there is a profit of −100, while for row 2 a profit of −20. Using the expected value formula we get:

$$\frac{\frac{10}{100}(-100)+\frac{10}{100}(-20)}{\frac{20}{100}}=-60.$$

Similarly for any value of q. We select as many rows starting from the top as are necessary to give a cumulative probability of q and then calculate an expectation over those cases. In general the last row selected may not be fully used (for example in calculating $-ES_{0.20}$ we used only 10 of the 30 cases per 100 provided by row 2).

As a final example, calculate $-ES_1$. This is the expectation over all cases, or:

$$0.1(-100)+0.3(-20)+0.4\cdot 0+0.2\cdot 50=-6.$$

The value at risk (VaR) is given below for comparison:

q	VaR_q
$0\% \le q < 10\%$	−100
$10\% \le q < 40\%$	−20
$40\% \le q < 80\%$	0
$80\% \le q \le 100\%$	50

Properties

The expected shortfall ES_q increases as q decreases.

The 100%-quantile expected shortfall $ES_{1.0}$ equals negative of the expected value of the portfolio.

For a given portfolio, the expected shortfall ES_q is greater than or equal to the Value at Risk VaR_q at the same q level.

Optimization of Expected Shortfall

Expected shortfall, in its standard form, is known to lead to a generally non-convex optimization problem. However, it is possible to transform the problem into a linear program and find the global solution. This property makes expected shortfall a cornerstone of alternatives to mean-variance portfolio optimization, which account for the higher moments (e.g., skewness and kurtosis) of a return distribution.

Suppose that we want to minimize the expected shortfall of a portfolio. The key contribution of Rockafellar and Uryasev in their 2000 paper is to introduce the auxiliary function $F_\alpha(w,\gamma)$ for the expected shortfall:

$$F_\alpha(w,\gamma) = \gamma + \frac{1}{1-\alpha}\int_{\ell(w,x)\geq\gamma}[\ell(w,x)-\gamma]p(x)dx$$

Where $\gamma = VaR_\alpha(X)$ and $\ell(w,x)$ is a loss function for a set of portfolio weights $w \in \mathbb{R}^p$ to be applied to the returns. Rockafellar/Uryasev proved that $F_\alpha(w,\gamma)$ is convex with respect to γ and is equivalent to the expected shortfall at the minimum point. To numerically compute the expected shortfall for a set of portfolio returns, it is necessary to generate J simulations of the portfolio constituents; this is often done using copulas. With these simulations in hand, the auxiliary function may be approximated by:

$$\tilde{F}_\alpha(w,\gamma) = \gamma + \frac{1}{(1-\alpha)J}\sum_{j=1}^{J}[\ell(w,x_j)-\gamma]_+$$

This is equivalent to the formulation:

$$\min_{\gamma,z,w} \gamma + \frac{1}{(1-\alpha)J}\sum_{j=1}^{J} z_j, \quad \text{s.t. } z_j \geq \ell(w,x_j)-\gamma \geq 0$$

Finally, choosing a linear loss function $\ell(w,x_j) = -w^T x_j$ turns the optimization problem into a linear program. Using standard methods, it is then easy to find the portfolio that minimizes expected shortfall.

Formulas for Continuous Probability Distributions

Closed-form formulas exist for calculating the expected shortfall when the payoff of a portfolio X or a corresponding loss $L = -X$ follows a specific continuous distribution. In the former case the expected shortfall corresponds to the opposite number of the left-tail conditional expectation below $-VaR_\alpha(X)$:

$$\text{ES}_\alpha(X) = E[-X \mid X \leq -\text{VaR}_\alpha(X)] = -\frac{1}{\alpha}\int_0^\alpha \text{VaR}_\gamma(X)d\gamma = -\frac{1}{\alpha}\int_{-\infty}^{-\text{VaR}_\alpha(X)} xf(x)dx.$$

Typical values of α in this case are 5% and 1%.

For engineering or actuarial applications it is more common to consider the distribution of losses $L = -X$, the expected shortfall in this case corresponds to the right-tail conditional expectation above $VaR_\alpha(L)$ and the typical values of α are 95% and 99%.

$$ES_{\alpha}(L) = E[L \mid L \geq VaR_{\alpha}(L)] = \frac{1}{1-\alpha}\int_{\alpha}^{1} VaR_{\gamma}(L)d\gamma = \frac{1}{1-\alpha}\int_{VaR_{\alpha}(L)}^{+\infty} yf(y)dy.$$

Since some formulas below were derived for the left-tail case and some for the right-tail case, the following reconciliations can be useful:

$$ES_{\alpha}(X) = -\frac{1}{\alpha}E[X] + \frac{1-\alpha}{\alpha}ES_{\alpha}(L) \text{ and } ES_{\alpha}(L) = \frac{1}{1-\alpha}E[L] + \frac{\alpha}{1-\alpha}ES_{\alpha}(X).$$

Normal Distribution

If the payoff of a portfolio X follows normal (Gaussian) distribution with the p.d.f. $f(x) = \frac{1}{\sqrt{2\pi}\sigma}e^{-\frac{(x-\mu)^2}{2\sigma^2}}$ then the expected shortfall is equal to $ES_{\alpha}(X) = \mu + \sigma\frac{\varphi(\Phi^{-1}(\alpha))}{\alpha}$, where $\varphi(x) = \frac{1}{\sqrt{2\pi}}e^{-\frac{x^2}{2}}$ is the standard normal p.d.f., $\Phi(x)$ is the standard normal c.d.f., so $\Phi^{-1}(\alpha)$ is the standard normal quantile.

If the loss of a portfolio L follows normal distribution, the expected shortfall is equal to

$$ES_{\alpha}(L) = \mu + \sigma\frac{\varphi(\Phi^{-1}(\alpha))}{1-\alpha}.$$

Generalized Student's t-Distribution

If the payoff of a portfolio X follows generalized Student's t-distribution with the p.d.f. $f(x) = \frac{\tilde{A}(\frac{\nu+1}{2})}{\tilde{A}(\frac{\nu}{2})\sqrt{\pi\nu}\sigma}\left(1+\frac{1}{\nu}\left(\frac{x-\mu}{\sigma}\right)^2\right)^{-\frac{\nu+1}{2}}$ then the expected shortfall is equal to $ES_{\alpha}(X) = \mu + \sigma\frac{\nu+(T^{-1}(\alpha))^2}{\nu-1}\frac{\tau(T^{-1}(\alpha))}{1-\alpha}$, where $\tau(x) = \frac{\tilde{A}(\frac{\nu+1}{2})}{\tilde{A}(\frac{\nu}{2})\sqrt{\pi\nu}}(1+\frac{x^2}{\nu})^{-\frac{\nu+1}{2}}$ is the standard t-distribution c.d.f., $T(x)$ is the standard t-distribution c.d.f., so $T^{-1}(\alpha)$ is the standard t-distribution quantile.

If the loss of a portfolio L follows generalized Student's t-distribution, the expected shortfall is equal to $ES_{\alpha}(L) = \mu + \sigma\frac{\nu+(T^{-1}(\alpha))^2}{\nu-1}\frac{\tau(T^{-1}(\alpha))}{1-\alpha}$.

Laplace Distribution

If the payoff of a portfolio X follows Laplace distribution with the p.d.f.

$$f(x) = \frac{1}{2b} e^{-|x-\mu|/b},$$

and the c.d.f.

$$F(x) = \begin{cases} 1 - \frac{1}{2} e^{-(x-\mu)/b} & \text{if } x \geq \mu, \\ [4pt]\frac{1}{2} e^{(x-\mu)/b} & \text{if } x < \mu. \end{cases}$$

then the expected shortfall is equal to:

$$\mathrm{E}S_\alpha(X) = -\mu + b(1 - \ln 2\alpha)\mathrm{E}S_\alpha(X) = -\mu + b(1 - \ln 2\alpha).$$

If the loss of a portfolio L follows Laplace distribution, the expected shortfall is equal to:

$$\mathrm{E}S_\alpha(L) = \begin{cases} \mu + b\frac{\alpha}{1-\alpha}(1 - \ln 2\alpha) & \text{if } \alpha < 0.5, \\ [4pt]\mu + b[1 - \ln(2(1-\alpha))] & \text{if } \alpha \geq 0.5. \end{cases}$$

Logistic Distribution

If the payoff of a portfolio X follows logistic distribution with the p.d.f.

$f(x) = \frac{1}{s} e^{-\frac{x-\mu}{s}} \left(1 + e^{-\frac{x-\mu}{s}}\right)^{-2}$ and the c.d.f. $F(x) = \left(1 + e^{-\frac{x-\mu}{s}}\right)^{-1}$

then the expected shortfall is equal to $\mathrm{E}S_\alpha(X) = -\mu + s \ln \frac{(1-\alpha)^{1-\frac{1}{\alpha}}}{\alpha}$

If the loss of a portfolio L follows logistic distribution, the expected shortfall is equal to $\mathrm{E}S_\alpha(L) = \mu + s\frac{-\alpha \ln \alpha - (1-\alpha)\ln(1-\alpha)}{1-\alpha}$.

Exponential Distribution

If the loss of a portfolio L follows exponential distribution with the p.d.f.

$f(x) = \begin{cases} \lambda e^{-\lambda x} & \text{if } x \geq 0, \\ 0 & \text{if } x < 0. \end{cases}$ and the c.d.f. $F(x) = \begin{cases} 1 - e^{-\lambda x} & \text{if } x \geq 0, \\ 0 & \text{if } x < 0. \end{cases}$ then the expected shortfall is equal to $\mathrm{E}S_\alpha(L) = \frac{-\ln(1-\alpha)+1}{\lambda}$

Pareto Distribution

If the loss of a portfolio L follows Pareto distribution with the p.d.f.

$f(x)=\begin{cases}\frac{ax_m^a}{x^{a+1}} & \text{if } x \geq x_m, \\ 0 & \text{if } x < x_m.\end{cases}$ and the c.d.f. $F(x)=\begin{cases}1-(x_m/x)^a & \text{if } x \geq x_m, \\ 0 & \text{if } x < x_m.\end{cases}$ then the expected shortfall is equal to $\text{ES}_\alpha(L)=\frac{x_m a}{(1-\alpha)^{1/a}(a-1)}$.

Generalized Pareto Distribution (GPD)

If the loss of a portfolio L follows GPD with the p.d.f.

$$f(x)=\frac{1}{s}\Big(1+\frac{\xi(x-\mu)}{s}\Big)^{\left(-\frac{1}{\xi}-1\right)}$$

and the c.d.f.

$$F(x)=\begin{cases}1-\Big(1+\frac{\xi(x-\mu)}{s}\Big)^{-\frac{1}{\xi}} & \text{if } \xi \neq 0, \\ 1-\exp\Big(-\frac{x-\mu}{s}\Big) & \text{if } \xi = 0.\end{cases}$$

then the expected shortfall is equal to:

$$\text{E}S_\alpha(L)=\begin{cases}\mu+s\Big[\frac{(1-\alpha)^{-\xi}}{1-\xi}+\frac{(1-\alpha)^{-\xi}-1}{\xi}\Big] & \text{if } \xi \neq 0, \\ \mu+s[1-\ln(1-\alpha)] & \text{if } \xi = 0,\end{cases}$$

and the VaR is equal to:

$$\text{VaR}_\alpha(L)=\begin{cases}\mu+s\frac{(1-\alpha)^{-\xi}-1}{\xi} & \text{if } \xi \neq 0, \\ \mu-s\ln(1-\alpha) & \text{if } \xi = 0.\end{cases}$$

Weibull Distribution

If the loss of a portfolio L follows Weibull distribution with the p.d.f.

$f(x)=\begin{cases}\frac{k}{\lambda}\Big(\frac{x}{\lambda}\Big)^{k-1}e^{-(x/\lambda)^k} & \text{if } x \geq 0, \\ 0 & \text{if } x < 0.\end{cases}$ and the c.d.f.

$$F(x)=\begin{cases}1-e^{-(x/\lambda)^k} & \text{if } x\geq 0,\\ 0 & \text{if } x<0.\end{cases}$$ then the expected shortfall is equal to,

$\mathrm{E}S_\alpha(L)-\frac{\lambda}{1-\alpha}\Gamma\left(1+\frac{1}{k},-\ln(1-\alpha)\right)$, where $\tilde{A}(s,x)$ is the upper incomplete gamma function.

Generalized Extreme Value Distribution (GEV)

If the payoff of a portfolio X follows GEV with the p.d.f.

$$f(x)=\begin{cases}\frac{1}{\sigma}\left(1+\xi\frac{x-\mu}{\sigma}\right)^{-\frac{1}{\xi}-1}\exp\left[-\left(1+\xi\frac{x-\mu}{\sigma}\right)^{-\frac{1}{\xi}}\right] & \text{if } \xi\neq 0,\\ \frac{1}{\sigma}e^{-\frac{x-\mu}{\sigma}}e^{-e^{-\frac{x-\mu}{\sigma}}} & \text{if } \xi=0.\end{cases}$$ and the c.d.f.

$$F(x)=\begin{cases}\exp\left(-\left(1+\xi\frac{x-\mu}{\sigma}\right)^{-\frac{1}{\xi}}\right) & \text{if } \xi\neq 0,\\ \exp\left(-e^{-\frac{x-\mu}{\sigma}}\right) & \text{if } \xi=0.\end{cases}$$ then the expected shortfall is equal to,

$$ES_\alpha(X)=\begin{cases}-\mu-\frac{\sigma}{\alpha\xi}\left[\Gamma(1-\xi,-\ln\alpha)-\alpha\right] & \text{if } \xi\neq 0,\\ -\mu-\frac{\sigma}{\alpha}\left[\mathrm{li}(\alpha)-\alpha\ln(-\ln\alpha)\right] & \text{if } \xi=0.\end{cases}$$ and the VaR is equal to,

$$\mathrm{VaR}_\alpha(X)=\begin{cases}-\mu-\frac{\sigma}{\xi}\left[(-\ln\alpha)^{-\xi}-1\right] & \text{if } \xi\neq 0,\\ -\mu+\sigma\ln(-\ln\alpha) & \text{if } \xi=0.\end{cases}$$, where $\tilde{A}(s,x)$ is the upper incomplete gamma function, $\mathrm{li}(x)=\int\frac{dx}{\ln x}$ is the logarithmic integral function.

If the loss of a portfolio L follows GEV, then the expected shortfall is equal to

$$\mathrm{E}S_\alpha(X)=\begin{cases}\mu+\frac{\sigma}{(1-\alpha)\xi}\left[\gamma(1-\xi,-\ln\alpha)-(1-\alpha)\right] & \text{if } \xi\neq 0,\\ \mu+\frac{\sigma}{1-\alpha}\left[y-\mathrm{li}(\alpha)+\alpha\ln(-\ln\alpha)\right] & \text{if } \xi=0.\end{cases}$$, where $\gamma(s,x)$ is the lower incomplete gamma function, y is the Euler-Mascheroni constant.

Generalized Hyperbolic Secant (GHS) Distribution

If the payoff of a portfolio X follows GHS distribution with the p.d.f.

$f(x) = \frac{1}{2\sigma} sech(\frac{\pi}{2}\frac{x-\mu}{\sigma})$ and the c.d.f.

$F(x) = \frac{2}{\pi}\arctan[\exp(\frac{\pi}{2}\frac{x-\mu}{\sigma})]$ then the expected shortfall is equal to

$\mathrm{ES}_\alpha(X) = -\mu - \frac{2\sigma}{\pi}\ln(\tan\frac{\pi\alpha}{2}) - \frac{2\sigma}{\pi^2\alpha} i[\mathrm{Li}_2(-i\tan\frac{\pi\alpha}{2}) - Li_2(i\tan\frac{\pi\alpha}{2})]$, where Li_2 is the Spence's function, $i = \sqrt{-1}$ is the imaginary unit.

Johnson's SU-distribution

If the payoff of a portfolio X follows Johnson's SU-distribution with the

c.d.f. $F(x) = \Phi[\gamma + \delta \sinh^{-1}(\frac{x-\xi}{\lambda})]$ then the expected shortfall is equal to,

$$\mathrm{E}S_\alpha(X) = -\xi - \frac{\lambda}{2\alpha}\left[\exp(\frac{1-2\gamma\delta}{2\delta^2})\Phi\left(\Phi^{-1}(\alpha) - \frac{1}{\delta}\right) - \exp(\frac{1+2\gamma\delta}{2\delta^2})\Phi\left(\Phi^{-1}(\alpha) + \frac{1}{\delta}\right)\right],$$

where Φ is the c.d.f. of the standard normal distribution.

Burr Type XII Distribution

If the payoff of a portfolio X follows the Burr type XII distribution with the p.d.f.

$f(x) = \frac{ck}{\beta}(\frac{x-\gamma}{\beta})^{c-1}[1 + (\frac{x-\gamma}{\beta})^c]^{-k-1}$ and the c.d.f.

$F(x) = 1 - [1 + (\frac{x-\gamma}{\beta})^c]^{-k}$, the expected shortfall is equal to,

$$\mathrm{E}S_\alpha(X) = -\gamma - \frac{\beta}{\alpha}\left((1-\alpha)^{-1/k} - 1\right)^{1/c}\left[\alpha - 1 + {}_2F_1\left(\frac{1}{c}, k; 1 + \frac{1}{c}; 1 - (1-\alpha)^{-1/k}\right)\right],$$

where ${}_2F_1$ is the hypergeometric function. Alternatively,

$$\mathrm{E}S_\alpha(X) = -\gamma - \frac{\beta}{\alpha}\frac{ck}{c+1}((1-\alpha)^{-1/k} - 1)^{1+\frac{1}{c}}{}_2F_1(1 + \frac{1}{c}, k+1; 2 + \frac{1}{c}; 1 - (1-\alpha)^{-1/k}).$$

Dagum Distribution

If the payoff of a portfolio X follows the Dagum distribution with the p.d.f.

$f(x) = \frac{ck}{\beta}(\frac{x-\gamma}{\beta})^{ck-1}[1+(\frac{x-\gamma}{\beta})^{c}]^{-k-1}$ and the c.d.f.

$F(x) = [1+(\frac{x-\gamma}{\beta})^{-c}]^{-k}$, the expected shortfall is equal to,

$$\mathrm{E}\,S_{\alpha}(X) = -\gamma - \frac{\beta}{\alpha}\frac{ck}{ck+1}\left(\alpha^{-1/k}-1\right)^{-k-\frac{1}{c}}{}_{2}F_{1}\left(k+1, k+\frac{1}{c}; k+1+\frac{1}{c}; -\frac{1}{\alpha^{-1/k}-1}\right),$$ where

${}_{2}F_{1}$ is the hypergeometric function.

Lognormal Distribution

If the payoff of a portfolio X follows lognormal distribution, i.e. the random variable $\ln(1+X)$ follows normal distribution with the p.d.f.

$f(x) = \frac{1}{\sqrt{2\pi}\sigma}e^{-\frac{(x-\mu)^2}{2\sigma^2}}$, then the expected shortfall is equal to,

$\mathrm{E}\,S_{\alpha}(X) = 1-\exp\left(\mu+\frac{\sigma^2}{2}\right)\frac{\Phi(\Phi^{-1}(\alpha)-\sigma)}{\alpha}$, where $\mathrm{\ddot{O}}(x)$ is the standard normal c.d.f., so $\mathrm{\ddot{O}}^{-1}(\alpha)$ is the standard normal quantile.

Log-logistic Distribution

If the payoff of a portfolio X follows log-logistic distribution, i.e. the random variable $\ln(1+X)$ follows logistic distribution with the p.d.f.

$f(x) = \frac{1}{s}e^{-\frac{x-\mu}{s}}(1+e^{-\frac{x-\mu}{s}})^{-2}$, then the expected shortfall is equal to,

$\mathrm{E}\,S_{\alpha}(X) = 1-\frac{e^{\mu}}{\alpha}I_{\alpha}(1+s, 1-s)\frac{\pi s}{\sin \pi s}$, where I_{α} is the regularized incomplete beta function, $I_{\alpha}(a,b) = \frac{\mathrm{B}_{\alpha}(a,b)}{\mathrm{B}(a,b)}$.

As the incomplete beta function is defined only for positive arguments, for a more generic case the expected shortfall can be expressed with the hypergeometric function:

$$ES_{\alpha}(X) = 1-\frac{e^{\mu}\alpha^{s}}{s+1}{}_{2}F_{1}(s, s+1; s+2; \alpha).$$

If the loss of a portfolio L follows log-logistic distribution with p.d.f.

$f(x) = \frac{\frac{b}{a}(x/a)^{b-1}}{(1+(x/a)^{b})^{2}}$ and c.d.f. $F(x) = \frac{1}{1+(x/a)^{-b}}$, then the expected shortfall is equal to $\mathrm{E}S_\alpha(L)=\frac{a}{1-\alpha}\left[\frac{\pi}{b}\csc\left(\frac{\pi}{b}\right)-\mathrm{B}_\alpha\left(\frac{1}{b}+1,1-\frac{1}{b}\right)\right]$, where B_α is the incomplete beta function.

Log-laplace Distribution

If the payoff of a portfolio X follows log-Laplace distribution, i.e. the random variable $\ln(1+X)$ follows Laplace distribution the p.d.f. $f(x)=\frac{1}{2b}e^{-\frac{|x-\mu|}{b}}$, then the expected shortfall is equal to $\mathrm{E}S_\alpha(X)=\begin{cases}1-\frac{e^{\mu}(2\alpha)^{b}}{b+1} & \text{if } \alpha\le 0.5,\\ 1-\frac{e^{\mu}2^{-b}}{\alpha(b-1)}\left[(1-\alpha)^{(1-b)}-1\right] & \text{if } \alpha>0.5.\end{cases}$

Log-generalized Hyperbolic Secant (log-GHS) Distribution

If the payoff of a portfolio X follows log-GHS distribution, i.e. the random variable $\ln(1+X)$ follows GHS distribution with the p.d.f.

$f(x)=\frac{1}{2\sigma}sech(\frac{\pi}{2}\frac{x-\mu}{\sigma})$, then the expected shortfall is equal to,

$$\mathrm{E}S_\alpha(X)=1-\frac{1}{\alpha(\sigma+\pi/2)}\left(\tan\frac{\pi\alpha}{2}\exp\frac{\pi\mu}{2\sigma}\right)^{2\sigma/\pi}\tan\frac{\pi\alpha}{2}\,{}_2F_1\left(1,\frac{1}{2}+\frac{\sigma}{\pi};\frac{3}{2}+\frac{\sigma}{\pi};-\tan\left(\frac{\pi\alpha}{2}\right)^2\right),$$

where ${}_2F_1$ is the hypergeometric function.

Dynamic Expected Shortfall

The conditional version of the expected shortfall at the time t is defined by:

$$\mathrm{E}S_\alpha^t(X)=\operatorname{ess\,sup}_{Q\in\mathcal{Q}_\alpha^t}E^Q[-X\mid\mathcal{F}_t],$$

where $\mathcal{Q}_\alpha^t=\{Q=P|_{\mathcal{F}_t}:\frac{dQ}{dP}\le\alpha_t^{-1}\text{ a.s.}\}$.

This is not a time-consistent risk measure. The time-consistent version is given by:

$$\rho_\alpha^t(X)=\operatorname{ess\,sup}_{Q\in\tilde{\mathcal{Q}}_\alpha^t}E^Q[-X\mid\mathcal{F}_t]$$

such that:

$$\tilde{\mathcal{Q}}_\alpha^t=\left\{Q\ll P:\mathrm{E}\left[\frac{dQ}{dP}\mid\mathcal{F}_{\tau+1}\right]\le\alpha_t^{-1}\mathrm{E}\left[\frac{dQ}{dP}\mid\mathcal{F}_\tau\right]\forall\tau\ge t\text{ a.s.}\right\}.$$

References

- Marketrisk: investopedia.com, Retrieved 22 June, 2019
- Holding-period-risk-definition: capital.com, Retrieved 15 May, 2019
- Homaifar, Ghassem A. (2004). Managing Global Financial and Foreign Exchange Risk. Hoboken, NJ: John Wiley & Sons. ISBN 978-0-471-28115-3
- Acharya, V; Pedersen, L (2005). "Asset pricing with liquidity risk". Journal of Financial Economics. 77 (2): 375–410. doi:10.1016/j.jfineco.2004.06.007
- What-is-reinvestment-risk-416902: thebalance.com, Retrieved 18 April, 2019
- Carlo Acerbi; Dirk Tasche (2002). "Expected Shortfall: a natural coherent alternative to Value at Risk" (PDF). Economic Notes. 31 (2): 379–388. arXiv:cond-mat/0105191. doi:10.1111/1468-0300.00091. Retrieved April 25, 2012

Financial Risk

5 CHAPTER

A few of the diverse aspects related to risk management are risk breakdown structure, network theory, event chain methodology, value at risk, control self-assessment, risk pool, contingency plan, etc. This chapter carefully examines these diverse aspects of risk management to provide an extensive understanding of the subject.

Financial risk is one of the high-priority risk types for every business. Financial risk is caused due to market movements and market movements can include a host of factors. Based on this, financial risk can be classified into various types such as Market Risk, Credit Risk, Liquidity Risk, Operational Risk, and Legal Risk.

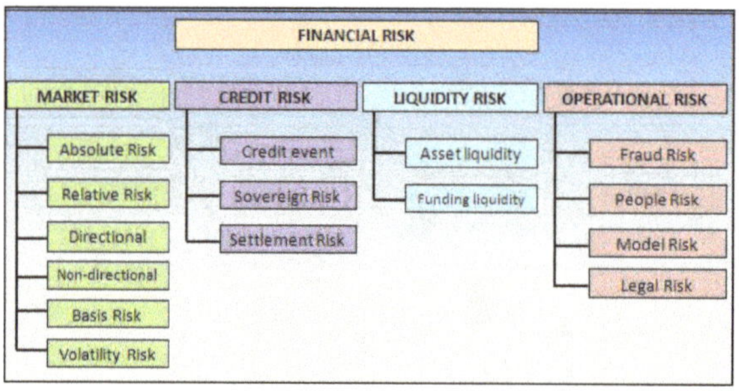

Market Risk

This type of risk arises due to the movement in prices of financial instrument. Market risk can be classified as Directional Risk and Non-Directional Risk. Directional risk is caused due to movement in stock price, interest rates and more. Non-Directional risk, on the other hand, can be volatility risks.

Credit Risk

This type of risk arises when one fails to fulfill their obligations towards their counterparties. Credit risk can be classified into Sovereign Risk and Settlement Risk. Sovereign risk usually arises due to difficult foreign exchange policies. Settlement risk, on the other hand, arises when one party makes the payment while the other party fails to fulfill the obligations.

Liquidity Risk

This type of risk arises out of an inability to execute transactions. Liquidity risk can be classified into Asset Liquidity Risk and Funding Liquidity Risk. Asset Liquidity risk arises either due to insufficient buyers or insufficient sellers against sell orders and buys orders respectively.

Operational Risk

This type of risk arises out of operational failures such as mismanagement or technical failures. Operational risk can be classified into Fraud Risk and Model Risk. Fraud risk arises due to the lack of controls and Model risk arises due to incorrect model application.

Legal Risk

This type of financial risk arises out of legal constraints such as lawsuits. Whenever a company needs to face financial loses out of legal proceedings, it is a legal risk.

DEPOSIT RISK

Deposit risk is one type of liquidity risk of a financial institution that is generated by deposits with the defined maturity dates (then such deposits are called time or term deposits) or without the ones (then such deposits are called demand or non-maturity deposits).

Types of Deposit Risk

Deposit risk is a risk of probable cash outflows from a financial institution that is caused by changes in depositors' behavior. In its turn, it consists of early withdrawal or redemption risk, rollover risk and run risk.

- Early withdrawal risk of time deposits is a risk that a depositor withdraws his or her deposit from an account before the agreed-upon maturity date. It might occur when the corresponding option was declared in a deposit agreement or determined by local laws. When an early withdrawal is made, the depositor usually incurs an early withdrawal fee or penalty.
- Rollover risk of time deposits is a risk that a depositor refuses to roll over his or her matured time deposit.
- Run risk of non-maturity deposits is a risk that a depositor takes back money from his or her accounts at any time. Thus, a run risk has characters of both early withdrawal and rollover risks. For instance, it occurs when depositors expect a bank to fail.

As a result, these risks might lead to dropping or even losing a liquidity of a financial institution if it cannot to attract new deposits instead of withdrawn ones. Wherein, the impossibility of the financial institution to refinance by borrowing in order to repay existing deposits is called a refinancing risk.

Exposures to Deposit Risk

- Exposure to early withdrawal risk at a given date is a sum of balances in time deposit accounts excluding those deposits that will be repaid at this date.
- Exposure to rollover risk at a given date is a sum of cash flows from deposits that will be matured at this date.
- Exposure to run risk at a given date is a sum of balances in non-maturity deposit accounts at this date.

An early withdrawal risk affects a rollover risk through decrease of cash flows that will be repaid in the future. The early withdrawal and rollover risks depend on a term to maturity of deposits. The more maturity, the more early withdrawal risk, and the lower rollover risk, and vice versa. The main financial determinants of the early withdrawal and rollover risks are interest rates of the financial institution and its competitors, term to maturity and age of deposit, credit rating of the financial institution, and amount of deposit insurance.

Evaluation of Deposit Risk

The considered types of deposit risk are usually evaluated by 'Cash Flow at Risk' (also CFaR) approach. Thus, 'Cash Flow at Deposit Risk' is possible cash outflows from a financial institution over a fixed period of time that are predicted with chosen confidence level.

MACRO RISK

Macro risk is financial risk that is associated with macroeconomic or political factors. There are at least three different ways this phrase is applied. It can refer to economic or financial risk found in stocks and funds, to political risk found in different countries, and to the impact of economic or financial variables on political risk. Macro risk can also refer to types of economic factors which influence the volatility over time of investments, assets, portfolios, and the intrinsic value of companies.

Macro risk associated with stocks, funds, and portfolios is usually of concern to financial planners, securities traders, and investors with longer time horizons. Some of the macroeconomic variables that generate macro risk include unemployment rates, price indexes, monetary policy variables, interest rates, exchange rates, housing starts, agricultural exports, and even commodity prices such as gold.

Models that incorporate macro risk are generally of two types. One type, used primarily by stock traders and institutions, focuses on how short-term changes in macro risk factors impact stock returns. These models include the arbitrage pricing theory and the modern portfolio theory families of models.

The other models that incorporate macro risk data are valuation models or the closely related fundamental analysis models. Used primarily by those focusing on longer term investments including wealth managers, financial planners, and some institutional investors, these models are examples of intrinsic value analysis. In such analysis, forecasts of future company earnings are used to estimate the current and expected value of the investment being studied. Macro risk factors include any economic variables that are used to construct these estimates.

Understanding that macro risk factors influence the intrinsic value of a particular investment is important because when the factors change values, errors can be introduced in the corresponding intrinsic value forecasts. Investors who follow the Black Swan Theory may try to reduce the overall exposure of their investments to different macro risk factors in order to reduce the impact of economic shocks. This may be accomplished using commercial portfolio optimization tools or by using mathematical programming methods.

Another way macro risk is used is to differentiate between countries as potential places to invest. In this meaning, the level of a country's macro risk differentiates its level of political stability and its general growth opportunities from those of other countries, and thus helps identify preferred countries for investment either directly or through country or regionally oriented funds. Such analysis of political risk is also used in the analysis of financial derivatives such as credit default swaps and other sophisticated financial products. International rankings of countries, often updated annually, provide insight into their relative political and social stability and economic growth.

A new application of macro risk is essentially a converse of the first two meanings; it refers to how macroeconomics and fluctuations in financial variables generate political risk. For example, economic turbulence that leads to higher or lower levels of approval for the president's policies would be a form of this macro risk.

VALUATION RISK

Valuation risk is the financial risk that an asset is overvalued and is worth less than expected when it matures or is sold. Factors contributing to valuation risk can include incomplete data, market instability, financial modeling uncertainties and poor data analysis by the people responsible for determining the value of the asset. This risk can be a concern for investors, lenders, financial regulators and other people involved in the financial markets. Overvalued assets can create losses for their owners and lead to reputational risks; potentially impacting credit ratings, funding costs and the management structures of financial institutions.

Valuation risks concern each stage of the transaction processing and investment management chain. From front office, to back office, distribution, asset management, private wealth and advisory services. This is particularly true for assets that have low liquidity and are not easily tradable in public exchanges. Moreover, issues associated with valuation risks go beyond the firm itself. With straight through processing and algorithmic trading, data and valuations must remain synchronized among the participants of the trade processing chain. The executing venue, prime brokers, custodian banks, fund administrators, transfer agents and audit share files electronically and try to automate such processes, raising potential risks related to data management and valuations.

To mitigate this risk it is important to provide transparency and ensure the integrity and consistency of the data, models and processes used to process and report calculations within valuations for all participants.

The growth and diversity made in financial engineering has led to highly creative and innovative strategies where new products and new structures are offered at very fast pace on the market. As most innovations are first proposed on over-the-counter (OTC) markets, they tend to rely on financial models, sometimes combining several models together. Financial models typically build on underlying assumptions and require calibration to a breadth of scenarios, business conditions and variations of the assumptions increasing the model risk.

The shock wave which affected the credit and capital markets following the burst of the US sub-prime mortgage crisis in late 2007, tested most underlying assumptions and had sweeping effects on a number of models that would unlikely be calibrated for extreme market conditions, or tail risk. This led to an emergency call for transparency and assessments of exposure from the financial institutions' clients, shareholders and managers, echoed by the regulators. In this process, it appears that market exposure and credit exposure intricately mix into a single notion of valuation risk.

Managing Valuation Risk

Valuation risks result from data management issues such as: Accuracy, integrity and consistency of static data. Accuracy and timeliness of information such as corporate events, credit events, or news potentially impact them. Streaming data, such as prices, rates, volatilities are even more vulnerable as they also depend on IT infrastructure and tools therefore adding a notion of technical and connectivity risk.

Some financial institutions have set up centralised data management platforms, open to multiple sources of static and streaming data where all financial instruments traded or held can possibly be defined, documented, priced, historised and distributed across the enterprise. Such centralisation facilitates data cleansing, historising and auditing, allow organisations to define and control pricing and valuation procedures as required for compliance. For OTC instruments, the platforms also involve the definition and storage of underlying information such as yield curves and credit curves, volatility surfaces, ratings and correlation matrices and probabilities of default.

In addition, an important aspect of managing valuation risk is associated with model risk. In search of transparency, market participants tend to adopt multiple model approaches and rely on consensus rather than science. In the absence of deep and liquid market transactions, and given the highly non-linear nature of some of the structured products, the mark-to-model process itself requires transparency. To achieve this, open pricing platforms may be linked to the centralised data warehouse. Those platforms are capable of using multiple models, scenarios, data sets with various distribution and dispersion models to price and re-price under ever-changing assumptions.

The final aspect of managing valuation risks relates to the actions that can be taken within the firm as a result of the assessments of exposures and sensitivities reported. The management of tail risks should also be reviewed so that allocating economic capital weighted by a very low probability of occurrence of an event amounted to considering a normal distribution of events or simply overlooking the tail risk.

ENDOGENOUS RISK

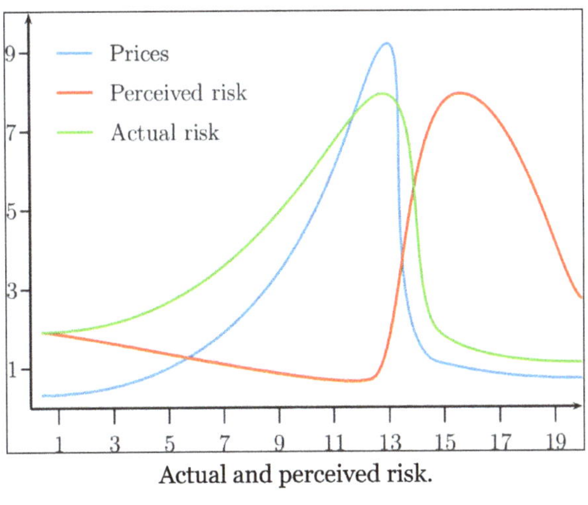

Actual and perceived risk.

Endogenous risk is a type of Financial risk that is created by the interaction of market participants. It was proposed by Jon Danielsson and Hyun-Song Shin in 2002.

Risk can be classified into the two categories of exogenous and endogenous risk. Under exogenous risk, shocks to the financial system arrived from outside the system, like an asteroid might hit the earth. Market participants react to the shock but do not influence it. By contrast, with endogenous risk, the interaction of market participants, each with their own abilities, biases, prejudices and resources, results in most market outcomes and all large outcomes. In particular, systemic risk is a form of endogenous risk.

As a practical interpretation of endogenous risk when applied to risk measurements, it can be further subdivided into actual risk, the underlying latent risk and perceived risk, what is reported by common risk measurement techniques, such as Value at risk and Expected shortfall. Shown in the figure on the right, as a financial asset enters into a bubble state, followed by a crash – up by the escalator, down by the lift – perceived risk, what is reported by typical risk measures, falls as the bubble builds up, sharply increasing after the bubble deflates. By contrast, actual risk increases along with the bubble, falling at the same time the bubble bursts. Perceived risk and actual risk are negatively correlated.

VOLATILITY RISK

Volatility risk is the risk of a change of price of a portfolio as a result of changes in the volatility of a risk factor. It usually applies to portfolios of derivatives instruments, where the volatility of its underlying is a major influencer of prices.

Sensitivity to Volatility

A measure for the sensitivity of a price of a portfolio (or asset) to changes in volatility is vega, the rate of change of the value of the portfolio with respect to the volatility of the underlying asset.

This kind of risk can be managed using appropriate financial instruments whose price depends on the volatility of a given financial asset (a stock, a commodity, an interest rate, etc.). Examples are Futures contracts such as VIX for equities, or caps, floors and swaptions for interest rates.

Risk management is the configuration and identification of analyzing, and or acceptance during investment decision-making. In essence this occurs whenever an investor or portfolio manager evaluates potential losses within an investment. Under certain investment objectives, appropriate solutions (or no solution) will occur to assess the investors goals and standards.

Improper risk management can and or will negatively affect companies as well as their individuals. For example, the recession that began in 2008 was largely caused by the loose credit risk management of financial firms.

MODEL RISK

In finance, model risk is the risk of loss resulting from using insufficiently accurate models to make decisions, originally and frequently in the context of valuing financial securities. However, model risk is more and more prevalent in activities other than financial securities valuation, such as assigning consumer credit scores, real-time probability prediction of fraudulent credit card transactions, and computing the probability of air flight passenger being a terrorist. Rebonato in 2002 defines model risk as "the risk of occurrence of a significant difference between the mark-to-model value of a complex and/or illiquid instrument, and the price at which the same instrument is revealed to have traded in the market".

Types

Burke regards failure to use a model (instead over-relying on expert judgment) as a type of model risk. Derman describes various types of model risk that arise from using a model:

Wrong Model

- Inapplicability of model.
- Incorrect model specification.

Model Implementation

- Programming errors.
- Technical errors.
- Use of inaccurate numerical approximations.

Model Usage

- Implementation risk.
- Data issues.
- Calibration errors.

Sources

Uncertainty on Volatility

Volatility is the most important input in risk management models and pricing models. Uncertainty on volatility leads to model risk. Derman believes that products whose value depends on a volatility smile are most likely to suffer from model risk.

Time Inconsistency

Buraschi and Corielli formalise the concept of 'time inconsistency' with regards to no-arbitrage models that allow for a perfect fit of the term structure of the interest rates. In these models the current yield curve is an input so that new observations on the yield curve can be used to update the model at regular frequencies. They explore the issue of time-consistent and self-financing strategies in this class of models. Model risk affects all the three main steps of risk management: specification, estimation and implementation.

Correlation Uncertainty

Uncertainty on correlation parameters is another important source of model risk. Cont and Deguest propose a method for computing model risk exposures in multi-asset equity derivatives and show that options which depend on the worst or best performances in a basket (so called rainbow option) are more exposed to model uncertainty than index options.

Gennheimer investigates the model risk present in pricing basket default derivatives. He prices these derivatives with various copulas and concludes that "unless one is very sure about the dependence structure governing the credit basket, any investors willing to trade basket default products should imperatively compute prices under alternative copula specifications and verify the estimation errors of their simulation to know at least the model risks they run".

Complexity

Complexity of a model or a financial contract may be a source of model risk, leading to incorrect identification of its risk factors. This factor was cited as a major source of model risk for mortgage backed securities portfolios during the 2007 crisis.

Illiquidity and Model Risk

Model risk does not only exist for complex financial contracts. Frey (2000) presents a study of how market illiquidity is a source of model risk. He writes "Understanding the robustness of models used for hedging and risk-management purposes with respect to the assumption of perfectly liquid markets is therefore an important issue in the analysis of model risk in general." Convertible bonds, mortgage-backed securities, and high-yield bonds can often be illiquid and difficult to value. Hedge funds that trade these securities can be exposed to model risk when calculating monthly NAV for its investors.

Quantitative Approaches

Model Averaging vs. Worst-case Approach

Rantala (2006) mentions that "In the face of model risk, rather than to base decisions on a single selected 'best' model, the modeller can base his inference on an entire set of models by using model averaging".

Another approach to model risk is the worst-case, or minmax approach, advocated in decision theory by Gilboa and Schmeidler. In this approach one considers a range of models and minimizes the loss encountered in the worst-case scenario. This approach to model risk has been developed by Cont.

Jokhadze and Schmidt propose several model risk measures using Bayesian methodology. They introduce superposed risk measures that incorporate model risk and enables consistent market and model risk management. Further, they provide axioms of model risk measures and define several practical examples of superposed model risk measures in the context of financial risk management and contingent claim pricing.

Quantifying Model Risk Exposure

To measure the risk induced by a model, it has to be compared to an alternative model, or a set of alternative benchmark models. The problem is how to choose these benchmark models. In the context of derivative pricing Cont (2006) proposes a quantitative approach to measurement of model risk exposures in derivatives portfolios: first, a set of benchmark models is specified and calibrated to market prices of liquid instruments, then the target portfolio is priced under all benchmark models. A measure of exposure to model risk is then given by the difference between the current portfolio valuation and the worst-case valuation under the benchmark models. Such a measure may be used as a way of determining a reserve for model risk for derivatives portfolios.

Position Limits and Valuation Reserves

Jokhadze and Schmidt introduce monetary market risk measures that covers model risk losses. Their methodology enables to harmonize market and model risk management and define limits and required capitals for risk positions.

Kato and Yoshiba discuss qualitative and quantitative ways of controlling model risk. They write "From a quantitative perspective, in the case of pricing models, we can set up a reserve to allow for the difference in estimations using alternative models. In the case of risk measurement models, scenario analysis can be undertaken for various fluctuation patterns of risk factors, or position limits can be established based on information obtained from scenario analysis." Cont advocates the use of model risk exposure for computing such reserves.

Mitigation

Theoretical Basis

- Considering key assumptions.
- Considering simple cases and their solutions (model boundaries).
- Parsimony.

Implementation

- Pride of ownership.
- Disseminating the model outwards in an orderly manner.

Testing

- Stress testing and backtesting.
- Avoid letting small issues snowball into large issues later on.
- Independent validation.
- Ongoing monitoring and against market.

Examples of Model Risk Mitigation

Parsimony

Taleb wrote when describing why most new models that attempted to correct the inadequacies of the Black–Scholes model failed to become accepted.

"Traders are not fooled by the Black–Scholes–Merton model. The existence of a 'volatility surface' is one such adaptation. But they find it preferable to fudge one parameter, namely volatility, and make it a function of time to expiry and strike price, rather than have to precisely estimate another".

However, Cherubini and Della Lunga describe the disadvantages of parsimony in the context of volatility and correlation modelling. Using an excessive number of parameters may induce overfitting while choosing a severely specified model may easily induce model misspecification and a systematic failure to represent the future distribution.

Model Risk Premium

Fender and Kiff note that holding complex financial instruments, such as CDOs, "translates into heightened dependence on these assumptions and, thus, higher model risk. As this risk should be expected to be priced by the market, part of the yield pick-up obtained relative to equally rated single obligor instruments is likely to be a direct reflection of model risk".

TOTAL RETURN SWAP

A Total Return Swap is a contract between two parties who exchange the return from a financial assetbetween them. In this agreement, one party makes payments based on a set rate while the other party makes payments based on the total return of an underlying asset. The underlying asset may be a bond, equity interest, or loan. Banks and other financial institutions use TRS agreements to manage risk exposurewith minimal cash outlay. However, in recent years, total return swaps are becoming more popular due to the increased regulatory scrutiny after the alleged manipulation of credit default swaps (CDS).

In a TRS contract, the party receiving the total return gets any income generated by the financial asset without actually owning it. The receiving party benefits from any price increases in the value of the assets during the lifetime of the contract. The receiver must then pay the asset owner the base interest rate during the life of the TRS. The asset owner forfeits the risk associated with the asset but absorbs the credit exposure risk that the asset is subjected to. For example, if the asset price falls during the lifetime of the TRS, the receiver will pay the asset owner a sum equal to the amount of the asset price decline.

Structure of a Total Return Swap Transaction

A TRS contract is made up of two parties, i.e., the payer and the receiver. The payer may be a bank, hedge fund, insurance company, or other cash-rich, fixed income portfolio manager. The total return payer agrees to pay the TRS receiver the total return on an underlying asset, while being paid LIBOR-based interest returns from the other party, the total return receiver. The underlying asset may be a corporate bond, bank loan, or sovereign bond.

The total return to the receiver includes interest payments on the underlying asset, plus any appreciation in the market value of the asset. The total return receiver pays the payer (asset owner) a LIBOR-based payment and the amount equal to any depreciation in the value of the asset (in the event that the value of the asset declines during the life of the TRS – no such payment occurs if the asset increases in value, as any appreciation in the asset's value goes to the TRS receiver). The TRS payer (asset owner) buys protection against a possible decline in the value of the asset by agreeing to pay all the future positive returns of the asset to the TRS receiver, in exchange for floating streams of payments.

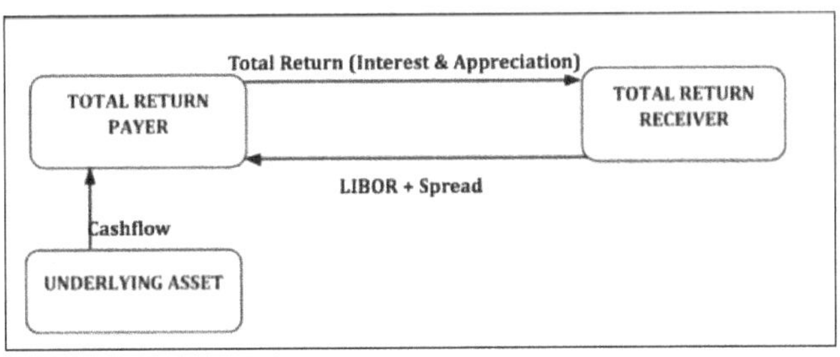

Requirements for Total Return Swaps

In a total return swap, the party receiving the total return collects any income generated by the asset and benefits if the price of the asset appreciates over the life of the swap. In exchange, the total return receiver must pay the asset owner the set rate over the life of the swap. If the asset's price falls over the swap's life, the total return receiver will be required to pay the asset owner the amount by which the asset has fallen. In a total return swap, the receiver assumes systematic, or market, risk and credit risk. Conversely, the payer forfeits the risk associated with the performance of the reference security but takes on the credit exposure to which the receiver may be subject.

Investing in Total Return Swaps

The major participants in the total return swap market include large institutional investors such as investment banks, mutual funds, commercial banks, pension funds, fund of funds, private equity funds, insurance companies, NGOs, and governments. Special Purpose Vehicles (SPVs) such as REITs and CDOs also participate in the market. Traditionally, TRS transactions were mostly between commercial banks, where bank (A) had already surpassed its balance sheet limits, while the other bank (B) still has available balance sheet capacity. Bank A could shift assets off its balance sheet and earn an extra income on these assets, while Bank B would lease the assets and make regular payments to Bank A, as well as compensate for depreciation or loss of value.

Hedge funds and SPVs are considered major players in the total return swap market, using TRS for leveraged balance sheet arbitrage. Usually, a hedge fund seeking exposure to particular assets pays for the exposure by leasing the assets from large institutional investors like investment banks and mutual funds. The hedge funds hope to earn high returns from leasing the asset, without having to pay the full price to own it, thus leveraging their investment. On the other hand, the asset owner expects to generate additional income in the form of LIBOR-based payments and getting a guarantee against capital losses. CDO issuers enter into a TRS agreement as protection sellers in order to gain exposure to the underlying asset without having to purchase it. The issuers receive interest on the underlying asset while the asset owner mitigates against credit risk.

Benefits of Total Return Swaps

One of the benefits of total return swaps is their operational efficiency. In a TRS agreement, the total return receiver does not have to deal with interest collection, settlements, payment calculations, and reports that are required in a transfer of ownership transaction. The asset owner retains ownership of the asset, and the receiver does not have to deal with the asset transfer process. The maturity date of the TRS agreement and the payment dates are agreed upon by both parties. The TRS contract maturity date does not have to correspond to the expiry date of the underlying asset.

The other major benefit of a total return swap is that it enables the TRS receiver to make a leveraged investment, thus making maximum use of its investment capital. Unlike in a repurchase agreement where there is a transfer of asset ownership, there is no ownership transfer in a TRS contract. This means that the total return receiver does not have to lay out substantial capital to purchase the asset. Instead, a TRS allows the receiver to benefit from the underlying asset without actually owning it, making it the most preferred form of financing for hedge funds and Special Purpose Vehicles (SPV).

Risks Associated with a Total Return Swap

There are several types of risk that parties in a TRS contract are subjected to. One of these is counterparty risk. When a hedge fund enters into multiple TRS contracts on similar underlying assets, any decline in the value of these assets will result in reduced returns as the fund continues to make regular payments to the TRS payer/owner. If the decline in the value of assets continues over an extended period and the hedge fund is not adequately capitalized, the payer will be at risk of the fund's default. The risk may be heightened by the high secrecy of hedge funds and the treatment of such assets as off-balance sheet items.

Both parties in a TRS contract are affected by interest rate risk. The payments made by the total return receiver equal to LIBOR +/- an agreed upon spread. An increase in LIBOR during the agreement increases the number of payments due to the payer, while a decrease in LIBOR decreases the payments to the payer. Interest rate risk is higher on the receiver's side, and they may hedge the risk through interest rate derivatives such as futures.

Total Return Swap Example

Assume that two parties enter into a one-year total return swap in which one party receives the London Interbank Offered Rate, or LIBOR, in addition to a fixed margin of 2%. The other party receives the total return of the Standard & Poor's 500 Index (S&P 500) on a principal amount of $1 million.

After one year, if LIBOR is 3.5% and the S&P 500 appreciates by 15%, the first party pays the second party 15% and receives 5.5%. The payment is netted at the end of the swap with the second party receiving a payment of $95,000, or $1 million x (15% - 5.5%). Conversely, consider that rather than appreciating, the S&P 500 falls by 15%. The first party would receive 15% in addition to the LIBOR rate plus the fixed margin, and the payment netted to the first party would be $205,000, or $1 million x (15% + 5.5%).

References

- Financial-risk-and-types-rar131-article: simplilearn.com, Retrieved 18 June, 2019
- Total-return-swap-trs: corporatefinanceinstitute.com, Retrieved 31 March, 2019
- Aretz, Kevin; Bartram, Söhnke M.; Pope, Peter F. (June 2010). "Macroeconomic Risks and Characteristic-Based Factor Models". Journal of Banking and Finance. 34 (6): 1383–1399. doi:10.1016/j.jbankfin.2009.12.006. SSRN 646522
- Totalreturnswap: investopedia.com, Retrieved 13 April, 2019
- Jokhadze, Valeriane; Schmidt, Wolfgang M. (2018). "Measuring model in financial risk management and pricing". SSRN. doi:10.2139/ssrn.3113139

Quality Related Risks

CHAPTER 6

Financial risk deals with various types of risks related to financial transactions of a company. Some of its concepts include macro risk, valuation risk, volatility risk, model risk, total return swap, etc. The topics elaborated in this chapter will help in gaining a better perspective of these concepts of financial risk.

QUALITY

Quality management is about making organisations perform for their stakeholders – from improving products, services, systems and processes, to making sure that the whole organisation is fit and effective.

Managing quality means constantly pursuing excellence: making sure that what your organisation does is fit for purpose, and not only stays that way, but keeps improving.

There's a lot more to managing quality than just manufacturing widgets without any defects or getting trains to run on time – although those things are certainly part of the picture.

What qualifies as an acceptable level of quality for an organisation is ultimately a question for stakeholders. And by stakeholders, we mean anyone who has an interest in the success of what your organisation does.

Customers will be the most important group of stakeholders for the majority of businesses, but investors, employees, suppliers and members of our wider society are stakeholders too. Delivering an acceptable level of quality in your organisation means knowing who your stakeholders are, understanding what their needs are and meeting those needs (or even better, exceeding expectations), both now and in the future.

This comes down to three things: strong governance to define the organisation's aims and translate them into action, robust systems of assurance to make sure things stay on track and a culture of improvement to keep getting better.

Importance of Quality for Organisations

To survive and thrive. Managing quality effectively can enhance your organisation's brand and reputation, protect it against risks, increase its efficiency, boost its profits and position it to keep on growing. All while making staff and customers happier.

Quality is not just a box to be ticked or something you pay lip service to. Failures resulting from poor governance, ineffective assurance and resistance to change can, and do, have dire consequences for businesses, individuals and society as a whole.

For example, the company BP faces a total bill of £35bn from the Gulf of Mexico oil spill of 2010, which left 11 people dead, the region's environment devastated and an indelible stain on BP's reputation.

Or Volkswagen, which will be dealing with the fallout from the 2015 emissions cheating scandal for years to come (it's still too early to know how much it will cost them, but the amount will run to 10 figures at least).

Or the retailers Tesco, Iceland, Aldi and Lidl, whose reputations took a battering in 2013 when beef products were found to contain horsemeat.

None of these things need have happened if the organisation had been managing the quality of its outputs more effectively. But quality isn't just about disaster prevention – it's about achieving great results, and seizing opportunities to get better and better.

Quality isn't just an issue for commercial enterprises. Every organisation has stakeholders of one kind or another whose needs they must strive to meet, which is what effective quality management is ultimately about.

Everything. Every product, service, process, task, action or decision in an organisation can be judged in terms of its quality – how good is it, is it good enough, how can we make it better?

The Person who is Responsible for Quality

Everyone from the CEO to the intern is responsible for the quality of what they do. Different people will have responsibility or influence over different things that affect the quality of an organisation's outputs, such as specifying requirements, meeting those requirements or determining the quality of something.

Having said that, it's important to have people who can provide the knowledge, tools and guidance to help everyone else play their part in determining and achieving the required level of quality. These people are quality professionals and their job is to make organisations better at producing outputs that satisfy the needs and expectations of their stakeholders.

They come in many guises: some are generalists, some are specialists. Many will have titles such as quality manager, quality engineer, quality director or assurance manager, while others deal with aspects of quality as part of a broader remit. Some are concerned with the delivery of products and services, while some are part of the leadership of their organisations. Some are employed in-house, while others work outside the organisations they deal with.

What unites quality professionals is their dedication to protecting and strengthening their organisations by making sure stakeholders' needs are met – and ideally, that their expectations are exceeded.

Quality Management

Quality management ensures that an organization, product or service is consistent. It has four main components: quality planning, quality assurance, quality control and quality improvement. Quality management is focused not only on product and service quality, but also on the means to achieve it. Quality management, therefore, uses quality assurance and control of processes as well as products to achieve more consistent quality. What a customer wants and is willing to pay for it determines quality. It is written or unwritten commitment to a known or unknown consumer in the market. Thus, quality can be defined as fitness for intended use or, in other words, how well the product performs its intended function.

Quality management is a recent phenomenon but important for an organization. Civilizations that supported the arts and crafts allowed clients to choose goods meeting higher quality standards rather than normal goods. In societies where arts and crafts are the responsibility of master craftsmen or artists, these masters would lead their studios and train and supervise others. The importance of craftsmen diminished as mass production and repetitive work practices were instituted. The aim was to produce large numbers of the same goods. The first proponent in the US for this approach was Eli Whitney who proposed (interchangeable) parts manufacture for muskets, hence producing the identical components and creating a musket assembly line. The next step forward was promoted by several people including Frederick Winslow Taylor, a mechanical engineer who sought to improve industrial efficiency. He is sometimes called "the father of scientific management." He was one of the intellectual leaders of the Efficiency Movement and part of his approach laid a further foundation for quality management, including aspects like standardization and adopting improved practices. Henry Ford was also important in bringing process and quality management practices into operation in his assembly lines. In Germany, Karl Benz, often called the inventor of the motor car, was pursuing similar assembly and production practices, although real mass production was properly initiated in Volkswagen after World War II. From this period onwards, North American companies focused predominantly upon production against lower cost with increased efficiency.

Walter A. Shewhart made a major step in the evolution towards quality management by creating a method for quality control for production, using statistical methods, first proposed in 1924. This became the foundation for his ongoing work on statistical quality control. W. Edwards Deming later applied statistical process control methods in the United States during World War II, thereby successfully improving quality in the manufacture of munitions and other strategically important products.

Quality leadership from a national perspective has changed over the past decades. After the second world war, Japan decided to make quality improvement a national imperative as part of rebuilding their economy, and sought the help of Shewhart, Deming and Juran, amongst others. W. Edwards Deming championed Shewhart's ideas in Japan from 1950 onwards. He is probably best known for his management philosophy establishing quality, productivity, and competitive position. He has formulated 14 points of attention for managers, which are a high level abstraction of many of his deep insights. They should be interpreted by learning and understanding the deeper insights. These 14 points include key concepts such as:

- Break down barriers between departments.
- Management should learn their responsibilities, and take on leadership.
- Supervision should be to help people and machines and gadgets to do a better job.
- Improve constantly and forever the system of production and service.
- Institute a vigorous program of education and self-improvement.

In the 1950s and 1960s, Japanese goods were synonymous with cheapness and low quality, but over time their quality initiatives began to be successful, with Japan achieving high levels of quality in products from the 1970s onward. For example, Japanese cars regularly top the J.D. Power customer satisfaction ratings. In the 1980s Deming was asked by Ford Motor Company to start a quality initiative after they realized that they were falling behind Japanese manufacturers. A number of highly successful quality initiatives have been invented by the Japanese. Many of the methods not only provide techniques but also have associated quality culture (i.e. people factors). These methods are now adopted by the same western countries that decades earlier derided Japanese methods.

Customers recognize that quality is an important attribute in products and services. Suppliers recognize that quality can be an important differentiator between their own offerings and those of competitors (quality differentiation is also called the quality gap). In the past two decades this quality gap has been greatly reduced between competitive products and services. This is partly due to the contracting (also called outsourcing) of manufacture to countries like China and India, as well internationalization of trade and competition. These countries, among many others, have raised their own standards of quality in order to meet international standards and customer demands. The ISO 9000 series of standards are probably the best known International standards for quality management.

Customer satisfaction is the backbone of Quality Management. Setting up a million dollar company without taking care of needs of customer will ultimately decrease its revenue.

There are many books available on quality management. Some themes have become more significant including quality culture, the importance of knowledge management, and the role of leadership in promoting and achieving high quality. Disciplines like systems thinking are bringing more holistic approaches to quality so that people, process and products are considered together rather than independent factors in quality management.

The influence of quality thinking has spread to non-traditional applications outside of walls of manufacturing, extending into service sectors and into areas such as sales, marketing and customer service.

QUALITY RISK MANAGEMENT

Quality Risk Management sits at the intersection of 3 different trends that are impacting many large industrial companies today: Quality, Sustainability, and Risk. In large companies, it would not be unusual to find director or vice president level positions in charge of each of these areas. There are also a lot of similarities between these three, including:

- The reporting structures and responsibilities of people in the areas of quality, sustainability, and risk are ill-defined. Many questions still exist as to if they are best served being part of finance, the supply chain, or reporting directly to the CEO.
- The business processes managed in each of these areas are also ill-defined and generally not managed as part of a traditional ERP system.
- Other than quality, these are relatively new positions. It is likely that VP of Sustainability or VP of Risk roles were created in the last year or two and it is very unlikely they would have been around more than five years ago.
- All three can not exist in a silo. By their very definition, they impact every major piece of the value chain: product development, suppliers, manufacturing, distribution, and service.

Quality

Although the language of risk is not always familiar to quality professionals, most of what they do and are responsible for can be understood as either risk identification or risk mitigation activities. Quality business processes like those in the below list can all be considered risk identification and risk mitigation processes by another name:

- Advanced Product Quality Planning (APQP).
- Failure Modes and Effect Analysis (FMEA).
- Supplier Quality Management.
- Non-Conformances / Corrective and Preventive Actions (NC/CAPA).

Other quality business processes can also be thought of in terms of risk. Many of the quality activities that are mandated by government regulations, like those in the below list, are just risk controls put in place to mitigate already identified risks that exist in manufacturing:

- Good Manufacturing Practices (GMP).
- Standard Operating Procedures (SOP).
- Statistical Process Control (SPC).
- Hazard Analysis and Critical Control Points (HACCP).

When thought about this way, almost everything we do in quality is connected to risk management in one way or another.

Sustainability

Many companies have many different definitions for Sustainability but more and more there is a common understanding across the industry.

Sustainability is the set of leadership, business process, culture, and technology capabilities an organizations establishes to maintain its social license for conducting business in a particular community.

For industrial settings, these capabilities generally fall into the below buckets:

- Energy,
- GHG.
- Environmental,
- Health and Safety,
- Operational Risk,
- Product Stewardship,
- Reporting.

Many of the same tools and issues that arise in quality are also used in managing Sustainability. In fact, for many companies it is still the quality department responsible for EH&S issues. It should also be noted that, as with Quality, much of what a Sustainability organization does is to manage risk. For example, improving performance in employee safety or environmental spills/releases is usually very tightly relate to reducing the risk profile of the firm in these areas.

Risk Management

Risk management plays a big role in both Quality and Sustainability. Unfortunately, most professionals in these areas are not subject matter experts in Risk Management. For these reasons, it is important for Risk Management organizations to collaborate with Quality and Sustainability organizations. But it is also not the case that Risk Management can just focus on these areas. Risk Management organizations are concerned with identifying, quantifying, and mitigating all types of risk across an organization including: financial, security, compliance, product, operational, supply chain, and more. It is by taking a broad perspective on risk that a company can balance needs in Quality or Sustainability with the many other needs an organization has.

Quality Risk Management is the set of leadership, business process, culture, and technology capabilities an organizations establishes to create a collaborative approach for for identifying, quantifying, and mitigating product, operational, supplier, and supply chain risks that can impact quality.

BENEFITS OF INTEGRATING QUALITY MANAGEMENT AND RISK MANAGEMENT

It's common for companies to think of quality management and risk management synonymously. In fact, in most industries, you cannot discuss quality management without also considering the impact of risk. Unfortunately, risk management is often isolated as a separate quality management project.

Although risk and quality management are distinct concepts, they require meaningful and intentional collaboration to capitalize on process improvements and product quality. In order to do that, it's important to use an enterprise quality management software (EQMS) solution that integrates risk management efforts to determine quality improvements and risk identification.

Risk Management vs. Quality Management

Quality management focuses on adherence to ISO standards, manufacturing requirements, and government regulations – both in domestic and international markets. These standards drive the fundamental framework of how a holistic quality management system should be implemented and maintained and ensures that a company's objectives are consistent.

Risk management focuses on the uncertainty, probability, and consequence of various threats to both a company's bottom line and its ability to deliver goods and services on time. Risk management enables companies to prepare for unexpected events – internally and externally –before they happen.

While quality management and risk management are different, they complement each other and must work together. Both disciplines rely on cause-and-effect analysis techniques to determine which corrective and preventative actions drive more efficient business practices. Risk management is an integral part of a complete quality management control system. It should be used as a mechanism to identify the risks and associated mitigations in the early stages of quality management activities.

As an example of how risk management and quality management complement one another, consider the challenges of managing a large, multi-tiered supplier base. Meeting both domestic and international compliance directives bears a complex set of processes for your organization to follow, which is why having a thorough quality management system is so critical. Comprehensive risk management and quality management systems allow companies to more easily anticipate and meet the demands of those processes, procedures, and responsibilities, and to simultaneously safeguard their assets.

Benefits of Merging Risk Management with Quality Management

Given the increasingly competitive nature of the manufacturing industry today, you know that risk management impacts every level of your quality management system. Thus, creating harmonization between quality management and risk management may not only give your company a competitive advantage over the long term but may also protect its assets and brand. After all, failure to recognize and address risks costs money, increases re-work and waste, and reduces customer satisfaction.

Including risk management strategies in a quality management system also allows you to thoroughly and systematically vet suppliers, which makes managing the quality of a globally-dispersed network of suppliers easier. Consider the trend of increasing the role of suppliers in daily quality management processes: as the quality of a supplier's products or parts decreases over time, the risk of delivering sub-par finished products increases. Taken a step further, without a systematic, integrated way to monitor quality and risk management collaboratively, the validity of a supplier's capabilities to deliver high-quality products comes into question.

As such, acknowledging risk is not only implicit to the responsibilities of a successful quality management professional, but it serves as an opportunity to learn, innovate, and improve products that satisfy your customer.

When Quality Management and Risk Management Work Well Together

The previous application of quality management and risk management activities took a reactive approach, whereas risk detection was performed after the fact. It's far more beneficial to consider risks upfront by having a well-constructed plan to address risks in the form of planning, managing, and driving actions that help control risk.

The integration of risk management into quality management is already evident in several industries today. One example is the use of failure modes and effects analysis used by automotive manufacturers today. Another example is the use of Six Sigma techniques for reducing product defects to lower risk.

Given the rapid pace of change in today's manufacturing industry, quality is the key to staying competitive and profitable in the global economy. Your competitiveness can be strengthened by responding to strategic opportunities to be successful, including recognizing the shift in the risk management and identification landscape.

In order for quality management to be effective, risk management data must be added to the equation. Furthermore, you must aim to challenge the culture within your company and work with your company's risk management professionals to find creative ways to embed risk management into quality management processes – and vice versa. By taking a comprehensive approach to quality and risk by deploying a combined solution, your company can achieve harmonization that improves quality early in the value chain, which in turn, instills confidence in your customers.

ASSESSING QUALITY RISKS IN AGILE METHODOLOGY

Risk is an event of uncertainty in projects. There are various testing challenges like proper selection, allocation and simulation of test environment. Often risks surface in determining the effort to cover various test conditions, and the way of sequencing resulting tests that optimizes the effectiveness and efficiency of the testing.

Agile projects embrace less quality risks than the traditional projects, if all the best engineering practices preached in Extreme Programming are put in use. Given the shorter time cycles, some techniques which improve the product quality may be put to use.

In Agile Projects, the quality risk is likely to take place at couple of places. In fact, it is the responsibility of every team member to rise risks in agile. Anyone in agile team can raise a risk during the scrum ceremonies and propose mitigation strategies for the same.

- Release planning: The Product Owner who knows the system functionality end-to-end explain the high level risk he/she foresee and the team assesses them.
- Iteration planning: the whole team goes through every user story and find out the quality risk associated with them.

Few examples of quality risks are:

- No test data or incorrect test data to test specific application (a functional risk related to accuracy).
- Slow system response to user input data (a non-functional risk related to efficiency and response time).
- Screens that with no boundary conditions and business logic (a non-functional risk related to usability and understandability).

In the iteration planning, the estimation of tasks take place in the task board which are prioritized in the order of the quality risks associated by them. Tasks with higher risks priority are one with high priority, need more effort. Similarly tasks with lower risk priority with less effort may be deferred to later part.

Listed below is an example of quality risk process during iteration planning:

- All team members, including testers get into iteration planning meeting.
- The prioritized backlog items are displayed on the task board for the current iteration.
- Considering the quality characteristics, identify the quality risks items with each of them.
- With each identified risk, categorize the level of risk and impact in terms of number of defects that may surface.
- Map the testing effort based on the level of risk.

- Based on the level of risk and its quality characteristic, select the appropriate technique to mitigate the risk.

The tester takes appropriate actions to address the risk during the iteration execution, which may include the aggregate number of features, their behaviors; quality attributes that affect customer or end user. The team may be mindful of any additional unknown information related to quality risks that was discovered during the execution and appropriate adjustments are made. Adjustments can also come in the form of new risks that shows up, evaluating and changing the level of existing risks and mitigation activities that support the adjustments.

Quality risks need to be planned for mitigation before the test execution. For example, if problems with the user stories are found during risk identification, the project team can thoroughly review user stories as a mitigating strategy.

References

- What-quality: quality.org, Retrieved 19 June, 2019
- Quality-risk-management-a-new-perspective-126119: blog.lnsresearch.com, Retrieved 26 April, 2019
- Common-ground-quality-management-risk-management: iqs.com, Retrieved 10 January, 2019
- How-to-assess-quality-risks-in-agile-methodology: tryqa.com, Retrieved 23 August, 2019
- Rose, Kenneth H. (July 2005). Project Quality Management: Why, What and How. Fort Lauderdale, Florida: J. Ross Publishing. p. 41. ISBN 978-1-932159-48-6

Diverse Aspects of Risk Management

7 CHAPTER

Quality refers to the value of a product. Quality risk is the potential loss of value of a product due to failure in adhering to minimum specifications. Quality Risk Management includes development, manufacturing, distribution and inspection of products. All these aspects of quality related risks have been carefully analyzed in this chapter.

CONTINGENCY PLAN

A contingency plan is a course of action designed to help an organization respond effectively to a significant future event or situation that may or may not happen.

A contingency plan is sometimes referred to as "Plan B," because it can be also used as an alternative for action if expected results fail to materialize. Contingency planning is a component of business continuity, disaster recovery and risk management.

The seven-steps outlined for an IT contingency plan in the NIST 800-34 Rev. 1 publication are:

- Develop the contingency planning policy statement. A formal policy provides the authority and guidance necessary to develop an effective contingency plan.
- Conduct the business impact analysis (BIA). The BIA helps identify and prioritize information systems and components critical to supporting the organization's mission/business functions.
- Identify preventive controls. Measures taken to reduce the effects of system disruptions can increase system availability and reduce contingency life cycle costs.
- Create contingency strategies. Thorough recovery strategies ensure that the system may be recovered quickly and effectively following a disruption.
- Develop an information system contingency plan. The contingency plan should contain detailed guidance and procedures for restoring a damaged system unique to the system's security impact level and recovery requirements.
- Ensure plan testing, training and exercises. Testing validates recovery capabilities,

whereas training prepares recovery personnel for plan activation and exercising the plan identifies planning gaps; combined, the activities improve plan effectiveness and overall organization preparedness.

- Ensure plan maintenance. The plan should be a living document that is updated regularly to remain current with system enhancements and organizational changes.

RISK POOL

A risk pool is one of the forms of risk management mostly practiced by insurance companies. Under this system, insurance companies come together to form a pool, which can provide protection to insurance companies against catastrophic risks such as floods or earthquakes. The term is also used to describe the pooling of similar risks that underlies the concept of insurance. While risk pooling is necessary for insurance to work, not all risks can be effectively pooled in a voluntary insurance bracket, unless there is a subsidy available to encourage participation.

Risk pooling is an important concept in supply chain management. Risk pooling suggests that demand variability is reduced if one aggregates demand across locations because as demand is aggregated across different locations, it becomes more likely that high demand from one customer will be offset by low demand from another. This reduction in variability allows a decrease in safety stock and therefore reduces average Inventory.

For example: in the centralized distribution system, the warehouse serves all customers, which leads to a reduction in variability measured by either the standard deviation or the coefficient of variation.

The three critical points to risk pooling are:

- Centralized inventory saves safety stock and average inventory in the system.
- When demands from markets are negatively correlated, the higher the coefficient of variation, the greater the benefit obtained from centralized systems; that is, the greater the benefit from risk pooling.
- The benefits from risk pooling depends directly on the relative market behavior. This is explained as follows: If we compare two markets and when demand from both markets are more or less than the average demand, we say that the demands from the market are positively correlated. Thus the benefits derived from risk pooling decreases as the correlation between demands from the two markets becomes more positive.

Basics of Risk Pooling

Whether insurance is covering health, a car, a home or a life, some people are at greater risk of actually needing the coverage. Most people decide to buy insurance -- even if they have very low risk of death, injury or property damage -- because the cost of insurance is typically less than what it would cost to cover these expenses out of pocket. Some types of insurance -- such as auto insurance -- are legally required. By insuring both low- and high-risk customers, insurance companies can transfer some of the costs of high-risk customers to lower-risk customers, thus reducing the overall cost to the insurance company of insuring high-risk people.

Coverage for High-risk Policyholders

Although insurance companies frequently insure high-risk people, their coverage might have limits. In health insurance, for example, some pre-existing conditions might traditionally have been excluded. Insurance companies commonly denied coverage to pregnant women and people with mental health conditions unless they have had coverage for a pre-established waiting period. When the Affordable Care Act took effect in 2014, it established a single risk pool for each state. It also prohibits insurance companies from denying coverage to people with pre-existing health conditions.

Higher Premiums for Higher Risk

High-risk people frequently pay more for insurance. This practice rewards low-risk people with lower insurance premiums and ensures that an insurance company gets sufficient money from high-risk people to justify covering their costs should they need to use their insurance. Insurance companies use actuarial tables to determine the risk of an individual based on both her individual choices and data about her demographic group. As a person's risk increases, her costs usually do, too. Life insurance, for example, tends to be more expensive for older people as well as people with significant health risks. Car insurance is often more expensive for teenagers since they are statistically more likely to get into auto accidents.

Benefits of Larger Insurance Pools

Larger insurance pools typically result in lower costs, which is why employer-funded health insurance with large companies is often less expensive: The employer can provide the insurer with a large pool of participants and negotiate a lower cost. Car insurance is required for drivers nationwide, which means that risk pools are very large and include drivers with a long history of moving violations as well as drivers who have never received a ticket. The Affordable Care Act, which is designed to make health care accessible and more affordable, began offering government-sponsored health-care exchanges from which individuals, families and small businesses could buy health insurance. These exchanges pool large groups of people together, thus reducing the cost to both buyers and the insurance company.

EVENT CHAIN METHODOLOGY

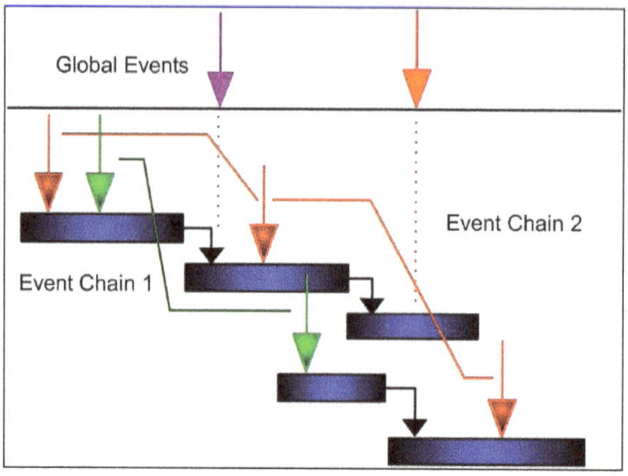

Event chain diagram.

Event chain methodology is a network analysis technique that is focused on identifying and managing events and relationship between them (event chains) that affect project schedules. It is an uncertainty modeling schedule technique. Event chain methodology is an extension of quantitative project risk analysis with Monte Carlo simulations. It is the next advance beyond critical path method and critical chain project management. Event chain methodology helps to mitigate the effect of motivational and cognitive biases in estimating and scheduling. It improves accuracy of risk assessment and helps to generate more realistic risk adjusted project schedules.

Principles

Moment of Risk and State of Activity

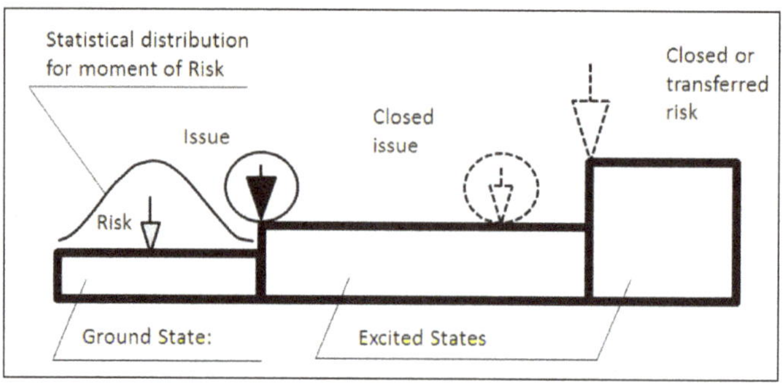

Event chain diagram for one activity.

Activities (tasks) are not a continuous uniform procedure. Tasks are affected by external events, which transform an activity from one state to another. One of the important properties of an event is the moment when an event occurs during the course of an activity. This moment, when an event occurs, in most cases is probabilistic and can be defined using statistical distribution. The original state is called a ground state, other states are called excited states. For example, if the team completes their job on activity, they can move to other activities. The notion of an activity's state is important because certain events can or cannot occur when activity is in certain state. It means that the state of an activity is subscribed to the events. Events can be local, affecting particular tasks or resources, or global affecting all tasks or resources.

Event Chains

Events can be related to other events, which will create event chains. These event chains can significantly affect the course of the project. For example, requirement changes can cause an activity to be delayed. To accelerate the activity, the project manager allocates a resource from another activity, which then leads to a missed deadline. Eventually, this can lead to the failure of the project. It could be different relationship between events. One event can trigger one or multiple events.

Events can be correlated with each other without one triggering another one. In this case if one risk has occurred, another one will occur and vice versa. One event assigned in one activity can execute another activity or group of activities. In many cases it the execution of risk response plans. For example, event "structural defect is discovered" can cause one or many activities "Repair". Events can cause other events to occur either immediately or with a delay. The delay is a property of the event subscription. The delay can be deterministic, but in most cases, it is probabilistic. Also risks can be transferred from one activity to another. To define event chains, we need to identify a "sender", the event that initiates the chain of events. The sender event can cause one or more events that effect multiple activities. These are called "receiver" events. In turn, the receiver events can also act as sender events.

Event Chain Diagrams

Event chain diagram is a visualization that shows the relationships between events and tasks and how the events affect each other. The simplest way to represent these chains is to depict them as arrows associated with certain tasks or time intervals on the Gantt chart. Here are a few important rules:

- Event chains diagrams present events as arrows on the Gantt charts.
- Arrows pointing down are threats. Arrows pointing up are opportunities.
- Issues are shown as an arrow within a circle. Color of the issue arrow is red (dark).
- Closed or transferred risks are shown using dashed lines. Color of arrow is white. Closed issue is shown in the circle with dashed border line.
- Excited states are represented by elevating the associated section of the bar on the Gantt chart.

- Colors represent the calculated impact of the risk. Higher impacts are red or darker shade. Low impacts are green or lighter shade. The size of the arrow represents probability.
- Event chains are shown as lines connecting arrows depicting events.
- Event chains may trigger another activity. In this case event chain line will be connected with the beginning of activity with optional arrow.
- Event chains may trigger a group of activities. In this case this group of activities will be surrounded by the box or frame and event chain line will be connected to the corner of the box or first activity within a frame.

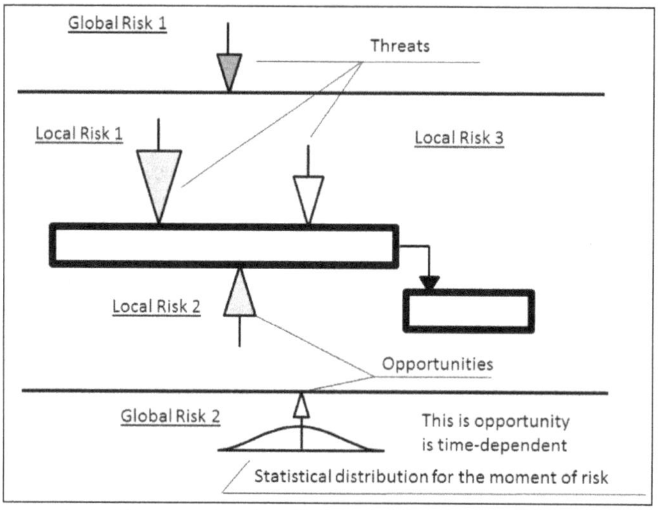

Example of event chain diagram: local and global threats and opportunities with different probabilities and impacts.

By using event chain diagrams to visualize events and event chains, the modeling and analysis of risks and uncertainties can be significantly simplified.

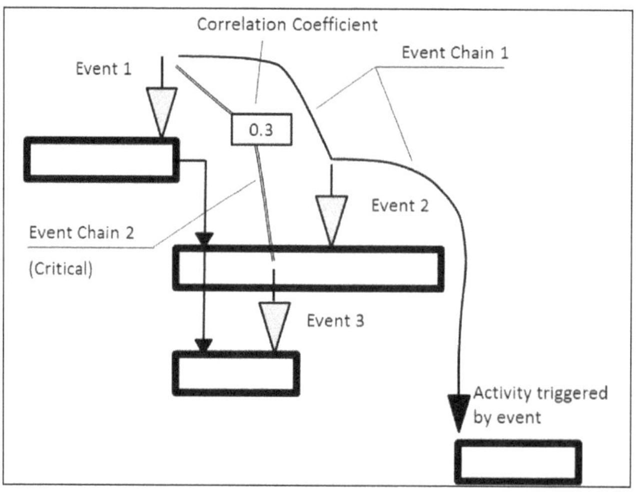

Example of event chain diagram with critical event chain and activity triggered by event.

Another tool that can be used to simplify the definition of events is a state table. Columns in the state table represent events; rows represent the states of an activity. Information for each event in each state includes four properties of event subscription: probability, moment of event, excited state, and impact of the event.

Monte Carlo Simulation

Once events and event chains are defined, quantitative analysis using Monte Carlo simulation can be performed to quantify the cumulative effect of the events. Probabilities and impacts of risks assigned to activities are used as input data for Monte Carlo simulation of the project schedule. In most projects it is necessary to supplement the event based variance with uncertainties as distributions related to duration, start time, cost, and other parameters.

In Event chain methodology, risk can not only affect schedule and cost, but also other parameters such as safety, security, performance, technology, quality, and other objectives. In other words, one event can belong to different categories. The result of the analysis would show risk exposure for different categories as well as integrated project risk score for all categories. This integrated project risk score is calculated based on relative weights for each risk category.

Critical Event Chains

Monte Carlo simulation provides the capability, through sensitivity analysis, to identify single or chains of events. These chains of events can be identified by analyzing the correlations between the main project parameters, such as project duration or cost, and the event chains. These are called "critical events" or "critical chains of events". By identifying critical events or critical chains of events, we can identify strategies to minimize their negative effects: Avoid, Transfer, Mitigate, or Accept. Event and event chain ranking is performed for all risk categories (schedule-related and non-schedule) as part of one process. Integrated risk probability, impact and score can be calculated using weights for each risk category.

Project Control with Event and Event Chains

Monitoring the activity's progress ensures that updated information is used to perform the analysis. During the course of the project, the probability and time of the events can be recalculated based on actual data. The main reason for performance tracking is forecasting an activity's duration and cost if an activity is partially completed and certain events are assigned to the activity. Event chain methodology reduces the risk probability and impact automatically based on the percent of work completed. Advanced analysis can be performed using a Bayesian approach. It is possible to monitor the chance that a project will meet a specific deadline. This chance is constantly updated as a result of the Monte Carlo analysis. Critical events and event chains can be different at the various phases of the project.

Phenomena

Repeated Activities

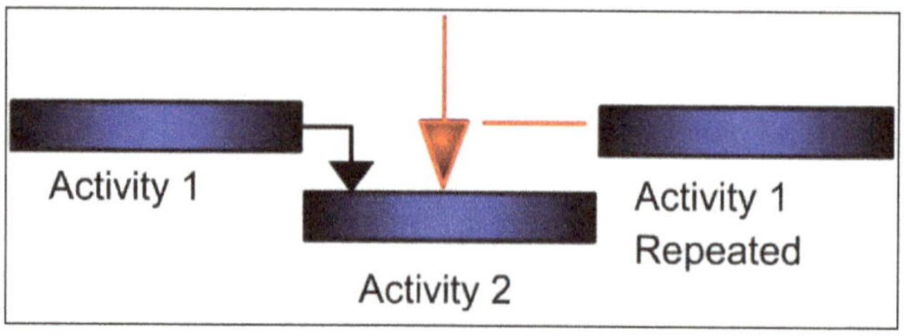

Repeated Activity

Sometimes events can cause the start of an activity that has already been completed. This is a very common scenario for real life projects; sometimes a previous activity must be repeated based on the results of a succeeding activity. Event chain methodology simplifies modeling of these scenarios The original project schedule does not need to be updated, all that is required is to define the event and assign it to an activity that points to the previous activity. In addition, a limit to the number of times an activity can be repeated must be defined.

Event Chains and Risk Response

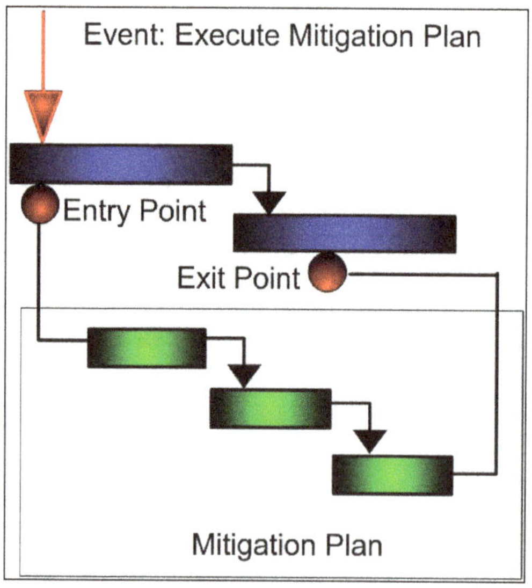

Mitigation plan.

If an event or event chain occurs during the course of a project, it may require some risk response effort.

Risk response plans execution are triggered by events, which occur if an activity is in an excited state. Risk response events may attempt to transform the activity from the excited state to the ground state. Response plans are an activity or group of activities (small schedule) that augment the project schedule if a certain event occurs. The solution is to assign the response plan to an event or event chain. The same response plan can be used for one or more events.

Resource Allocation based on Events

One potential event is the reassignment of a resource from one activity to another, which can occur under certain conditions. For example, if an activity requires more resources to complete it within a fixed period, this will trigger an event to reallocate the resource from another activity. Reallocation of resources can also occur when activity duration reaches a certain deadline or the cost exceeds a certain value. Events can be used to model different situations with resources, e.g. temporary leave, illness, vacations, etc.

CURRENCY ANALYTICS

Companies that do business in more than one currency are exposed to exchange rate risk – that is, changes in the value of one currency versus another. Exchange rate risk (also known as foreign exchange risk, FX risk, or currency risk) is especially high in periods of high currency volatility.

Currency analytics are technology tools that enable global companies to manage the risk associated with currency volatility. Currency analytics often involve automation that helps companies access and validate currency exposure data and make decisions that mitigate currency risk.

Currency volatility can impact a company's balance sheet and/or cash flow. Corporate currency analytics help companies manage currency risk in both areas.

Balance Sheet Risk

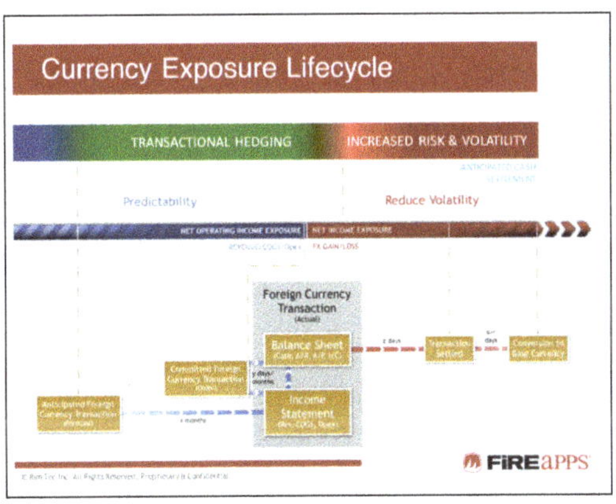

Currency Exposure Lifecycle.

In the process of remeasuring transaction currency monetary assets and liability account balances, the difference between the exchange rate when the transaction was posted and exchange rate when the transaction was cleared goes to the functional entity's income statement as an FX gain or loss. Then in the process of translating the functional entity's income statement for the reporting entity's consolidated income statement, that FX gain/loss gets translated at current income statement rate to reporting currency and appears on the consolidated income statement.

Managing balance sheet risk can involve organic (natural) hedging such as using cash positions or intercompany loans to create exposure offsets. It can also involve external hedging such as buying a forward contract to offset FX exposure.

In both cases, efficient hedging depends on being able to drill down into the balance sheet to see the currencies of the transactions sitting on the company's books around the world. Currency analytics automates that drill-down process and presents balance sheet exposure data in an easy-to-use dashboard that allows companies to efficiently manage balance sheet risk and minimize FX gain/loss.

Cash Flow Risk

In the process of translating the functional entity's income statement, revenue, cost of goods sold (COGS), and operating expenses (OpEx) get translated at the current income statement rate to reporting currency and appear on the consolidated income statement. Currency impact to revenue, COGS, and OpEx arises from differences between the current income statement rate and the forecasted rate.

Managing cash flow risk is fundamentally about protecting the economic value of the company's future flow of cash from being eroded by currency volatility. It can involve organic (natural) hedging such as pricing contracts in a particular currency. It can also involve external hedging, but accounting rules require matching hedges to forecasted cash flows and don't allow hedging economic risk.

Currency analytics allow companies to mitigate cash flow risk by uncovering accounting exposures to match the economic exposures so the company can hedge the accounting exposure as a proxy. Currency analytics enable what/if scenario analysis so companies can model how volatility in particular currencies could impact their revenue and expenses in the future.

VALUE AT RISK

Value at risk (VaR) is a measure of the risk of loss for investments. It estimates how much a set of investments might lose (with a given probability), given normal market conditions, in a set time period such as a day. VaR is typically used by firms and regulators in the financial industry to gauge the amount of assets needed to cover possible losses.

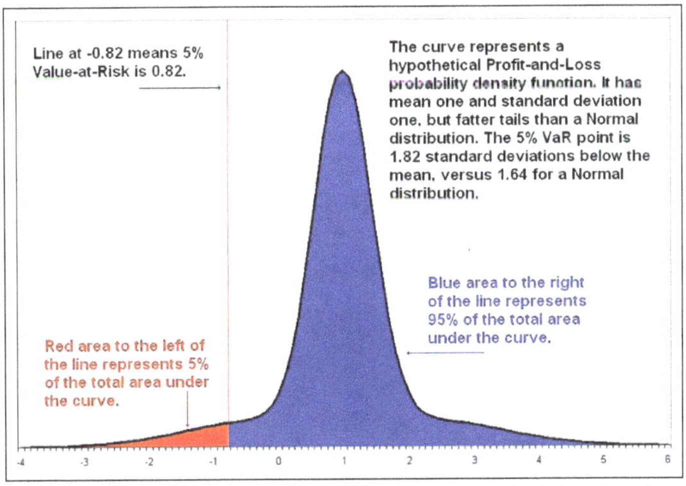

The 5% Value at Risk of a hypothetical profit-and-loss probability density function.

For a given portfolio, time horizon, and probability *p*, the *p* VaR can be defined informally as the maximum possible loss during that time after we exclude all worse outcomes whose combined probability is at most *p*. This assumes mark-to-market pricing, and no trading in the portfolio.

For example, if a portfolio of stocks has a one-day 5% VaR of $1 million, that means that there is a 0.05 probability that the portfolio will fall in value by more than $1 million over a one-day period if there is no trading. Informally, a loss of $1 million or more on this portfolio is expected on 1 day out of 20 days (because of 5% probability).

More formally, *p* VaR is defined such that the probability of a loss greater than VaR is (at most) *p* while the probability of a loss less than VaR is (at least) *1–p*. A loss which exceeds the VaR threshold is termed a "VaR breach".

It is important to note that, for a fixed *p*, the *p* VaR does not assess the magnitude of loss when a VaR breach occurs and therefore is considered by some to be a questionable metric for risk management. For instance, assume someone makes a bet that flipping a coin seven times will not give seven heads. The terms are that they win $100 if this does not happen (with probability 127/128) and lose $12,700 if it does (with probability 1/128). That is, the possible loss amounts are $0 or $12,700. The 1% VaR is then $0, because the probability of any loss at all is 1/128 which is less than 1%. They are, however, exposed to a possible loss of $12,700 which can be expressed as the *p* VaR for any *p* <= *0.78%*.

VaR has four main uses in finance: risk management, financial control, financial reporting and computing regulatory capital. VaR is sometimes used in non-financial applications as well. However, it is a controversial risk management tool.

Important related ideas are economic capital, backtesting, stress testing, expected shortfall, and tail conditional expectation.

Details

Common parameters for VaR are 1% and 5% probabilities and one day and two week horizons, although other combinations are in use.

The reason for assuming normal markets and no trading, and to restricting loss to things measured in daily accounts, is to make the loss observable. In some extreme financial events it can be impossible to determine losses, either because market prices are unavailable or because the loss-bearing institution breaks up. Some longer-term consequences of disasters, such as lawsuits, loss of market confidence and employee morale and impairment of brand names can take a long time to play out, and may be hard to allocate among specific prior decisions. VaR marks the boundary between normal days and extreme events. Institutions can lose far more than the VaR amount; all that can be said is that they will not do so very often.

The probability level is about equally often specified as one minus the probability of a VaR break, so that the VaR in the example above would be called a one-day 95% VaR instead of one-day 5% VaR. This generally does not lead to confusion because the probability of VaR breaks is almost always small, certainly less than 50%.

Although it virtually always represents a loss, VaR is conventionally reported as a positive number. A negative VaR would imply the portfolio has a high probability of making a profit, for example a one-day 5% VaR of negative $1 million implies the portfolio has a 95% chance of making more than $1 million over the next day.

Another inconsistency is that VaR is sometimes taken to refer to profit-and-loss at the end of the period, and sometimes as the maximum loss at any point during the period. The original definition was the latter, but in the early 1990s when VaR was aggregated across trading desks and time zones, end-of-day valuation was the only reliable number so the former became the *de facto* definition. As people began using multiday VaRs in the second half of the 1990s, they almost always estimated the distribution at the end of the period only. It is also easier theoretically to deal with a point-in-time estimate versus a maximum over an interval. Therefore, the end-of-period definition is the most common both in theory and practice today.

Varieties

The definition of VaR is nonconstructive; it specifies a property VaR must have, but not how to compute VaR. Moreover, there is wide scope for interpretation in the definition. This has led to two broad types of VaR, one used primarily in risk management and the other primarily for risk measurement. The distinction is not sharp, however, and hybrid versions are typically used in financial control, financial reporting and computing regulatory capital.

To a risk manager, VaR is a system, not a number. The system is run periodically (usually daily) and the published number is compared to the computed price movement in opening positions over the time horizon. There is never any subsequent adjustment to the published VaR, and there is no distinction between VaR breaks caused by input errors (including Information Technology breakdowns, fraud and rogue trading), computation errors (including failure to produce a VaR on time) and market movements.

A frequentist claim is made, that the long-term frequency of VaR breaks will equal the specified probability, within the limits of sampling error, and that the VaR breaks will be independent in time and independent of the level of VaR. This claim is validated by a backtest, a comparison of published VaRs to actual price movements. In this interpretation, many different systems could produce VaRs with equally good backtests, but wide disagreements on daily VaR values.

For risk measurement a number is needed, not a system. A Bayesian probability claim is made, that given the information and beliefs at the time, the subjective probability of a VaR break was the specified level. VaR is adjusted after the fact to correct errors in inputs and computation, but not to incorporate information unavailable at the time of computation. In this context, "backtest" has a different meaning. Rather than comparing published VaRs to actual market movements over the period of time the system has been in operation, VaR is retroactively computed on scrubbed data over as long a period as data are available and deemed relevant. The same position data and pricing models are used for computing the VaR as determining the price movements.

Although some of the sources listed here treat only one kind of VaR as legitimate, most of the recent ones seem to agree that risk management VaR is superior for making short-term and tactical decisions today, while risk measurement VaR should be used for understanding the past, and making medium term and strategic decisions for the future. When VaR is used for financial control or financial reporting it should incorporate elements of both. For example, if a trading desk is held to a VaR limit, that is both a risk-management rule for deciding what risks to allow today, and an input into the risk measurement computation of the desk's risk-adjusted return at the end of the reporting period.

In Governance

VaR can also be applied to governance of endowments, trusts, and pension plans. Essentially trustees adopt portfolio Values-at-Risk metrics for the entire pooled account and the diversified parts individually managed. Instead of probability estimates they simply define maximum levels of acceptable loss for each. Doing so provides an easy metric for oversight and adds accountability as managers are then directed to manage, but with the additional constraint to avoid losses within a defined risk parameter. VaR utilized in this manner adds relevance as well as an easy way to monitor risk measurement control far more intuitive than Standard Deviation of Return. Use of VaR in this context, as well as a worthwhile critique on board governance practices as it relates to investment management oversight in general can be found in *Best Practices in Governance.*

Mathematical Definition

Let X be a profit and loss distribution (loss negative and profit positive). The VaR at level $\alpha \in (0,1)$ is the smallest number y such that the probability that $Y := -X$ does not exceed y is at least $1-\alpha$. Mathematically, $\mathrm{VaR}_\alpha(X)$ is the $(1-\alpha)$-quantile of Y, i.e.,

$$\mathrm{VaR}_\alpha(X) = -\inf\{x \in \mathbb{R} : F_X(x) > \alpha\} = F_Y^{-1}(1-\alpha).$$

This is the most general definition of VaR and the two identities are equivalent (indeed, for any random variable X its cumulative distribution function F_X is well defined). However this formula cannot be used directly for calculations unless we assume that X has some parametric distribution.

Risk managers typically assume that some fraction of the bad events will have undefined losses, either because markets are closed or illiquid, or because the entity bearing the loss breaks apart or loses the ability to compute accounts. Therefore, they do not accept results based on the assumption of a well-defined probability distribution. Nassim Taleb has labeled this assumption, "charlatanism". On the other hand, many academics prefer to assume a well-defined distribution, albeit usually one with fat tails. This point has probably caused more contention among VaR theorists than any other.

Value of Risks can also be written as a distortion risk measure given by the distortion function $g(x) = \begin{cases} 0 & \text{if } 0 \le x < 1-\alpha \\ 1 & \text{if } 1-\alpha \le x \le 1 \end{cases}$.

Risk Measure and Risk Metric

The term "VaR" is used both for a risk measure and a risk metric. This sometimes leads to confusion. Sources earlier than 1995 usually emphasize the risk measure, later sources are more likely to emphasize the metric.

The VaR risk measure defines risk as mark-to-market loss on a fixed portfolio over a fixed time horizon. There are many alternative risk measures in finance. Given the inability to use mark-to-market (which uses market prices to define loss) for future performance, loss is often defined (as a substitute) as change in fundamental value. For example, if an institution holds a loan that declines in market price because interest rates go up, but has no change in cash flows or credit quality, some systems do not recognize a loss. Also some try to incorporate the economic cost of harm not measured in daily financial statements, such as loss of market confidence or employee morale, impairment of brand names or lawsuits.

Rather than assuming a static portfolio over a fixed time horizon, some risk measures incorporate the dynamic effect of expected trading (such as a stop loss order) and consider the expected holding period of positions.

The VaR risk metric summarizes the distribution of possible losses by a quantile, a point with a specified probability of greater losses. A common alternative metrics is expected shortfall.

VaR Risk Management

Supporters of VaR-based risk management claim the first and possibly greatest benefit of VaR is the improvement in systems and modeling it forces on an institution. In 1997, Philippe Jorion wrote:

The greatest benefit of VAR lies in the imposition of a structured methodology for critically thinking about risk. Institutions that go through the process of computing their VAR are forced to confront their exposure to financial risks and to set up a proper risk management function. Thus the process of getting to VAR may be as important as the number itself.

Publishing a daily number, on-time and with specified statistical properties holds every part of a trading organization to a high objective standard. Robust backup systems and default assumptions must be implemented. Positions that are reported, modeled or priced incorrectly stand out, as do data feeds that are inaccurate or late and systems that are too-frequently down. Anything that affects profit and loss that is left out of other reports will show up either in inflated VaR or excessive VaR breaks. "A risk-taking institution that *does not* compute VaR might escape disaster, but an institution that *cannot* compute VaR will not".

The second claimed benefit of VaR is that it separates risk into two regimes. Inside the VaR limit, conventional statistical methods are reliable. Relatively short-term and specific data can be used for analysis. Probability estimates are meaningful, because there are enough data to test them. In a sense, there is no true risk because you have a sum of many independent observations with a left bound on the outcome. A casino doesn't worry about whether red or black will come up on the next roulette spin. Risk managers encourage productive risk-taking in this regime, because there is little true cost. People tend to worry too much about these risks, because they happen frequently, and not enough about what might happen on the worst days.

Outside the VaR limit, all bets are off. Risk should be analyzed with stress testing based on long-term and broad market data. Probability statements are no longer meaningful. Knowing the distribution of losses beyond the VaR point is both impossible and useless. The risk manager should concentrate instead on making sure good plans are in place to limit the loss if possible, and to survive the loss if not.

One specific system uses three regimes:

- One to three times VaR are normal occurrences. You expect periodic VaR breaks. The loss distribution typically has fat tails, and you might get more than one break in a short period of time. Moreover, markets may be abnormal and trading may exacerbate losses, and you may take losses not measured in daily marks such as lawsuits, loss of employee morale and market confidence and impairment of brand names. So an institution that can't deal with three times VaR losses as routine events probably won't survive long enough to put a VaR system in place.
- Three to ten times VaR is the range for stress testing. Institutions should be confident they have examined all the foreseeable events that will cause losses in this range, and are prepared to survive them. These events are too rare to estimate probabilities reliably, so risk/return calculations are useless.
- Foreseeable events should not cause losses beyond ten times VaR. If they do they should be hedged or insured, or the business plan should be changed to avoid them, or VaR should be increased. It's hard to run a business if foreseeable losses are orders of magnitude larger than very large everyday losses. It's hard to plan for these events, because they are out of scale with daily experience. Of course there will be unforeseeable losses more than ten times VaR, but it's pointless to anticipate them, you can't know much about them and it results in needless worrying. Better to hope that the discipline of preparing for all foreseeable three-to-ten times VaR losses will improve chances for surviving the unforeseen and larger losses that inevitably occur.

"A risk manager has two jobs: make people take more risk the 99% of the time it is safe to do so, and survive the other 1% of the time. VaR is the border".

Another reason VaR is useful as a metric is due to its ability to compress the riskiness of a portfolio to a single number, making it comparable across different portfolios (of different assets). Within any portfolio it is also possible to isolate specific position that might better hedge the portfolio to reduce, and minimise, the VaR. An example of market-maker employed strategies for trading linear interest rate derivatives and interest rate swaps portfolios is cited.

Computation Methods

VaR can be estimated either parametrically (for example, variance-covariance VaR or delta-gamma VaR) or nonparametrically (for examples, historical simulation VaR or resampled VaR).

A McKinsey report published in May 2012 estimated that 85% of large banks were using historical simulation. The other 15% used Monte Carlo methods.

Backtesting

A key advantage to VaR over most other measures of risk such as expected shortfall is the availability of several backtesting procedures for validating a set of VaR forecasts. Early examples of backtests can be found in Christoffersen, later generalized by Pajhede, which models a "hit-sequence" of losses greater than the VaR and proceed to tests for these "hits" to be independent from one another and with a correct probability of occurring. E.g. a 5% probability of a loss greater than VaR should be observed over time when using a 95% VaR, these hits should occur independently.

A number of other backtests are available which model the time between hits in the hit-sequence, see Christoffersen, Haas, Tokpavi, and Pajhede As pointed out in several of the papers, the asymptotic distribution is often poor when considering high levels of coverage, e.g. a 99% VaR, therefore the parametric bootstrap method of Dufour is often used to obtain correct size properties for the tests. Backtest toolboxes are available in Matlab , or R—though only the first implements the parametric bootstrap method.

The second pillar of Basel II includes a backtesting step to validate the VaR figures.

RISK BREAKDOWN STRUCTURE

Risk Breakdown Structure (RBS) - A hierarchically organised depiction of the identified project risks arranged by category.

When planning a project to meet targets for cost, schedule, or quality, it is useful to identify likely risks to the success of the project. A risk is any possible situation that is not planned for, but that, if it occurs, is likely to divert the project from its planned result. For example, an established project team plans for the work to be done by its staff, but there is the risk that an employee may unexpectedly leave the team.

In Project Management, the *Risk Management Process* has the objectives of identifying, assessing, and managing risks, both positive and negative. All too often, project managers focus only on negative risk, however, good things can happen in a project, "things" that were foreseen, but not expressly planned.

The objective of Risk Management is to predict risks, assess their likelihood and impact, and to actively plan what should be done ahead of time to best deal with situations when they occur.

The risk management process usually occurs in five distinct steps: plan risk management, risk identification, qualitative and quantitative risk analysis, risk response planning, and risk monitoring and control. The central point of risk identification and assessment in risk management is understanding the risk. However, this is also where project managers and risk subject matter experts (SMEs) get the least help from recognized references, best practices, or work standards.

Currently, the Project Management Institute (PMIr) has a team of SMEs working on a Practice Standard for Risk Management. This team has identified one very good tool: the Risk Breakdown Structure (RBS). The RBS helps the project manager, the risk manager, and almost any stakeholder to understand, and therefore be able to identify and assess risk.

The RBS will prove extremely valuable to better grasp when a project needs to receive special scrutiny, in other words, when risk might happen. The RBS can also help the project manager and the risk manager to better understand recurring risks and concentrations of risk that could lead to issues that affect the status of the project.

Following the concept of the Work Breakdown Structure (WBS), the Risk Breakdown Structure provides a means for the project manager and risk manager to structure the risks being addressed or tracked. Just as PMI defines the Work Breakdown Structure as a "deliverable-oriented grouping of project elements that organizes and defines the total work scope of the project" the RBS could be considered as a "hierarchically organized depiction of the identified project risks arranged by risk category".

In project management language, risks include anything unplanned and unforeseen that can have a negative impact on the project's costs, timing or quality. [This does not conform to the ISO 31000 view of Risk] A good project manager should be able to manage the risks effectively and get the project on track.

Many project managers and risk managers currently use "home-grown" methods for listing, identifying, assessing, and tracking risks in their projects. These methods include: spreadsheets, listing, generic risk taxonomy, based somewhat loosely on various standards and guidelines.

An approach that simply places the risks in a list, a simple table, or even in a database does not provide the strength of using a structured, organized method similar to a Work Breakdown Structure. To fully understand the risks and better identify and assess the risk, a "deep-dive" into each risk, recording as many levels of identification as necessary, may be required. The project value of placing risks in a structure such as this lies in the ability of the project manager and risk manager to then quickly and easily identify and assess the risk, identify the potential risk triggers, and develop a more robust risk response plan . If all risks are placed in a hierarchical structure as they are identified, and the structure is organized by source, the total risk exposure to the project can be more easily understood, and planning for the risk more easily accomplished.

Templates for creating a Risk Breakdown Structure

The concept of the RBS is new. The PMBoK (2004), barely references its use; however, the PMI Standards team has incorporated the RBS in the *Practice Standard for Risk Management*. Dr. David Hillson, in the proceedings of the Project Management Institute Annual Seminars and Symposium, on Oct. 3-10, 2002, provided several different RBS Structure examples, with topics similar to those already shown. Dr. Hillson broke out two different examples, an RBS for Software Development, which had the following major topics: Product Engineering, Development Environment, Program Constraints; and an RBS for Construction Design, which has these major topics: Environment, Industry, Client, Project.

Each RBS is broken into "levels", with each level providing a more in-depth "view" of the identified risk. As an example, in creating a RBS for software development, Level 1 of the RBS might be Technical, followed by Level 2, Requirements, followed by Level 3, Functional Requirements, Informational Requirements, Non-functional Requirements, etc. If desired, Level 3 can be further refined with Level 4, Stability, Completeness, Functionality, Interfaces, Testability, etc., Level 5, etc.

Once the project team has created its RBS, then individual risks can be identified. Several different techniques for defining the individual risks are available, including brain-storming, surveys, workshops, etc. Each identified risk needs to be categorized, and placed in the RBS under a specific topic (or topics) if the risk spans two or more topics, such as a risk in gathering requirements might span Technical, organizational and project management.

After the RBS has completed its first "pass" in the creation phase, it can then become an input to qualitative risk analysis, where probabilities, priorities, and impacts are determined.

Creation of Tailor-made Risk Breakdown Structures

Construction projects, like all complex activities, involve many partners with different objectives, who are subjected to many risks in an uncertain environment. In practice, different project stakeholders have different understanding and perception of project risks. Each one identifies and analyzes the project risks regarding his objectives, risk attitude and special perspective to project risks without relying on a common and shared methodology. This is why in most of construction projects, discussing the project risks and making risk based decisions are of common difficulties which may also cause to disputes between project parties. Also, the project risk management is a scalable activity and should be commensurate with the size, level of available information and complexity of the project under consideration. Furthermore, this process is iterative, since in each phase of the project, new information is available and some predicted risks events occur while others will not, new unpredicted risk events may occur or may be identified, and the characteristics of those already identified may change. Thus, an iterative risk management should be carried out at all stages of the project life cycle. As consequence, the project risk management process has to be tailored for each particular case and project.

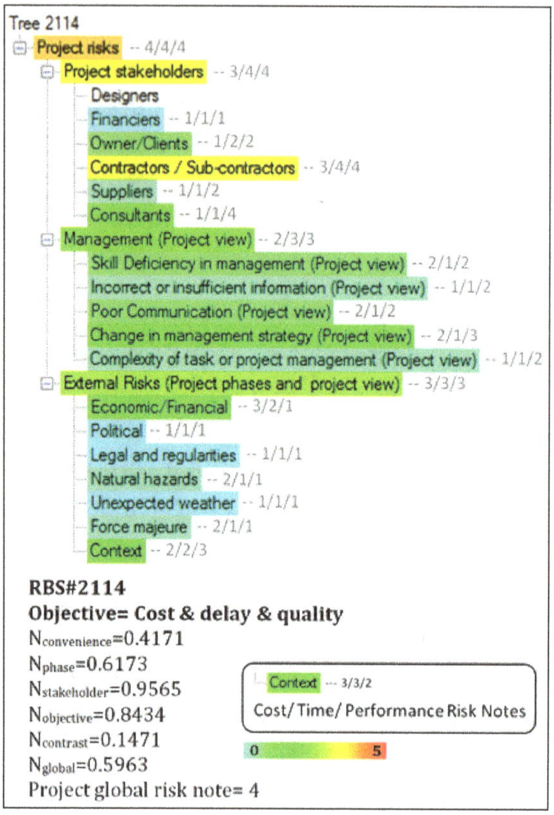

An example of designed tailor-made Risk Breakdown Structure, with results of a multi-objective risk analysis.

Dr. Rasool Mehdizadeh has developed a methodology for a dynamic, multi-scale and multi-perspective risk management of construction projects. This method is based on the application of tailor-made risk breakdown structures (RBS) which are well adapted to: (1) the stage and degree of development of project, (2) specific requirements and objectives of project stakeholders, and (3) required level of details. Using this method, each of the project stakeholders, at each stage of the project, considering his/her special view to project risks, can build his/her own specific RBS. Moreover, the RBS can also be tailored as a shared support for all the project stakeholders in order to facilitate understanding and discussing project risks. Using these tailored RBSs which are all generated using a unique procedure and knowledge database, each of project stakeholders can identify, analyze and represent the project risks regarding his/her point of view and requirements. The method ensures the consistency of all these perspectives.

Using the Hierarchical Risk Breakdown Structure

The RBS serves as more than just a "database" for identifying risks to the project. When created, the RBS provides a vehicle for risk analysis and reporting, and risk comparison across projects. Most importantly, the RBS is "the" tool for risk identification.

Risk Identification and Classification

Risk identification will be the first step in determining which risks may affect a project. Identification also provides documentation of the risk characteristics. The first level (Level 1) of the RBS can be used as a sanity check to make certain that all topics that might include risk are covered during the risk identification process. Using the RBS, an iterative process can be initiated that will persist throughout the project life-cycle. The frequency and applicability of this iterative process will be different in each phase of the life-cycle

Using a risk identification checklist that is focused on the RBS, using Levels 2, 3 and below, assists in identifying specific and generic risks. This checklist can then become a part of the project managers' and risk managers' tool set for future projects.

Risk identification leads to quantitative risk analysis, conducted by the Project Risk Manager. Sometimes merely identifying the risk will suggest the proper response, which can be entered into the Risk Response Plan.

Risk Analysis

Qualitative Risk Analysis

Risk analysis is more easily achieved if, after identification, the risks are placed in proper perspective within the RBS by categorizing the risks in the various levels. Risk analysis involves the use of techniques for prioritizing the risk, determining the probability of the risk, and calculating the impact of the risk. At no point should the project manager or risk manager decide that the total number of identified risks should cause the cancellation of the project. The total number does not take into account the probability with which the risk will occur, nor the impact to the project, should the risk occur. A few risks, with high probabilities and high impact, are far more critical to the overall success of the project than a large number of risks with low probability and minimal impact. Using the RBS, the project manager and the risk manager should create a "risk score" based on the priority, probability and impact of each risk, and with each "group" of risks (according to the appropriate Level of the RBS).

Using the RBS also offers other valuable understanding into the analysis of the identified risks. Some of these new understandings are:

- Risk exposure type.
- Dependencies between risks.
- Root causality of risks.

- Most significant and least significant risks.
- Correlations between risks.

Another benefit of the RBS is the ability to focus risk responses to the high probability, high impact, high priority risks using the risk topic groupings.

A specific method was developed by Dr. Mehdizadeh in order to: (1) calculate risk values of risk events regarding different project objectives, (2) aggregate the risk values through the RBS branches and also (3) to calculate global risk score of project. The method combines consistently the quantitative and qualitative approaches, allowing the user to choose the best one for risk assessment at any level, based on the available information and required accuracy. In this method, at the first step, the probability and impact factors of risk events are assessed quantitatively or qualitatively. Two concomitant scales are used: a continuous cardinal scale and a discrete ordinal scale ranging from 1 to 5. Each scale has its own advantage. Continuous scale is closer to physical reality and has a more concrete meaning while discrete scale has a strong symbolic value. The assessments based on each of these scales can be converted to the other one following a defined process. At the second step, the risk values of risk events are calculated and then aggregated through the RBS branches in order to calculate the risk values of risk categories. Finally, application of a multi-criteria decision method allows calculating the global risk score of each category. This method provides a more consistent approach to get more realistic results without suffering from the usual weaknesses of available methods cited in literature.

PRECAUTIONARY PRINCIPLE

The precautionary principle (or precautionary approach) generally defines actions on issues considered to be uncertain, for instance applied in assessing risk management. The principle is used by policy makers to justify discretionary decisions in situations where there is the possibility of harm from making a certain decision (e.g. taking a particular course of action) when extensive scientific knowledge on the matter is lacking. The principle implies that there is a social responsibility to protect the public from exposure to harm, when scientific investigation has found a plausible risk. These protections can be relaxed only if further scientific findings emerge that provide sound evidence that no harm will result.

In some legal systems, as in law of the European Union, the application of the precautionary principle has been made a statutory requirement in some areas of law.

Regarding international conduct, the first endorsement of the principle was in 1982 when the World Charter for Nature was adopted by the United Nations General Assembly, while its first international implementation was in 1987 through the Montreal Protocol. Soon after, the principle integrated with many other legally binding international treaties such as the Rio Declaration and Kyoto Protocol.

The concept "precautionary principle" is generally considered to have arisen in English from a translation of the German term *Vorsorgeprinzip* in the 1980s. In 1988, Konrad von Moltke described the German concept for a British audience, which he translated into English as the precautionary principle.

The concepts underpinning the precautionary principle pre-date the term's inception. For example, the essence of the principle is captured in a number of cautionary aphorisms such as "an ounce of prevention is worth a pound of cure", "better safe than sorry", and "look before you leap". The precautionary principle may also be interpreted as the evolution of the "ancient-medical principle" of "first, do no harm" to apply to institutions and institutional decision-making processes rather than individuals.

In economics, the Precautionary Principle has been analysed in terms of "the effect on rational decision-making", of "the interaction of irreversibility" and "uncertainty". Authors such as Epstein and Arrow and Fischer show that "irreversibility of possible future consequences" creates a "quasi-option effect" which should induce a "risk-neutral" society to favour current decisions that allow for more flexibility in the future. Gollier et al. conclude that "more scientific uncertainty as to the distribution of a future risk – that is, a larger variability of beliefs – should induce society to take stronger prevention measures today".

Formulations

Many definitions of the precautionary principle exist: Precaution may be defined as "caution in advance", "caution practised in the context of uncertainty", or informed prudence. Two ideas lie at the core of the principle:

- An expression of a need by decision-makers to anticipate harm before it occurs. Within this element lies an implicit reversal of the onus of proof: under the precautionary principle it is the responsibility of an activity-proponent to establish that the proposed activity will not (or is very unlikely to) result in significant harm.
- The concept of proportionality of the risk and the cost and feasibility of a proposed action.

One of the primary foundations of the precautionary principle, and globally accepted definitions, results from the work of the Rio Conference, or "Earth Summit" in 1992. The principle 15 of the Rio Declaration notes: "In order to protect the environment, the precautionary approach shall be widely applied by States according to their capabilities. Where there are threats of serious or irreversible damage, lack of full scientific

Wcertainty shall not be used as a reason for postponing cost-effective measures to prevent environmental degradation".

The 1998 Wingspread Statement on the Precautionary Principle summarises the principle this way: "When an activity raises threats of harm to human health or the environment, precautionary measures should be taken even if some cause and effect relationships are not fully established scientifically." The Wingspread Conference on the Precautionary Principle was convened by the Science and Environmental Health Network.

In February 2000, the Commission of the European Communities noted in a *Communication from the Commission on the Precautionary Principle* that, "The precautionary principle is not defined in the Treaties of the European Union, which prescribes it [the Precautionary Principle] only once – to protect the environment. But in practice, its scope is much wider, and specifically where preliminary-objective-scientific-evaluation indicates that there are reasonable grounds for concern that potentially dangerous effects on the environment, human, animal or [and] plant health may be inconsistent with the high level of protection [for what] chosen for the Community".

The January 2000 Cartagena Protocol on Biosafety says, in regard to controversies over GMOs: "Lack of scientific certainty due to insufficient relevant scientific information shall not prevent the Party of [I]mport, in order to avoid or minimize such potential adverse effects, from taking a decision, as appropriate, with regard to the import of the living modified organism in question".

Application

The application of the precautionary principle is hampered by both lack of political will, as well as the wide range of interpretations placed on it. One study identified 14 different formulations of the principle in treaties and nontreaty declarations. R.B. Stewart reduced the precautionary principle to four basic versions:

- Scientific uncertainty should not automatically preclude regulation of activities that pose a potential risk of significant harm (Non-Preclusion PP).
- Regulatory controls should incorporate a margin of safety; activities should be limited below the level at which no adverse effect has been observed or predicted (Margin of Safety PP).
- Activities that present an uncertain potential for significant harm should be subject to best technology available requirements to minimise the risk of harm unless the proponent of the activity shows that they present no appreciable risk of harm (BAT PP).
- Activities that present an uncertain potential for significant harm should be prohibited unless the proponent of the activity shows that it presents no appreciable risk of harm (Prohibitory PP).

In deciding how to apply the principle, one may use a cost-benefit analysis that factors in both the opportunity cost of not acting, and the option value of waiting for further information before acting.One of the difficulties of the application of the principle in modern policy-making is that there is often an irreducible conflict between different interests, so that thc debate necessarily involves politics.

Strong vs. Weak

Strong precaution holds that regulation is required whenever there is a possible risk to health, safety, or the environment, even if the supporting evidence is speculative and even if the economic costs of regulation are high. In 1982, the United Nations World Charter for Nature gave the first international recognition to the strong version of the principle, suggesting that when "potential adverse effects are not fully understood, the activities should not proceed". The widely publicised Wingspread Declaration, from a meeting of environmentalists in 1998, is another example of the strong version. Strong precaution can also be termed as a "no-regrets" principle, where costs are not considered in preventative action.

Weak precaution holds that lack of scientific evidence does not preclude action if damage would otherwise be serious and irreversible. Humans practice weak precaution every day, and often incur costs, to avoid hazards that are far from certain: we do not walk in moderately dangerous areas at night, we exercise, we buy smoke detectors, we buckle our seatbelts.

According to a publication by the New Zealand Treasury Department:

The weak version of the Precautionary Principle is the least restrictive and allows preventive measures to be taken in the face of uncertainty, but does not require them (eg, Rio Declaration 1992; United Nations Framework Convention of Climate Change 1992). To satisfy the threshold of harm, there must be some evidence relating to both the likelihood of occurrence and the severity of consequences. Some, but not all, require consideration of the costs of precautionary measures. Weak formulations do not preclude weighing benefits against the costs. Factors other than scientific uncertainty, including economic considerations, may provide legitimate grounds for postponing action. Under weak formulations, the requirement to justify the need for action (the burden of proof) generally falls on those advocating precautionary action. No mention is made of assignment of liability for environmental harm. Strong versions justify or require precautionary measures and some also establish liability for environmental harm, which is effectively a strong form of "polluter pays". For example, the Earth Charter states: "When knowledge is limited apply a precautionary approach Place the burden of proof on those who argue that a proposed activity will not cause significant harm, and make the responsible parties liable for environmental harm." Reversal of proof requires those proposing an activity to prove that the product, process or technology is sufficiently "safe" before approval is granted. Requiring proof of "no environmental harm" before any action proceeds implies the public is not prepared to acccpt any environmental risk, no matter what economic or social benefits may arise. At the extreme, such a requirement could involve bans and prohibitions on entire classes of potentially threatening activities or substances. Over time, there has been a gradual transformation of the precautionary principle from what appears in the Rio Declaration to a stronger form that arguably acts as restraint on development in the absence of firm evidence that it will do no harm.

International Agreements and Declarations

The World Charter for Nature, which was adopted by the UN General Assembly in 1982, was the first international endorsement of the precautionary principle. The principle was implemented in an international treaty as early as the 1987 Montreal Protocol, and among other international treaties and declarations is reflected in the 1992 Rio Declaration on Environment and Development (signed at the United Nations Conference on Environment and Development).

Principle vs. Approach

No introduction to the precautionary principle would be complete without brief reference to the difference between the precautionary principle and the precautionary approach. Principle 15 of the Rio Declaration 1992 states that: "in order to protect the environment, the precautionary approach shall be widely applied by States according to their capabilities. Where there are threats of serious or irreversible damage, lack of full scientific certainty shall be not used as a reason for postponing cost-effective measures to prevent environmental degradation." As Garcia pointed out, "the wording, largely similar to that of the principle, is subtly different in that: (1) it recognizes that there may be differences in local capabilities to apply the approach, and (2) it calls for cost-effectiveness in applying the approach, e.g., taking economic and social costs into account." The 'approach' is generally considered a softening of the principle.

"As Recuerda has noted, the distinction between the 'precautionary principle' and a 'precautionary approach' is diffuse and, in some contexts, controversial. In the negotiations of international declarations, the United States has opposed the use of the term 'principle' because this term has special connotations in legal language, due to the fact that a 'principle of law` is a source of law. This means that it is compulsory, so a court can quash or confirm a decision through the application of the precautionary principle. In this sense, the precautionary principle is not a simple idea or a desideratum but a source of law. This is the legal status of the precautionary principle in the European Union. On the other hand, an 'approach' usually does not have the same meaning, although in some particular cases an approach could be binding. A precautionary approach is a particular 'lens' used to identify risk that every prudent person possesses.

The Swiss Federal Act on the Protection of the Environment, dated Oct. 1983, stipulates in its Art. 1 as its Aim:

This act intends to protect people, animals and plants, their biological communities and habitats against harmful effects or nuisances and to preserve the natural foundations of life sustainably, in particular biological diversity and the fertility of the soil. Early preventive measures must be taken in order to limit effects which could become harmful or a nuisance.

On 2 February 2000, the European Commission issued a Communication on the precautionary principle, in which it adopted a procedure for the application of this concept, but without giving a detailed definition of it. Paragraph 2 of article 191 of the Lisbon Treaty states that:

> Union policy on the environment shall aim at a high level of protection taking into account the diversity of situations in the various regions of the Union. It shall be based on the precautionary principle and on the principles that preventive action should be taken, that environmental damage should as a priority be rectified at source and that the polluter should pay.

After the adoption of the European Commission's Communication on the precautionary principle, the principle has come to inform much EU policy, including areas beyond environmental policy. As of 2006 it had been integrated into EU laws "in matters such as general product safety, the use of additives for use in animal nutrition, the incineration of waste, and the regulation of genetically modified organisms". Through its application in case law, it has become a "general principle of EU law".

In Case T-74/00 *Artegodan*, the General Court (then Court of First Instance) appeared willing to extrapolate from the limited provision for the precautionary principle in environmental policy in Article 191(2) TFEU to a general principle of EU law.

In France, the Charter for the Environment contains a formulation of the precautionary principle:

> When the occurrence of any damage, albeit unpredictable in the current state of scientific knowledge, may seriously and irreversibly harm the environment, public authorities shall, with due respect for the principle of precaution and the areas within their jurisdiction, ensure the implementation of procedures for risk assessment and the adoption of temporary measures commensurate with the risk involved in order to preclude the occurrence of such damage.

On 18 July 2005, the City of San Francisco passed a Precautionary Principle Purchasing ordinance, which requires the city to weigh the environmental and health costs of its $600 million in annual purchases – for everything from cleaning supplies to computers. Members of the Bay Area Working Group on the Precautionary Principle including the Breast Cancer Fund, helped bring this to fruition.

In 1997, Japan tried to use the consideration of the precautionary principle in a WTO

SPS Agreement on the Application of Sanitary and Phytosanitary Measures case, as Japan's requirement to test each variety of agricultural products (apples, cherries, peaches, walnuts, apricots, pears, plums and quinces) for the efficacy of treatment against codling moths was challenged.

This moth is a pest that does not occur in Japan, and whose introduction has the potential to cause serious damage. The United States claimed that it was not necessary to test each variety of a fruit for the efficacy of the treatment, and that this varietal testing requirement was unnecessarily burdensome.

The most important Australian court case so far, due to its exceptionally detailed consideration of the precautionary principle, is Telstra Corporation Limited v Hornsby Shire Council.

The Principle was summarised by reference to the NSW *Protection of the Environment Administration Act 1991*, which itself provides a good definition of the principle:

"If there are threats of serious or irreversible environmental damage, lack of full scientific certainty should not be used as a reasoning for postponing measures to prevent environmental degradation. In the application of the principle decisions should be guided by: (i) careful evaluation to avoid, wherever practicable, serious or irreversible damage to the environment; and (ii) an assessment of risk-weighted consequence of various options".

The most significant points of Justice Preston's decision are the following findings:

- The principle and accompanying need to take precautionary measures is "triggered" when two prior conditions exist: a threat of serious or irreversible damage, and scientific uncertainty as to the extent of possible damage.
- Once both are satisfied, "a proportionate precautionary measure may be taken to avert the anticipated threat of environmental damage, but it should be proportionate".
- The threat of serious or irreversible damage should invoke consideration of five factors: the scale of threat (local, regional etc.); the perceived value of the threatened environment; whether the possible impacts are manageable; the level of public concern, and whether there is a rational or scientific basis for the concern.
- The consideration of the level of scientific uncertainty should involve factors which may include: what would constitute sufficient evidence; the level and kind of uncertainty; and the potential to reduce uncertainty.
- The principle shifts the burden of proof. If the principle applies, the burden shifts: "a decision maker must assume the threat of serious or irreversible

environmental damage is a reality [and] the burden of showing this threat is negligible reverts to the proponent".

- The precautionary principle invokes preventative action: "the principle permits the taking of preventative measures without having to wait until the reality and seriousness of the threat become fully known".
- "The precautionary principle should not be used to try to avoid all risks".
- The precautionary measures appropriate will depend on the combined effect of "the degree of seriousness and irreversibility of the threat and the degree of uncertainty the more significant and uncertain the threat, the greater the precaution required". "measures should be adopted proportionate to the potential threats".

A petition filed 17 May 2013 by environmental group Greenpeace Southeast Asia and farmer-scientist coalition Masipag (*Magsasaka at Siyentipiko sa Pagpapaunlad ng Agrikultura*) asked the Appellate court to stop the planting of Bt eggplant in test fields, saying the impacts of such an undertaking to the environment, native crops and human health are still unknown. The Court of Appeals granted the petition, citing the precautionary principle stating "when human activities may lead to threats of serious and irreversible damage to the environment that is scientifically plausible but uncertain, actions shall be taken to avoid or diminish the threat." Respondents filed a motion for reconsideration in June 2013 and on 20 September 2013 the Court of Appeals chose to uphold their May decision saying the *bt talong* field trials violate the people's constitutional right to a "balanced and healthful ecology." The Supreme Court on 8 December 2015 permanently stopped the field testing for Bt (Bacillus thuringiensis) talong (eggplant), upholding the decision of the Court of Appeals which stopped the field trials for the genetically modified eggplant. The court is the first in the world to adopt the precautionary principle regarding GMO products in its decision.

Corporate

The Body Shop International, a UK-based cosmetics company, included the precautionary principle in their 2006 Chemicals Strategy.

Environment and Health

Fields typically concerned by the precautionary principle are the possibility of:

- Global warming or abrupt climate change in general.
- Extinction of species.
- Introduction of new and potentially harmful products into the environment, threatening biodiversity (e.g., genetically modified organisms).

- Threats to public health, due to new diseases and techniques (e.g., HIV transmitted through blood transfusion).
- Long-term effects of new technologies (e.g. health concerns regarding radiation from cell phones and other electronics communications devices).
- Persistent or acute pollution (e.g., asbestos, endocrine disruptors).
- Food safety (e.g., Creutzfeldt–Jakob disease).
- Other new biosafety issues (e.g., artificial life, new molecules).

The precautionary principle is often applied to biological fields because changes cannot be easily contained and have the potential of being global. The principle has less relevance to contained fields such as aeronautics, where the few people undergoing risk have given informed consent (e.g., a test pilot). In the case of technological innovation, containment of impact tends to be more difficult if that technology can self-replicate. Bill Joy emphasised the dangers of replicating genetic technology, nanotechnology, and robotic technology in his report, "Why the future doesn't need us", though he does not specifically cite the precautionary principle. The application of the principle can be seen in the public policy of requiring pharmaceutical companies to carry out clinical trials to show that new medications are safe.

Oxford based philosopher Nick Bostrom discusses the idea of a future powerful superintelligence, and the risks that we/it face should it attempt to gain atomic level control of matter.

Application of the principle modifies the status of innovation and risk assessment: it is not the risk that must be avoided or amended, but a potential risk that must be prevented. Thus, in the case of regulation of scientific research, there is a third party beyond the scientist and the regulator: the consumer.

In an analysis concerning application of the precautionary principle to nanotechnology, Chris Phoenix and Mike Treder posit that there are *two forms* of the principle, which they call the "strict form" and the "active form". The former "requires inaction when action might pose a risk", while the latter means "choosing less risky alternatives when they are available, and taking responsibility for potential risks." Thomas Alured Faunce has argued for stronger application of the precautionary principle by chemical and health technology regulators particularly in relation to Tio_2 and ZnO nanoparticles in sunscreens, biocidal nanosilver in waterways and products whose manufacture, handling or recycling exposes humans to the risk of inhaling multi-walled carbon nanotubes.

Resource Management

Several natural resources like fish stocks are now managed by precautionary approach, through Harvest Control Rules (HCR) based upon the precautionary principle. The figure indicates how the principle is implemented in the cod fisheries management proposed by the International Council for the Exploration of the Sea.

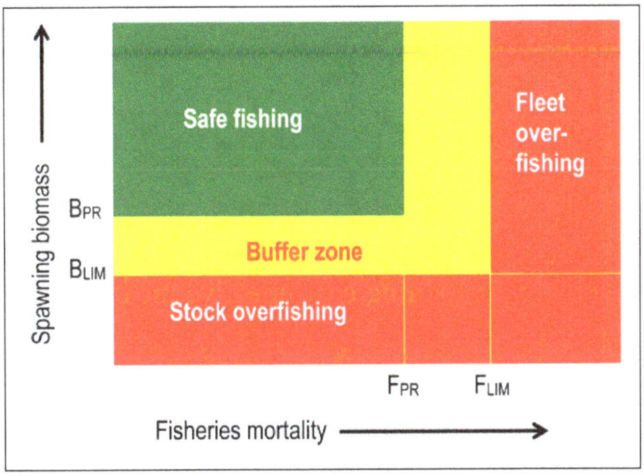

The Traffic Light colour convention, showing the concept of Harvest Control Rule (HCR), specifying when a rebuilding plan is mandatory in terms of precautionary and limit reference points for spawning biomass and fishing mortality rate.

In classifying endangered species, the precautionary principle means that if there is doubt about an animal's or plant's exact conservation status, the one that would cause the strongest protective measures to be realised should be chosen. Thus, a species like the silvery pigeon that might exist in considerable numbers and simply be under-recorded or might just as probably be long extinct is not classified as "data deficient" or "extinct" (which both do not require any protective action to be taken), but as "critically endangered" (the conservation status that confers the need for the strongest protection), whereas the increasingly rare, but probably not yet endangered emerald starling is classified as "data deficient", because there is urgent need for research to clarify its status rather than for conservation action to save it from extinction.

If, for example, a large ground-water body that people use for drinking water is contaminated by bacteria (e-coli 0157 H7, campylobacter or leptospirosis) and the source of contamination is strongly suspected to be dairy cows but the exact science is not yet able to provide absolute proof, the cows should be removed from the environment until they are proved, by the dairy industry, not to be the source or until that industry ensures that such contamination will not recur.

Animal Sentience Precautionary Principle

Appeals to the precautionary principle have often characterized the debates concerning animal sentience – that is, the question of whether animals are able to feel "subjective experiences with an attractive or aversive quality", such as pain, pleasure, happiness, or joy – in relation to the question of whether we should legally protect sentient animals.

A version of the precautionary principle suitable for the problem of animal sentience has been proposed by LSE philosopher Jonathan Birch: "The idea is that when the evidence of sentience is inconclusive, we should 'give the animal the benefit of doubt' or 'err on the side of caution' in formulating animal protection legislation." Since we cannot reach absolute certainty with regards to the fact that some animals are sentient, the precautionary principle has been invoked in order to grant potentially sentient animals "basic legal protections". Birch's formulation of the Animal Sentience Precautionary Principle runs as follows:

> Where there are threats of serious, negative animal welfare outcomes, lack of full scientific certainty as to the sentience of the animals in question shall not be used as a reason for postponing cost-effective measures to prevent those outcomes.

This version of the precautionary principle consists of an epistemic and a decision rule. The former concerns the "evidential bar" that should be required for animal sentience. In other words, how much evidence of sentience is necessary before one decides to apply precautionary measures? According to Birch, only *some* evidence would be sufficient, which means that the evidential bar should be set at low levels. Birch proposes to consider the evidence that certain animals are sentient sufficient whenever "statistically significant evidence of the presence of at least one credible indicator of sentience in at least one species of that order" has been obtained. For practical reasons, Birch says, the evidence of sentience should concern the order, so that if one species meets the conditions of sentience, then all the species of the same order should be considered sentient and should be thus legally protected. This is due to the fact that, on the one hand, "to investigate sentience separately in different orders" is feasible, whereas on the other hand, since some orders include thousands of species, it would be unfeasible to study their sentience separately.

What is more, the evidential bar should be so low that only *one* indicator of sentience in the species of a specific order will be sufficient in order for the precautionary principle to be applied. Such indicator should be "an observable phenomenon that experiments can be designed to detect, and it must be credible that the presence of this indicator is explained by sentience". Lists of such criteria already exist for detecting animal pain. The aim is to create analogous lists for other criteria of sentience, such as happiness, fear, or joy. The presence of one of these criteria should be demonstrated by means of experiments which must meet "the normal scientific standards".

Regarding the second part of the animal sentience precautionary principle, the decision rule concerns the requirement that we have to act once we have sufficient evidence of a seriously bad outcome. But what counts as sufficient evidence? According to Birch, "we should aim to include within the scope of animal protection legislation all animals for which the evidence of sentience is sufficient, according to the standard of sufficiency outlined [above]". In other words, the decision rule states that once the aforementioned low evidential bar is met, then we *should* act in a precautionary way. Finally, Birch's proposal "deliberately leaves open the question of how, and to what extent, the treatment of these animals should be regulated", thus also leaving open the content of the regulations, as this will largely depend on the animal in question.

CONTROL SELF-ASSESSMENT

Control self-assessment is a technique developed in 1987 that is used by a range of organisations including corporations, charities and government departments, to assess the effectiveness of their risk management and control processes.

A "control process" is a check or process performed to reduce or eliminate the risk of error. Since its introduction the technique has been widely adopted in the United States, European Union and other countries. There are a number of ways a control self-assessment can be implemented but its key feature is that, in contrast to a traditional audit, the tests and checks are made by staff whose normal day-to-day responsibilities are within the business unit being assessed. A self-assessment, by identifying the higher risk processes within the organisation, allows internal auditors to plan their work more effectively. A number of governmental organisations require the use of control self-assessment. In the United States it is a requirement of the FFIEC that control self-assessments are performed on IT systems and operational processes on a regular basis. Benefits claimed for control self-assessment include creating a clear line of accountability for controls, reducing the risk of fraud and the creation of an organisation with a lower risk profile.

In certain circumstances control self-assessment is not always effective. For example, it can be difficult to implement in a decentralised environment, in organisations where there is high employee turnover, where the organisation goes through frequent change or where the senior management of the organisation does not foster a culture of open communication.

Performing the Control Self-assessment

The first step in control self-assessment is to document the organisation's control processes with the aim of identifying suitable ways of measuring or testing each control. The actual testing of the controls is performed by staff whose day-to-day role is within the area of the organisation that is being examined as they have the greatest knowledge of how the processes operate. The two common techniques for performing the evaluations are:

- Workshops, that may be but do not have to be independently facilitated, involving some or all staff from the business unit being tested.
- Surveys or questionnaires completed independently by the staff.

Both approaches are the opposite of formal audits where the auditors, not the business unit staff, will perform the assessment.

Transit Board Self-Assessment Tool Level I

Level I Survey Tool: Please rate each measure below, using the rating system of 1 = Strongly Disagree through 5 = Strongly Agree	Strongly Disagree				Strongly Agree
	1	2	3	4	5
I. Board Processes					
1. The Board sets policy; management implements policy. Board members do not become involved in specific management, personnel, or service issues except in a predetermined oversight role.					
2. a. Board members devote sufficient time to fulfilling their responsibilities.					
b. Board members attend meetings well prepared and participate fully in all matters.					
3. Board members work cohesively and cooperatively to try to minimize miscommunication and confusion.					
4. There is an orientation process for new board members.					
II. Strategic Planning					
5. Board creates and communicates the agency's strategic direction; this is achieved by regularly evaluating core values and strategic mission.					
III. Fiduciary and Legal Responsibilities					
6. Board provides effective monitoring, evaluation, and oversight of the agency's fiscal concerns, including understanding of the funding mechanisms.					
7. Board supports a code of conduct and ethical practices; each board member is committed to ethical practices and guards against conflicts of interest.					
8. Board approves annual operating and capital goals and budgets.					

Section 1 of the control self-assessment form used by the Federal Transit Administration.

On completion of the assessment each control may be rated based on the responses received to determine the probability of its failure and the impact if a failure occurred. These ratings can be mapped to produce a heatmap showing potential areas of vulnerability.

Methodologies

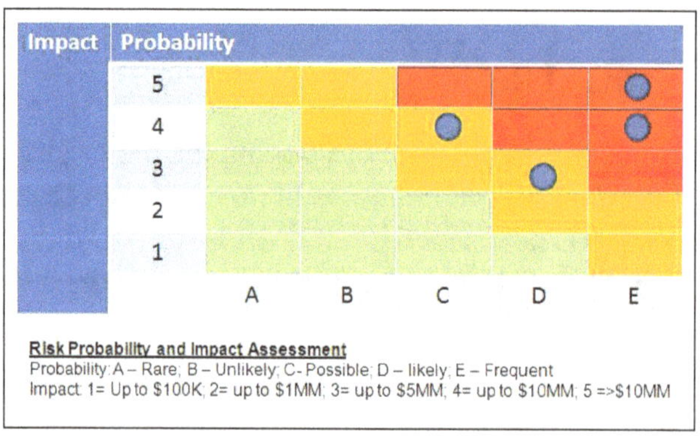

A heatmap produced from the information captured in a control self-assessment. The cluster of issues in the red and amber sections of the heatmap indicate that this is a high risk area and probably in need of new or changed control processes.

Six basic methodologies for control self-assessment have been defined:

- Internal Control Questionnaire (ICQ) self-audit.
- Customised questionnaires.
- Control guides.
- Interview techniques.
- Control model workshops.
- Interactive workshops.

The National Institute of Standards and Technology control self-assessment methodology is based on customised questionnaires. It is an IT focused methodology suitable for assessing system based controls. It provides a cost-effective technique to determine the status of information security controls, identify any weaknesses and, where necessary, define an improvement plan. The methodology uses a questionnaire that contains specific control objectives and techniques against a system or group of systems can be tested and measured. The methodology was designed for United States federal agencies but can also be valuable for private sector organisations.

The COBIT methodology can be used for control self-assessment; like the NIST methodology it was designed for IT focused assessments. COBIT's Process Description component provides a reference model of an organisation's processes and their ownership. Its Control Objectives component provides a set of requirements considered necessary for effective control of each IT process with the organisation. Assessment and evaluation of these components using the Management Guidelines component provides an assessment mechanism that generates a maturity model indicating if the organisation is meeting its control objectives.

The Institute of Internal Auditors based its control self-assessment methodology on the Total Quality Management approaches of the 1990s as well as the COSO's framework. The methodology became part of the *International Standards for Professional Practice of Internal Auditing* and was adopted by a large number of major organisations.

A number of other methodologies to standardise the control self-assessment have been published. The Institute of Internal Auditors offers a certification in control self-assessment practice.

Software Tools

A number of software packages are available to support the control self-assessment process. These are typically modified versions of software developed originally for internal use by audit and accountancy firms such as Deloitte or by niche vendors specialising in business or financial management tools.

Benefits

Control self-assessment creates a clear line of accountability for controls, reduces the risk of fraud (by examining data that may flag unusual patterns of transactions) and results in an organisation with a lower risk profile.

A number of other soft benefits have been claimed for organisations performing control self-assessment. These include a better understanding of business operations (by both management and operational staff); stronger awareness of risk practices; a reinforced corporate governance regime and internal audit efficiency improvements.

NETWORK THEORY IN RISK ASSESSMENT

A network is an abstract structure capturing only the basics of connection patterns and little else. Because it is a generalized pattern, tools developed for analyzing, modeling and understanding networks can theoretically be implemented across disciplines. As long as a system can be represented by a network, there is an extensive set of tools – mathematical, computational, and statistical – that are well-developed and if understood can be applied to the analysis of the system of interest.

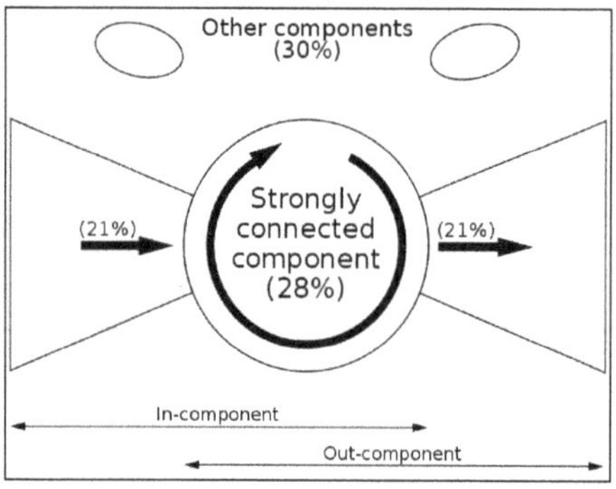

A "bow-tie" diagram of components in a directed network.

Tools that are currently employed in risk assessment are often sufficient, but model complexity and limitations of computational power can tether risk assessors to involve more causal connections and account for more Black Swan event outcomes. By applying network theory tools to risk assessment, computational limitations may be overcome and result in broader coverage of events with a narrowed range of uncertainties.

Decision-making processes are not incorporated into routine risk assessments; however, they play a critical role in such processes. It is therefore very important for risk assessors to minimize confirmation bias by carrying out their analysis and publishing their results with minimal involvement of external factors such as politics, media, and advocates. In reality, however, it is nearly impossible to break the iron triangle among politicians, scientists (in this case, risk assessors), and advocates and media. Risk

Wassessors need to be sensitive to the difference between risk studies and risk perceptions. One way to bring the two closer is to provide decision-makers with data they can easily rely on and understand. Employing networks in the risk analysis process can visualize causal relationships and identify heavily-weighted or important contributors to the probability of the critical event.

A "bow-tie" diagram, cause-and-effect diagram, Bayesian network (a *directed acyclic* network) and fault trees are few examples of how network theories can be applied in risk assessment.

In epidemiology risk assessments once a network model was constructed, we can visually see then quantify and evaluate the potential exposure or infection risk of people related to the well-connected patients or high-traffic places. In ecological risk assessments, through a network model we can identify the keystone species and determine how widespread the impacts will extend from the potential hazards being investigated.

Risk Assessment Key Components

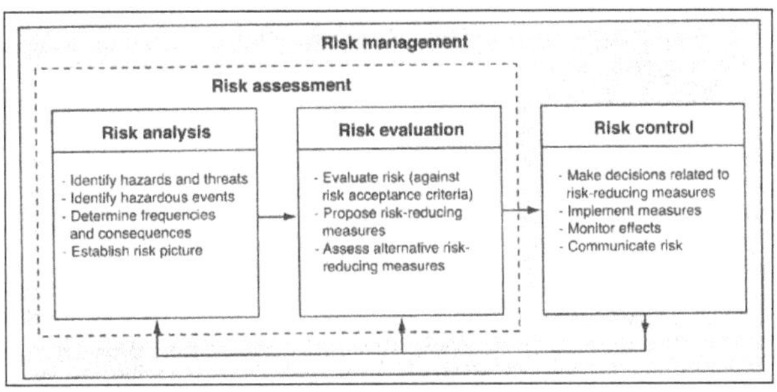

Risk Analysis, evaluation, assessment, and management.

Risk assessment is a method for dealing with uncertainty. For it to be beneficial to the overall risk management and decision making process, it must be able to capture extreme and catastrophic events. Risk assessment involves two parts: risk analysis and risk evaluation, although the term "*risk assessment*" can be seen used indistinguishable with "*risk analysis*". In general, risk assessment can be divided into these steps:

- Plan and prepare the risk analysis.
- Define and delimit the system and the scope of the analysis.
- Identify hazards and potential hazardous events.
- Determine causes and frequency of each hazardous event.
- Identify accident scenarios (i.e. even sequences) that may be initiated by each hazardous event.
- Select relevant and typical accident scenarios.

- Determine the consequences of each accident scenario.
- Determine the frequency of each accident scenario.
- Assess the uncertainty.
- Establish and describe the risk picture.
- Report the analysis.
- Evaluate the risk against risk acceptance criteria
- Suggest and evaluate potential risk-reducing measures.

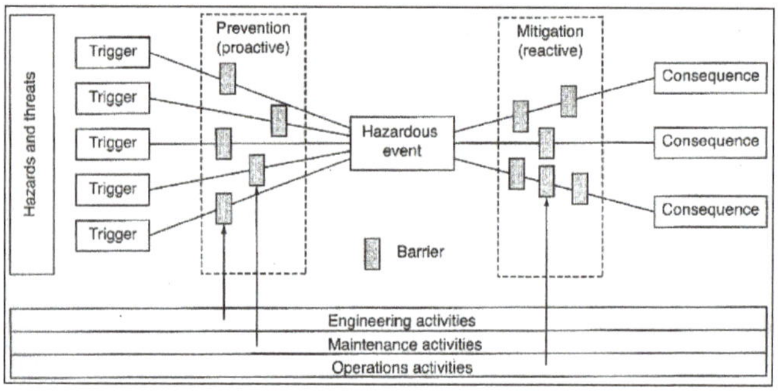

Bow-tie diagram of risk management.

Naturally, the number of steps required varies with each assessment. It depends on the scope of the analysis and the complexity of the study object. Because these is always varies degrees of uncertainty involved in any risk analysis process, sensitivity and uncertainty analysis are usually carried out to mitigate the level of uncertainty and therefore improve the overall risk assessment result.

Network Theory Key Components

A network is a simplified representation that reduces a system to an abstract structure. Simply put, it is a collection of points linked together by lines. Each point is known as a "vertex" (multiple: "vertices") or "nodes", and each line as "edges" or "links". Network modeling and studying have already been applied in many areas, including computer, physical, biological, ecological, logistical and social science. Through the studying of these models, we gain insights into the nature of individual components (i.e. vertices), connections or interactions between those components (i.e. edges), as well as the pattern of connections (i.e. network).

Undoubtedly, modifications of the structure (or pattern) of any given network can have a big effect on the behavior of the system it depicts. For example, connections in a social network affect how people communicate, exchange news, travel, and, less obviously, spread diseases. In order to gain better understanding of how each of these systems functions, some knowledge of the structure of the network is necessary.

Small-world Effect

The small-world effect is one of the most remarkable network phenomena. It describes a finding that in many (perhaps most) networks the mean path distances between vertices are surprisingly small. It has many implications in various areas of network studies. For instance, in social network, one can ruminate how fast a rumor (or a contagious disease) is spread in a community. From a mathematical point of view, since path lengths in networks are typically scale as log n (where n = number of network vertices), it is only logical it remains a small number even with large complex networks.

Another idea comes along with the small-world effect is called *funneling*. It was derived from a social network experiment conducted by the experimental psychologist Stanley Milgram in the 1960s. In that experiment he concluded, along with the small-world effect phenomenon, that in any given social network, there were always few that were especially well connected. These few individuals were therefore responsible for the connection between any members and the rest of the world.

Degree, Hubs and Paths

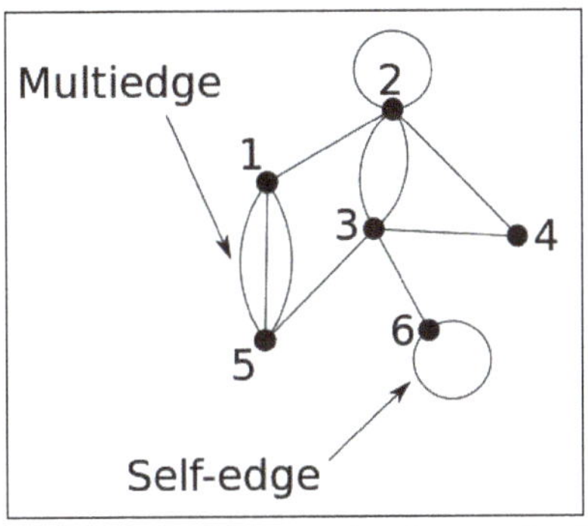

A small network with both multiedges and self-edges.

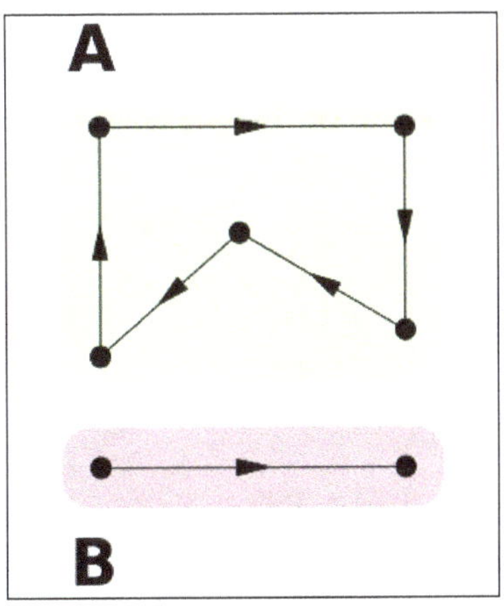

A disconnected directed network with two components (shaded).

Degree of a vertex is the number of edges connected to it. For example, on vertex 3 has a degree of five. Hubs are vertices in a network with a relatively higher degree. Vertex 3 again is a good example. In a social network, hubs can mean individuals with many acquaintances. In risk assessment, it can mean a hazardous event with multiple triggers (or the causal part of a bow-tie diagram). A path in a network is a route between a vertex and another across the network. From the same figure, an example of a path from vertex 1 to 6 can be 1→5→3→6.

Centrality

Centrality is a measure of how important (or *central*) certain vertices are in a network. It can be measured by counting the number of edges connected to it (i.e its *degree*). The vertices with the highest degree therefore have a high *degree centrality.*

Degree centrality can have many implications. In a social network, a person with high degree centrality may have more influence over others, more access to information, or more opportunities than those with fewer connections. In a citation network, a paper with high degree centrality may suggest it is more influential and thus has a greater impact on its respective area of research.

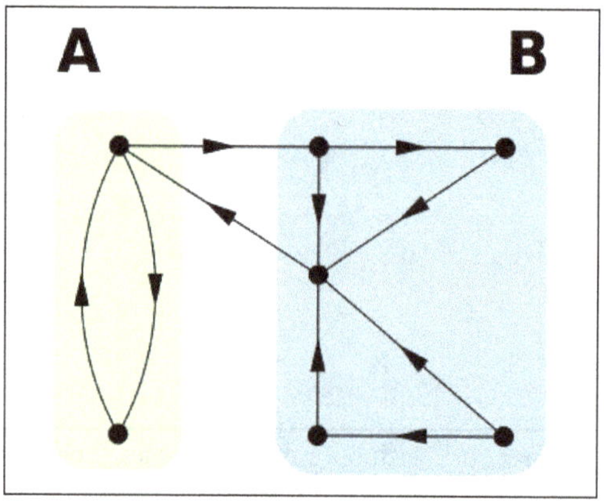

A connected directed network with two components (shaded).

Eigenvector centrality is an extension of the concept of degree centrality, based on the fact that in many networks not all vertices have the same weight or importance. A vertex's importance in its network increases if it has more connections to important vertices. Eigenvector centrality, therefore, can be view as a centrality scoring system for not just one but its neighboring vertices as well.

Components

Subgroups, or subsets of vertices, in a disconnected network. *Disconnected network* means in such network, there is at least a pair of vertices that no path connecting between them at all. Vice verse is known as a *connected network*, where all vertices within are connected by at least one path. One can therefore say a connected network has only one component.

Directed Networks

FIGURE 2. Probable cases of severe acute respiratory syndrome, by reported source of infection* — Singapore, February 25–April 30, 2003

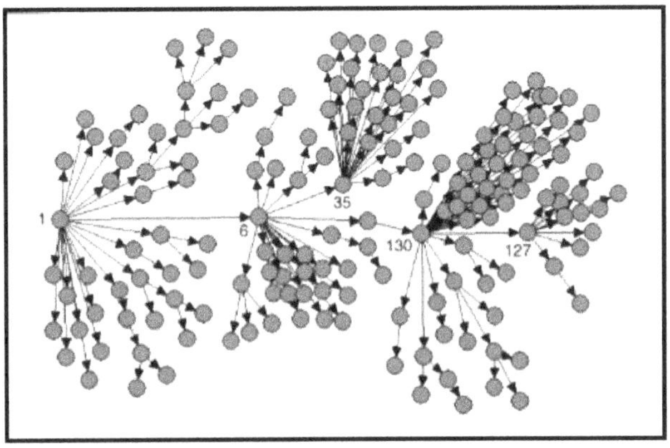

* Patient 1 represents Case 1; Patient 6, Case 2; Patient 35, Case 3; Patient 130, Case 4; and Patient 127, Case 5. Excludes 22 cases with either no or poorly defined direct contacts or who were cases translocated to Singapore and the seven contacts of one of these cases.
Reference: Bogatti SP. Netdraw 1.0 Network Visualization Software.

An example of acyclic directed network in epidemiology by CDC.

Networks of which each edge has a direction from one vertex to another. The edges are therefore known as *directed edges*. Example of such network include a link from the reference section on this page which will leads you to another, but not the other way around. In terms of food web, a prey eaten by a predator is another example.

Directed networks can be *cyclic* or *acyclic*. A *cyclic* directed network is one with a closed loop of edges. An *acyclic* directed network does not contain such loop. Since a *self-edge* – an edge connecting a vertex to itself – is considered a cycle, it is therefore absent from any acyclic network.

A Bayesian network is an example of an acyclic directed network.

Weighted Network

In reality, not all edges shares the same importance or weight (connections in a social network and keystone species in a food web, for example). A weighted network adds such element to its connections. It is widely used in genomic and systems biologic applications.

Trees

Undirected networks with no closed loops. A *tree* can be part of a network but isolated as a separate component. If all parts of a network are trees, such network is called a *forest*. An administrative body can sometime be viewed as a forest.

RISK REGISTER

Purpose of Risk Registers

Risk registers provide project managers with a list of risks identified, stated clearly and assessed as to their importance to meeting project objectives. The risk register can lead directly to risk handling, such as risk mitigation. The risk register is also used in a focused quantified risk analysis such as schedule risk analysis based on driving the Monte Carlo simulation with specific risks. This latter use is called the Risk Driver Method of schedule and cost risk analysis.

Identifying Risks

The risk register starts with a list of risks that may affect the project's ability to achieve its objectives. Risk identification starts with the risk breakdown structure. Often there is a discussion between the risk consultant and the project leadership including the project manager and team leadership about where the risks to the project may originate. A generalized risk breakdown structure is shown below:

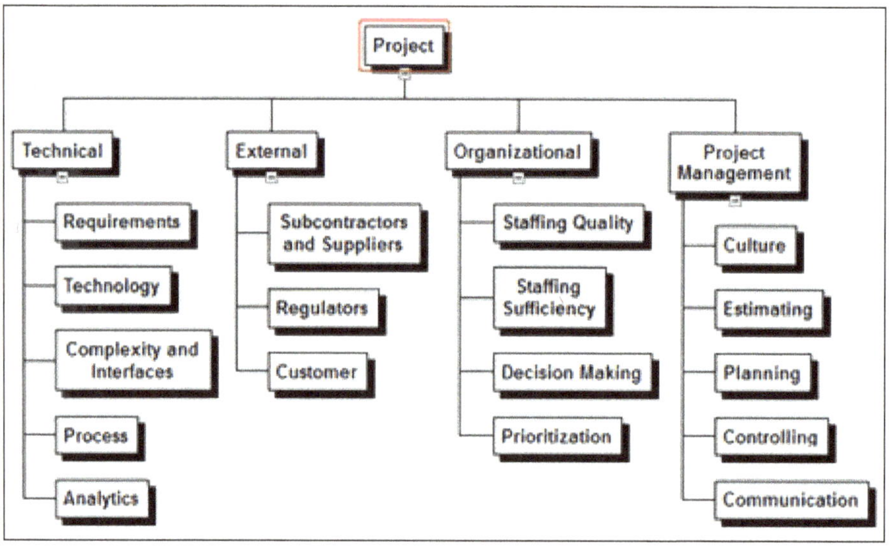

The purpose of the risk breakdown structure (RBS) is to encourage people to think of risks that may originate outside of their "stovepipe." Most people will think of the specific risks, often technical risks, that are impeding their getting their specific assignment done, and it is good to identify those risks. However, project team members have been involved with the project and have seen risks to success arising from other causes. In particular, external elements including regulators or the customer may be causing problems with the project. And there are barriers to success from the performing organization as well. These particular risks may be unpopular to discuss and to recognize, so the RBS helps people confront those sources of risks.

The risks should be discussed in a structured way, such as: "Because of (some cause that is true), a risk (an uncertain event or condition that, if it occurs will affect an objective in a positive or negative way), leading to (an impact, sometimes a range of possible impacts on a project objective). Distinguishing a risk from its cause and impact is important so that a mitigation of the true risk can be developed. For instance, do not say; "We have 12 schedule risks." We might say, we have 4 external risks that affect schedule if they were to occur, distinguishing the source of the risk from its impact. Also, do not say; "Our risk is that the mineral deposit is in an inaccessible location in a mountainous jungle." That fact may be a cause of logistical risks, but it is not an uncertainty at all.

We do include so-called "uncertainties," risks that are 100 likely to happen but with uncertain impacts. Hence, there is uncertainty to these risks, just not to their occurring or not.

Defining the Terms for Qualitative Risk Analysis

The discipline of assessing the probability and impact of a risk on a project depends on defining the terms used and them applying those terms to each risk assessed. Someone in authority, probably the project manager who is responsible for delivering the project objectives, needs to provide these definitions. The terms defined include:

- Probability the risk will occur with some noticeable impact on the project. The project manager needs to determine which probabilities would be scored between very low to very high, inclusive.
- The definitions of impact should be set by the Project Manager for the levels of very low, low, moderate, high and very high impact, by objective (time, cost, scope and quality).
- The structure of the probability – impact matrix is also the responsibility of the project manager. That means which combinations of probability and impact will cause a risk to be assessed red, yellow or green.

The probability measures such as those shown below will serve, but sometimes the project leadership wants to provide more detail in the lower (‹ 50%) probabilities:

Probability %	Score
Very High (81 - 100)	5
High (61 - 80)	4
Mod (41 - 60)	3
Low (21 - 40)	2
Very Low (1 - 20)	1

The impact scales are applied to individual risks. Looking at the definitions, we recognize, that successful overall project delivery is affected by many individual risks and that if any one of them would cause a 1-month delay or an increase of $100,000 it would be deemed to have a high-impact. On quality and scope "very high" impacts result if the risk makes the "project end item is effectively useless". For a large, lengthy project such as the construction of an oil refinery the definitions may be something like these:

Defined Conditions for Impact Scales of a Risk on Major Project Objectives Examples for Negative Impacts Only					
Project Objective	Cost	Time	Scope	Quality	Score
Very Low	Less than $100,000	$100,000 - $250.000	$250,000 - $500,000	$500,000 - $1,000,000	Greater than $1,000,000
Low	Insignificant Time increase	Less than 1 month	1 - 2 months	2 - 4 months	Greater than 4 months
Moderate	Scope Decreases are barely Noticeable	Minor Areas of Scope Affected	Major Areas of Scope Affected	Scope Reduction Unacceptable to Customer	Project End Item is Effectively Useless
High	Quality Degradation Barely Noticeable	Only Very Demanding Applications are Affected	Quality Reduction Requires Customer Approval	Quality Reduction Unacceptable to Customer	Project End Item is Effectively Useless
Very High	1	2	3	4	5

Notice that we provide defined impacts for each of the project objectives. In many risk register exercises the participants just try to assess risk to the entire project. That is too vague and does not answer the question: "What are the main (red) risks to my schedule?" "What is likely to affect my ability to achieve the scope I have committed to deliver?" Only if the risks are assessed against specific objectives will there be clarity in the exercise and usefulness in the results. We often find, for instance, risks to schedule that have little impact on cost and no impact on scope or quality.

Often there are attempts at risk analysis that do not use any definitions at all, assuring management that "we will be able to distinguish high impact from moderate impact when we see it." This approach is bound to fail, and any Risk Register based on this approach cannot have any credibility.

In addition, the probability and impact matrix is developed by the project manager and will be used to determine which combinations of probability and impact would warrant a risk being assessed as "low" "moderate" or "high". A representative matrix is shown below for threats.

There are also opportunities. Opportunities are those uncertainties that, if they occur, will help the project achieve its objectives. We should look for opportunities or we will never find them, since most people think of risk as the possibility of bad things (scope shortfalls, cost or schedule overruns) occurring. There are usually more threats than opportunities.

Probability and Impact Matrix for an Objective (e.g., Time, Cost, Scope, Quality)						
Probability (%)	**Prob. Score**	**Impact**				
Very High (81 - 100)	5	5	10	15	20	25
High (61 - 80)	4	4	8	12	16	20
Mod (41 - 60)	3	3	6	9	12	15
Low (21 - 40)	2	2	4	6	8	10
Very Low (1 - 20)	1	1	2	3	4	5
Impact Score		1	2	3	4	5
		Very Low	Low	Moderate	High	Very High

These assessments provide relative rankings particularly of impacts. It is not true that a "high" impact with a score of 4 can be described as being twice as impactful as a "low" impact with a score of 2. However, multiplying the probability and impact scores does put the risks in the right cells. Hence, a conditional formatting in a spreadsheet might show:

- Any score below 5 is green or low risk to the objective in question.
- Any score between 5 and 10 is yellow or moderate risk to the objective.
- Any score above 10 is red or high risk to the objective (notice the "10" in the right-hand column is red. We can fix this by scoring "very high" impacts as 5.1 and the rule will apply).

Collecting Data for the Risk Assessments

- Workshops usually involve many participants who discuss the risks individually and arrive at a consensus conclusion about impact and probability. If there are many risks, for instance more than 50, the participants can be formed into teams of 4 or more, and each assigned to provide assessments of a portion of the risk list. If this is the approach, each team should report back to the entire workshop for discussion and confirmation or adjustment of their assessment.

- Individual interviews require team members to meet individually with the facilitator to provide their input probability and impact assessment on those risks they feel comfortable discussing. In this approach multiple different assessments are gathered for most of the risks and the facilitator needs to review these to arrive at one specific probability and impact value for each risk.

There are benefits and limitations of each of these methods. The first factor to consider is that the qualitative assessment of risks' probability and impact relies on the project team's expert judgment. This is why one needs to be careful in choosing the participants and also to encourage them to contribute about a risk only if they feel comfortable in doing so.

- Workshops can contribute to a rich discussion of the risks that will get people thinking of new facts or concepts to consider. Sometimes, however, the workshop can be hijacked by a strong personality or someone in authority, and others in the workshop may feel it is better not to voice their own concerns. People have been criticized from mentioning risks that are true but sensitive in nature, such as those risks involving the customer or a lack of qualified people in the performer's organization. Also, if there are 20 people in a 1-day workshop, some 160 staff hours are used, with many of those hours focusing on a few individuals' ideas.
- Interviews take longer in calendar time than workshops but they can unearth important risks that might not be discussable in a workshop. Usually confidentiality is pledged so that an individual's contributions are never identified as coming from that individual. A difficulty of this approach is that several people will comment on an identified risk and have different opinions that ultimately have to be consolidated into one probability and one impact. If there are 20 people and the interviews take on average 2 hours each, approximately 40 staff hours will be expended on this exercise, although the hours of the facilitator will be greater than it is with the workshop approach.

Pre-mitigation Risk Register Results

The identified risks with names and source areas (from the Risk Breakdown Structure) could be shown in a spreadsheet with conditional formatting (red, yellow or green) as shown below.

The risks can be described individually or sorted by objective or source. Below the risks are sorted by their impact on schedule (we have eliminated the Quality columns to make the presentation feasible.)

This sort of the Risk Register answers the question; What are the most important risks to my schedule?

	Probability and Impacts				Resulting Risk Score			Risk Action	
Risk Description	Probability Risk Occurs	On Schedule	On Cost	On Scope	Risk on Schedule	Risk on Cost	Risk on Scope	Risk Owner	Risk Mitigation Actions
PM5	4	5	4	3	18	15	10		
TECH2	4	5	4	3	17	16	13		
ORG6	3	4	3	3	14	11	10		
EXT12	3	5	4	3	13	12	10		
ORG5	3	4	3	3	13	9	8		
ORG9	3	4	3	3	13	10	9		
EXT5	3	4	3	2	12	11	7		
PM3	3	4	4	3	12	12	8		
TECH15	2	5	5	3	12	12	7		
TECH6	3	5	4	3	12	10	7		
PM1	3	4	3	2	11	8	7		
TECH1	3	3	3	3	10	11	10		
EXT1	2	4	3	3	7	7	5		
TECH5	2	4	3	3	6	6	6		
EXT4	2	4	4	2	6	5	3		
PM7	3	2	4	2	6	12	6		
TECH14	1	5	5	2	5	5	2		
TECH8	1	5	3	1	5	3	1		
EXT9	1	3	3	1	3	3	1		
TECH3	1	3	3	1	3	3	1		

Risk Owner, Mitigations and Post-mitigation Risk Register Assessments

To be taken seriously, certain actions are needed before the Risk Register is considered done:

- Assign a risk owner to each risk.
- The risk owner is responsible for getting people together to identify and plan risk mitigation steps. The risk owner does not need to be the owner of the risk mitigation action but he or she needs to be responsible to see that the action is identified, planned (including cost, resources, timing and approvals if needed), implemented and monitored for effectiveness.
- Identify and plan risk mitigations, at least for the high or red risks: Mitigation actions often take money and resources and sometimes take top management approvals. Some risks will be managed by more than one mitigation step. The mitigation measures need to be specific and actionable, appropriate to the risk and reasonably likely to be effective.

- Implement the risk mitigation actions On some projects risk mitigations are discussed but never implemented.
- Risk mitigations need to be planned, budgeted, staffed, scheduled and managed like any other important project activity.
- Assess the risks' probability and impact after mitigation, using the same discipline and definitions that have been used to rank the risks initially.
- A comparison can be made with the pre-mitigated risk scores to see how effective the team thinks the mitigations will be.
- It is possible that even after mitigation there will still remain risks judged to be high or red risk, especially to the schedule. In some industries projects go ahead with red risks, where in other industries there can be an expectation that red risks can be mitigated to yellow or green conditions.

References

- Contingency-plan: whatis.techtarget.com, Retrieved 19 July, 2019
- Risk-pooling-insurance-2491: pocketsense.com, Retrieved 11 May, 2019
- Gollier, Christian, Bruno Jullien & Nicolas Treich (2000). "Scientific Progress and Irreversibility: An Economic Interpretation of the 'Precautionary Principle'". Journal of Public Economics. 75 (2): 229–253. doi:10.1016/S0047-2727(99)00052-3
- Risk-register-development: projectrisk.com, Retrieved 23 June, 2019
- Jorion, Philippe (2006). Value at Risk: The New Benchmark for Managing Financial Risk (3rd ed.). McGraw-Hill. ISBN 978-0-07-146495-6

Risk Management Software

CHAPTER 8

There are many software that are used to increase the working efficiency of risk management and optimization of business performance. GRC Envelop, Avanon, Lockpath, SAS, Qualys, Cura, Optial, etc. are some examples of these software. This chapter has been carefully written to provide an easy understanding of these risk management software.

Risk management software is a type of enterprise software that helps companies to actively manage risk. Many of these tools are analytical in nature, and use existing data or projections to help human decision makers identify risk and take measures to avoid potential crises.

Different companies offer various kinds of risk management software tools. Some are based on predictive analytics, where data filters provide educated predictions about the future. Others compare and contrast specific business processes to understand where a business's strengths are. Experts also talk about "risk drivers" where software can identify and analyze key factors in enterprise vulnerability.

Many risk management tools involve transparent dashboards that help human decision makers to handle a great deal of information in a transparent way. These can include the use of best practices information, along with data about existing operations. Many of these tools are based on creating a useful and user-friendly graphical user interface that helps end users to understand their goals and how to reach them.

Risk analysis and management tools serve multiple purposes and come in many shapes and sizes. Some risk analysis and management tools include those used for:

- Strategic and Capability Risk Analysis: Focuses on identifying, analyzing, and prioritizing risks to achieve strategic goals, objectives, and capabilities.
- Threat Analysis: Focuses on identifying, analyzing, and prioritizing threats to minimize their impact on national security.
- Investment and Portfolio Risk Analysis: Focuses on identifying, analyzing, and prioritizing investments and possible alternatives based on risk.
- Program Risk Management: Focuses on identifying, analyzing, prioritizing, and managing risks to eliminate or minimize their impact on a program's objectives and probability of success.

- Cost Risk Analysis: Focuses on quantifying how technological and economic risks may affect a system's cost. Applies probability methods to model, measure, and manage risk in the cost of engineering advanced systems.

Each specialized risk analysis and management area has developed tools to support its objectives with various levels of maturity.

Selecting the Right Tool

It is important that the organization define the risk analysis and management process before selecting a tool. Ultimately, the tool must support the process. When selecting a risk analysis and management tool, consider these criteria:

- Aligned to risk analysis objectives: Does the tool support the analysis that the organization is trying to accomplish? Is the organization attempting to implement an ongoing risk management process or conduct a one-time risk analysis?
- Supports decision making: Does the tool provide the necessary information to support decision making?
- Accessibility: Is the tool accessible to all users and key stakeholders? Can the tool be located/hosted where all necessary personnel can access it?
- Availability of data: Is data available for the tool's analysis?
- Level of detail: Is the tool detailed enough to support decision making?
- Integration with other program management / systems engineering processes: Does the tool support integration with other program management / systems engineering processes?

GRC ENVELOP

GRC Envelop is a risk management and audit management software tool. It enables process control managers, auditors and risk managers to document and manage their work. The entire tool is web based and is built using the Python/Django. The idea behind GRC Envelop is to help risk managers and auditors with a standard work flow and framework to help capture the process details within an organisation. This tool is mainly used for internal and external audits focused on financial, IT, HR and sales processes within firms.

Since, this tool has an open source license, it has been listed on a few sites.

Throughout GRC Envelop, the fundamental data structure is as follows:

Processes → Objectives → Risks → Controls → Tests → Findings → Actions.

Processes are the basic starting point for the entire tool. Objectives, risks and controls are the most important part that this tool intends to handle. Sometimes this part is also referred to as the risk control matrix in some organisations.

Features

- Audit management: There are three basic areas for the audit management:
    - Creating audits - Title, description, start and end dates are of some of the features that are available while creating an audit. You can also attached work papers to an Audit. While creating an audit, you can create the processes, the objectives, the risks, the controls and the tests. At each of these levels you can attach work papers too.
    - Managing and executing audits - to manage or execute an Audit, the GRC Envelop tool provides a separate workflow to ensure that auditors can only enter test results and test descriptions. While executing the audit you can create findings and actions. The ability to make control and test assessment is only available in the enterprise version.
    - Report generation - the main use of this tool is to provide easy report generation at the end of an auditing exercise. report generation template can be modified according to your needs. The community version has only one default report generation template. The enterprise version has the ability to have multiple templates.
- Risk Management: The risk management module looks at providing the basic structure for capturing the risk assessment process and documentation. The module is generally based around ISO/IEC 27001:2013.
    - Risk register: A register is a collection of risks. Registers may be used to group risks in any manner that is convenient to the firm. A Register report can be generated to show risk register details and an overview of all the risks and stakeholder opinions.
    - Risk: A risk is a clear definition of some kind of uncertainty that will affect the firm in future. An uncertainty can occur on many different dimensions, for example, financial risk or reputation risk. There are two aspects to consider when modeling risk, likelihood and impact. Likelihood and Impact are presented as scales in the risk management module.
    - The risk owner: any user on the system.

- Risk Opinion: The most powerful feature of this module is to generate a survey link which can be sent to all the stakeholders associated with the risk (or risk register). GRC Envelop with capture all the responses on the survey and present the report based on a template.
- Risk Summary: The risk summary provides an overview of all the responses from the stakeholders to the Risk Manager. There is a table that provides the detailed view of each stakeholder and their responses. The last row of the table has the average values of the likelihood and impacts across all the stakeholders.
- Report generation: reports can be generated based on a changeable template. The template can be designed to aggregate the responses in numerous ways.
- Scales: Scales are to be defined for likelihood and impact of a risk. Each scale has numeric range (minimum and maximum values), the units that the scale deals with and the type of scale (whether Likelihood or Impact scale). Each scale has a title and description too.

- Repository: The repository module is a store or library of processes, objectives, risks, controls and tests. The structure under a process group is the same as that in the audit module. However, there are no findings or actions in the repository module.
- Planning: Planning module helps managers to see on a calendar format the different audits and resources that are planned for a time period. For example, conflicts of assignment of auditors can be quickly recognised

Users and Roles

Restricting users to their areas is an important task for a tool. The community version has only one user type (auditor) whereas the enterprise version has the following seven user types:

- Auditor,
- Audit manager,
- Risk manager,
- Repository manager,
- Internal business user,
- External viewer,
- System administrator,

Licenses

There are two types of licenses that with which GRC Envelop is available:

- Open source MIT license (limited features).
- Enterprise license.

ACTIVE RISK

Active Risk (LSE:ARI) formerly known as Strategic Thought Group, is a software company that specialises in enterprise-wide risk management (ERM) and governance, risk and compliance (GRC) software. It is a subsidiary of Sword Group.

Strategic Thought was founded in 1987 as a specialist technology company in London, England. In 2001, Active Risk Manager (ARM), enterprise-wide risk management (ERM) and governance, risk and compliance (GRC) software was launched and today is the company's flagship product.

The company is publicly listed on the London Stock Exchange Alternative Investment Market and has offices in Maidenhead, England and Herndon, Virginia.

Active Risk Manager is used by major global organizations such as NASA, US Air Force, London Underground, EADS and Nestlé. ARM was awarded "Risk Management Application of the Year" in 2010 at the global Risk Management Awards run in conjunction with the Institute of Risk Management.

AVANON

Avanon is operational risk control software, founded in Zurich, Switzerland. In October 2012 it was acquired by Thomson Reuters and integrated into the Thomson Reuters Accelus suite, to form the risk component of their governance, risk and compliance (GRC) division. The majority of clients operate in the financial services industry.

Avanon is an application which helps to manage client companies enterprise risk and compliance programs. The application is not limited to a specific industry, but deals in industries like banking, insurance and energy. Avanon provides clients continuously monitoring and feedback which enables them to manage operational risk and control. The application can be customized to support different risk and regulatory requirements (Basel Accord).

The primary customer base is Europe but has recently expanded into Africa and Asia.

LOCKPATH

Lockpath is a provider of governance, risk management, and compliance and information security software. Its Keylight platform integrates business processes to simplify risk management and regulatory compliance challenges. Common business areas Lockpath target are policy and procedure management, risk assessment, incident management, vulnerability management, vendor management, business continuity planning and internal audit preparation.

Lockpath was founded by Chris Caldwell and Chris Goodwin in 2010 to develop and sell governance, risk management and compliance software. Today, Lockpath's client base included global organizations ranging from small and midsize companies to Fortune 10 enterprises in over 15 industries. Lockpath is headquartered in Overland Park, Kansas.

On August 6th 2019 leading ethics and compliance software and services company NAVEX Global announced that it has acquired Lockpath, Inc., a recognized leader in Integrated Risk Management (IRM) software solutions.

Products

Keylight Platform

Lockpath launched the Keylight Platform and their first application, Compliance Manager, in October 2010. The initial launch consisted of a regulatory content and controls library fully integrated with the Unified Compliance Framework (UCF), workflow capabilities and a reporting engine. Keylight 1.2 introduced the Threat Manager and Vendor Manager applications. Keylight 2.0 launched the Dynamic Content Framework and introduced two new applications, Incident Manager and Risk Manager. SE Magazine's Peter Stephenson described Keylight as a "family of applications [that] helps organizations manage enterprise risks and demonstrate compliance by providing visibility into corporate risk and security controls. The ready-to-use toolset integrates all applications under a single user interface, unifies and correlates any amount of security content, exposes vulnerabilities throughout the organization by tracking and recording key information about secured assets, and creates an iron-clad audit history". Keylight 2.4 introduced the Business Continuity Manager application and gave users the ability to create business continuity plans, conduct Business Impact Analyses, and perform tabletop exercises to test business continuity plans. Keylight 3.0 included an integration with the Health Information Trust Alliance (HITRUST) Common Security Framework (CSF), a framework designed for healthcare organizations. Keylight 3.3 introduced the Audit Manager application and renamed Threat Manager to Security Manager. Keylight 3.5 included a hybrid-cloud delivery method for Vendor Manager and the Anonymous Incident Portal. Keylight 4.0 added the Advanced Analytics Engine to the product portfolio.

On October 28, 2014, Lockpath received U.S. patent number 8,874,621 for the Dynamic Content Framework (DCF). The DCF is a highly scalable and flexible content engine that gives users the ability to create custom tables and fields. With DCF's drag-and-drop functionality, users can efficiently import and modify large sets of records. It gives users the ability to generate their own reports without requiring the assistance of developers and report writers.

Keylight 4.1 introduced the Keylight Ambassador. It was the first GRC platform to allow for both SAML and LDAP integration, the first to perform bulk tasks on data records, including data edits, workflow and record deletion, and the first to create ad-hoc reports on historical content. Keylight 4.1 also added support for syslog data collection.

Blacklight Platform

In 2018 Lockpath launched Blacklight, Blacklight brings automation to the configuration assessment of servers and corporate devices. The platform utilizes agent technology that continuously assesses devices and systems against Center for Internet Security (CIS) configuration benchmarks, as well as custom benchmarks, to detect misconfigurations that put organizations at risk for breaches or noncompliance.

The Keylight Ambassador

The launch of Keylight 4.1 in November 2014 introduced the Keylight Ambassador, the first hybrid connector on the market to allow users to securely automate data collection processes from on-premise applications, custom applications, applications without APIs, and applications where ad-hoc data is created.

nTask

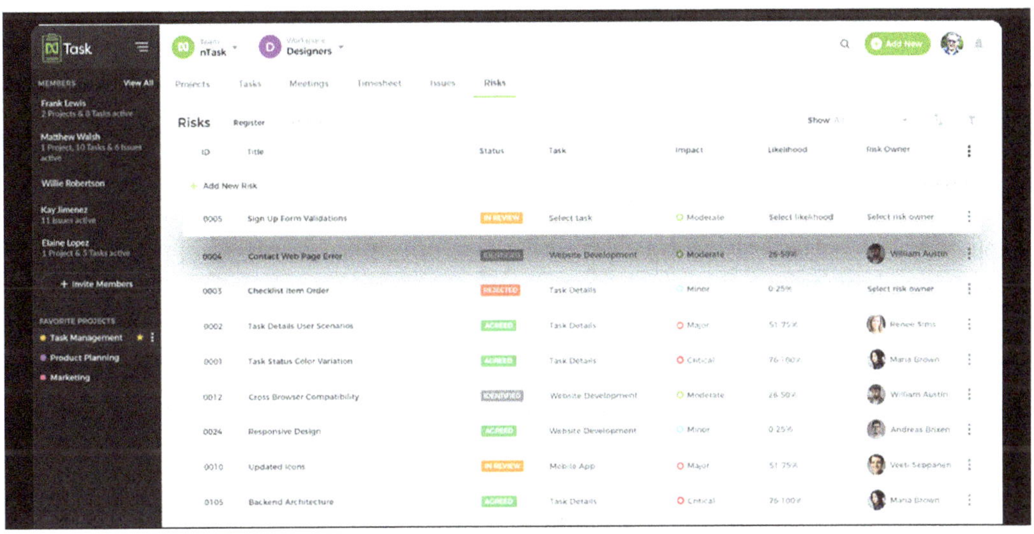

If your risk management software is clunky and complex to use, it will only aggravate your ability to track and assess harmful risks rather than simplifying the process of risk management.

In nTask, the prospect of having to deal with and resolve identified risks doesn't seem too formidable. And the credit for which is single-handedly accounted to the extremely friendly, and pleasantly neutral tones of its risk management board.

The strongest suit that elevates nTask to a higher pedestal than it's fellow contenders is that it is a fully-featured project management tool. So, whether you're working on a task or conducting a meeting, nTask lets you keep one eagle eye on risk updates. Benefits & Features:

- Proficient Risk Reporting – Made to please Agile Teams, in particular, nTask lets you create a plethora of risks whenever the need arises. Each risk is meant to have a specified Risk Owner that is accountable for coming up with ways to resolve the risk and monitor its progress.
- Easy Visibility – Identifying risks is not enough. You have to be able to view each risk whenever you require and locate them without having to lose precious time. Using the List view, gain quick visibility of an entire set of risks, where each risk is currently standing and who is responsible for handling them.
- Determine Risk Impact – Risks of any nature, in any department are at times uncertain and other times fairly predictable. Either way, to keep project stability intact, it is vital that the best risk management software offers the advantage of presaging the likelihood of the risk and how severe is it. Select from three different severity options to let everyone know how urgent a risk is.
- Risk Matrix – A self-generating risk matrix that provides a tabular summary of the probability of each risk in cross-reference with its frequency of occurring. So instead of sifting through each risk individually, access the risk matrix in a single click.

Resolver

There's no knowing when a risk will erupt and jeopardize the foundation of your project, leaving you with nothing but remorse. The only panacea to this predicament is constructive planning.

Resolver is one such tool that focuses primarily on risk planning and preparation. It supports early planning of risk identification, in stages when project objectives and regulatory requirements are still in the making.

There's an entire set of consolidated products offered by Resolver that are specific to organizations of all sizes and from all industries.

Corporations like Delta Airlines make use of Resolver's Enterprise Risk Management solution for Global Security challenges. On a different front, clients like Farmer Mutual Hail chose Resolver's Internal Audit and Risk Compliance software for efficient reporting of risks to their management team.

Benefits and Features

- Effective Assessment – Resolver Ballot facilitates a data-driven approach for conducting the risk assessment.
- Flexible & Custom Reporting – Visualize your security data, risk matrix summaries and trending threats in customizable reports and heat maps that can be exported into spreadsheets and presentations.
- Real-time accessibility & Insight – A centralized dashboard, that allows easy tracking of total risks assigned, resolved and unresolved.
- Incident Management – Establish links between risks associated with external events from a third-party source.
- Prioritize Risk Analysis – Use risk-scoring algorithms to rank each threat based on various attributes such as priority and severity level.
- Rapid Risk Retrieval – Resolver integrates with 40+ apps that let you share and transfer your risk inventory with outside parties or on your favorite project management tool.
- Risk Response Management – Manage and monitor your team's thoughts on each vulnerability assessment and mitigation technique used to resolve it.

TimeCamp

Sometimes the simplest of vulnerabilities are the most injurious, silently weakening the integrity of the project until it suddenly collapses, resulting in complete and utter project failure. Simple management tools such as TimeCamp, are the perfect fit for addressing such seemingly benign risks.

Though TimeCamp is fundamentally a time tracking tool made to assist teams in delivering on time, users can also conduct a risk assessment with special built-in features for multiple facets of their workflow.

Benefits and Features

- Determine Financial Risk – Allows users to monitor when their project budget is falling out of proportion. In such cases, users can sort and control leaky expenses with simple and easy editing options.

- Evaluate Time Management Risk – Owing to its chief feature of time management, TimeCamp enables teams to reach project and task completion on set deadlines with the help of due date options, instant alerts, inactivity tracking and a weekly summary of how each employee is spending their time.
- Curb Project Failure — In TimeCamp, project managers enjoy the ability to track and monitor the likelihood of a project reaching its completion.Options such as the state of the project and status allow teams to keep a solid check on any impending risks that may be festering beneath the surface and keeping the project from meeting its deliverable deadline.

Integrum

Trusted by many, Integrum is one of the best risk management software in the world.

Winner of multiple awards and appreciated for being the most configurable system on the market, Integrum helps companies accelerate their business by helping them manage and reduce risks creeping out at any stage of a project.

Integrum's strongest suit is that it is particularly built for the health and safety management of an organization.

Australia's largest water supplying facility renders successful in supplying safe water and wastewater services to over 500,000 people with the help of Integrum's Quality, Health and Safety Management system. Integrum proffers a sophisticated range of integrations to help a legion of legacy systems streamline their processes and business growth.

Benefits and Features

- Governance Risk & Compliance – Equipped with features such as incident, investigation and document management, Integrum aims to help companies in identifying potential risks before, during and at the end of a project.
- Business Optimization – Integrum takes great pride in being the most customizable software on the market. You can use their intelligent built-in tools such as the SMARTForms that extracts your data to generate comprehensive forms. A similar inbuilt tool responsible for designing workflows helps ensures that company work is up to speed and whether any roadblocks are imminent.
- Business Intelligence – Risk identification is incomplete without a proper reporting system. Integrum BI reporting system is a world-class reporting system that allows users to create as many dashboards, reports and graphical analysis of their mitigation plans. On top of efficient reporting, an easily maneuverable interface is a cherry on top. All and any members from a team can access a complete list of potential and identified risks from a centralized hub where data can be moved from one board to another via drag and drop option.

Qualys

Every Project scope is different from the previous project and the one next in line. With differing projects, arises differing vulnerabilities in the system as well.

The small and menial ones are often captured and dealt with little fuss. It is the highly specialized ones that need a mechanized system of host scanning to avoid any sneaky loopholes that may later damage the entire project development.

Qualys is one of the most advanced tools that offers vulnerability scanning, malware detection, and remediation tracking.

Qualys has a generous compilation of security solutions included but not limited to: asset management, IT security, Cloud security, Web App Security and Policy Compliance. It is because of its simpler, safer and cost-effective suite of features, that Qualys is used across 130 countries and is trusted by major global brands like Microsoft and Deloitte Inc.

Benefits and Features

- Vulnerability Management –Vulnerability Management works with additional Qualys tools such as Continuous Monitoring that provides teams with a hacker's-eye view of their business empire. This feature proactively sends alerts to whenever there is a risk-breach anywhere within the system. These alerts can be tailored and altered according to user preference or circumstance.
- Host Scanning – Qualys VM conducts a comprehensive scan of the entire business perimeter and protects all fronts of a company by identifying any vulnerabilities and bringing them to surface for remediation. Remediation details and the entire security posture of a project or a company domain can be easily viewed in the executive dashboard. Users can obtain role-based reports and documentation of identified or unresolved risks through VM report generator.
- Malware Detection – Companies can use Web Application scanning to detect viruses roaming close by, faulty website policies and technical infections. The scanner also performs behavioral analysis, that demonstrates visual reports of malware trends, scan activity, and risk-prone pages.
- Threat Protection – Use Qualys powerful search engine to search and retrieve specific vulnerabilities and risk history from the inventory, and fine-tune your results with the help of various filters and sorting options.

CURA

Some risks are fairly predictable, some are hidden, and some are recurring. Which is why the monitoring of risks that keep re-surfacing or that are on-going, should be a vital part of the risk management software that you choose.

CURA provides companies with the expertise of supervising each risk, in accordance with its impact and probability.

It offers solutions, to multiple industries ranging from banks, healthcare, insurance firms, utility firms, and telecommunication, in the form of project risk management, enterprise risk management, operational risk management, and incident risk management.

Organizations all across the world, rely on CURA to manage risks. Kellogg's one of the world's leading cereal producer uses CURA's automation system to manage their SOX Section 404 compliance.

Benefits and Features

- Risk Identification – With the help of Governance Risk Compliance, users can identify risks and regulatory requirements at any stage of the project from the beginning to the very end.CURA's project risk management is extremely flexible. You can link risks to projects to ensure vulnerability assessment is a major part of your decision-making process. Once the risks have been identified, you communicate the update on the risk management process with teams within the organization and with outside sources such as stakeholders or clients.
- Risk Monitoring – Using the Goals & Objectives features, project managers can examine and monitor each member's performance and activity, related to risk remediation.
- Risk Reporting – In CURA, companies enjoy the highly configurable feature of risk reporting facilitated with flexible dashboards. Users can formulate reports in the form of lists, tables or even visually interactive graphs. Once created, all reports can be exported to a third party via email, Word Doc, Excel Spreadsheets, and PDF.

A1 Tracker by A1 Enterprise

It is very user-friendly and powerful. Some of its inbuilt features include a web portal, risk audits and log history, alerts and notifications, dashboard metrics and charts, threat assessments, threat response, and risk ratings as well as documentation. It caters to the integration with financial software and provides modules to track events, incidents, contracts, insurance, claims, projects, and assets.

Benefits and Features

Some of the processes this risk management tool can address include:

- Auditing.
- Business Process Control.

- Compliance Management.
- Corrective Actions (CAPA).
- Dashboard.
- Incident Management.
- Internal Controls Management.
- Risk Assessment.

Synergi Life

Synergi Life is a risk management tool by DNV GL. It comes as a complete business solution for risk as well as QHSE (quality, health, safety, environment) management.

With this tool, you can manage risk assessments and analyses, non-conformances, audits and provide a channel for suggestions for improvement. It also helps teams communicate, report, manage corrective actions and experience transfer, trends and KPI monitoring.

Synergi Life is among the best risk management software you can use to manage projects and business risks.

Benefits and Features

Some of the key features you can avail with this risk management tool are:

- Auditing.
- Compliance Management.
- Dashboard.
- Incident Management.
- Risk Assessment.

Audits.io

The unique feature of this risk management software is that it is customizable. You can make use of this tool on devices, online and offline. It helps you assign work and notify responsible people, attach images and share files, conduct inspections and audits on the go with your mobile or tablets or in one place, on a computer.

You can even transfer automated PDF reports to stakeholders, assess bottlenecks and trends with real-time statistics.

Benefits and Features

Here are some features and processes this tool provides:

- Auditing.
- Business Process Control.
- Compliance Management.
- Corrective Actions (CAPA).
- Dashboard.
- Incident Management.
- Internal Controls Management.
- Risk Assessment.

MasterControl Risk Analysis

MasterControl complies with FDA regulations as well as with ISO quality standards. An alluring feature about this tool is that it helps in recovering documents that may have been lost in unforeseen situations.

You can easily restore them and continue the project. Moreover, this tool establishes risk evaluation as a separate process. This significantly helps the quality departments in quality decision making.

Benefits and Features:

MasterControl comes with the following salient features:

- Auditing.
- Business Process Control.
- Compliance Management.
- Corrective Actions (CAPA).
- Dashboard.
- Incident Management.
- Risk Assessment.

Predict360 by 360factors

This cloud-based Enterprise Risk and Compliance Management Technology specializes in the sectors of Banking and Financial Services, Oil and Gas, and Power and Utility.

Predict360 comes with a user-friendly interface and offers a single platform to integrate audits and inspections, policies and procedures, regulatory information, risks as well as online training.

Moreover, this tool also has pre-configured content to assist functional managers and staff in managing daily risk and compliance matters.

Benefits and Features

Here is a list of features you can avail with this risk management software:

- Archiving and Retention.
- Audit Trail.
- Environmental Compliance.
- FDA Compliance.
- HIPAA Compliance.
- ISO Compliance.
- OSHA Compliance.
- Risk Alerts.
- Sarbanes-Oxley Compliance.
- Version Control.

Pims Risk Management by Omega.no

Pims is one of the best risk management software helping teams with risk identification, mitigation, and management. It comes with a simplified interface that users can swiftly learn and be able to work. You can retrieve relevant information regarding risks, add risks or perform editing.

You can even store documentation, assess past risks and accordingly work on historic risk development.

Benefits and Features

This tool facilitates risk management through the following features:

- Auditing.
- Corrective Actions (CAPA).

- Dashboard.
- Risk Assessment.

Opture ERM

The Opture Risk Management Software is an integrated risk management software that facilitates the entire risk management process. With this risk management tool, you can manage risks efficiently by boosting risk data quality and conducting risk analysis individually. Moreover, it is flexible, easy to incorporate, modularly extendable and simple to work with.

Benefits and Features

Opture provides the following features and usability in your risk management process:

- Auditing.
- Business Process Control.
- Compliance Management.
- Dashboard.
- Incident Management.
- Internal Controls Management.
- Risk Assessment.

ARC Cyber Risk Management

ARC Risk is one of the best risk management software available. It is a Cyber Security Risk Management tool. This tool lets you assess risks, report, and track, manage assets, gap analysis, supports incident management and provides results that can be audited annually.

It complies with the ISO 27001:2013. It saves time spent on information risk management and gives you results that can be audited on a yearly basis.

ARC is a web-based risk management software that can be accessed from anywhere.

Benefits and Features:

This risk management tool gives you the following key features:

- Auditing.
- Compliance Management.

- Dashboard.
- Incident Management.
- Risk Assessment.

PERMISSIONS

All chapters in this book are published with permission under the Creative Commons Attribution Share Alike License or equivalent. Every chapter published in this book has been scrutinized by our experts. Their significance has been extensively debated. The topics covered herein carry significant information for a comprehensive understanding. They may even be implemented as practical applications or may be referred to as a beginning point for further studies.

We would like to thank the editorial team for lending their expertise to make the book truly unique. They have played a crucial role in the development of this book. Without their invaluable contributions this book wouldn't have been possible. They have made vital efforts to compile up to date information on the varied aspects of this subject to make this book a valuable addition to the collection of many professionals and students.

This book was conceptualized with the vision of imparting up-to-date and integrated information in this field. To ensure the same, a matchless editorial board was set up. Every individual on the board went through rigorous rounds of assessment to prove their worth. After which they invested a large part of their time researching and compiling the most relevant data for our readers.

The editorial board has been involved in producing this book since its inception. They have spent rigorous hours researching and exploring the diverse topics which have resulted in the successful publishing of this book. They have passed on their knowledge of decades through this book. To expedite this challenging task, the publisher supported the team at every step. A small team of assistant editors was also appointed to further simplify the editing procedure and attain best results for the readers.

Apart from the editorial board, the designing team has also invested a significant amount of their time in understanding the subject and creating the most relevant covers. They scrutinized every image to scout for the most suitable representation of the subject and create an appropriate cover for the book.

The publishing team has been an ardent support to the editorial, designing and production team. Their endless efforts to recruit the best for this project, has resulted in the accomplishment of this book. They are a veteran in the field of academics and their pool of knowledge is as vast as their experience in printing. Their expertise and guidance has proved useful at every step. Their uncompromising quality standards have made this book an exceptional effort. Their encouragement from time to time has been an inspiration for everyone.

The publisher and the editorial board hope that this book will prove to be a valuable piece of knowledge for students, practitioners and scholars across the globe.

INDEX

www.ingramcontent.com/pod-product-compliance
Lightning Source LLC
LaVergne TN
LVHW080056220926
848484LV00006BB/1555
* 9 7 8 1 6 8 2 8 5 9 8 9 6 *